"Full of lively illustrations, wise warnings, and hard-hitting application for everyday life, Bond's latest book addresses all of the strong temptations and difficult trials that young men face today. Ideal for personal study or father-son discussion, *Fathers and Sons* is an invitation to pursue manly godliness in the adventure of life."

—Philip Graham Ryken, senior minister,
Tenth Presbyterian Church, Philadelphia

"Douglas Bond has written the book that many dads will wish their father had read with them, and that they will be so thankful to have for prayerful discussion with their own sons now. . . . Fathers, get this book, sit down with your son, pray, and get started. Your son will understand the engaging language and powerful illustrations; you will be thanking God for the help in talking about so many topics you know will benefit your son as he reaches for manhood. Very edifying; don't miss out on this!"

—Paul Walker, pastor and hospital chaplain
(retired), Vancouver, BC

"Douglas Bond's engaging study will help us as men know how to think about our world and our responsibilities as sons and fathers and leaders. I would encourage dads and sons to read it together, to discuss it, to pray over what you've learned, and to memorize the key Scripture verses together."

—Bently B. Rayburn, United States Air Force
Major General (retired)

"Douglas Bond doesn't write for the faint-hearted. This is for men who want the next generation—including their very own sons—to be more stalwart than they were themselves. . . . Douglas Bond calls you to set your plow shares deep, do the hard work of parenting while it is yet day, and look to a faithful heavenly Father for a rewarding harvest."

—Joel Belz, founder, *World* magazine

Fathers and Sons, Volume 1

Fathers and Sons, Volume 1

Stand Fast in the Way of Truth

Douglas Bond

PUBLISHING
P.O. BOX 817 • PHILLIPSBURG • NEW JERSEY 08865-0817

Printed in the United States of America

Library of Congress Cataloging-in-Publication Data

Bond, Douglas, 1958-
Fathers and sons / Douglas Bond.
    p. cm.
Includes bibliographical references.
ISBN 978-1-59638-076-9 (pbk.)
1. Teenage boys—Religious life. 2. Teenage boys—Conduct of life. 3. Conduct of life—Biblical teaching. 4. Christian life—Biblical teaching. I. Title.
BV4541.3.B65 2007
248.8'32—dc22

                 2007030982

In Grateful Memory of
My Father,
Douglas Elwood Bond
September 21, 1933–June 12, 2006
"Serve the Lord with Gladness"

For my sons
Rhodri, Cedric, Desmond, Giles

and for the sons that my daughters,
Brittany and Gillian,
God willing, will someday marry

"Watch, stand fast in the faith, be brave, be strong. Let all that you do be done with love."

1 Corinthians 16:13-14 (NKJV)

"Stand fast in Christ, keep the faith, contend for Christ. Wrestle for Him."

Samuel Rutherford, 1637

"I am going now to see that head that was crowned with thorns, and that face which was spit upon for me. I have formerly lived by hearsay and faith: but now I go where I shall live by sight, and shall be with Him in whose company I delight myself."

John Bunyan's Mr. Standfast, from *Pilgrim's Progress*

CONTENTS

FOREWORD

Major General Bentley Rayburn

I am a fighter pilot. I spent nearly thirty-one years as an officer in the United States Air Force and have flown jet fighter aircraft all over the world. I've spent my whole professional life working with men in a dangerous and demanding profession. Since entering the United States Air Force Academy in 1971, I have also been a student of leadership. In thirty-one years in the military I have been led by great commanders, have led men myself, and have taught other men to lead, including many young men who claim to be Christians. My biggest leadership challenge, however, did not come in combat operations. It came in being a father to my son, Micah.

My son is grown now. He is married and has started his own family, but as I look back on raising my son, I see the importance of the relationship with my own father. It is an enormous responsibility being fathers who must train our sons to be the men God commands them to be and that our families, our churches, and our country need them to be.

As men, the one thing we have in common is that we all have a father. We've learned from our fathers—for good or for ill. Many of us have or will have sons ourselves. Sons that will learn from us—good lessons for life or bad ones.

My own dad was a hero. A real hero. Two days after volunteering to be a chaplain for an airborne unit in the Korean War, Dad found himself jumping into combat behind the enemy lines. With no formal parachute training, and fully aware that no one would have thought it cowardly for him to skip the jump and join the unit later once they had linked up on the ground, he knew that his responsibility was to be with his men who needed the ministry of a chaplain on such a dangerous mission. Of course my father wasn't perfect, but in so many ways I now realize how much I learned from him. He was courageous in physical combat and he was courageous in spiritual warfare as well. In all, he was a wonderful role model for me. But, have I always been that kind of role model for my own son?

Men, we are in trouble. Collectively, we are not doing a very good job of raising our next generation of young men. Statistics tell us that the average dad spends less than five minutes a day with his kids. The number of homes in America without a father is reaching catastrophic levels. Our teen boys are becoming more and more irresponsible—happy to hang out, waste time on video games, TV, and mindless activities. Today's young man is far less likely to take responsibility and pour himself into preparation for life as an adult and as a future father. We desperately need our boys to grow up to be strong men and leaders in our society and especially in our churches.

This is our great challenge. To pass on to our sons what they need from their fathers to be leaders in their own right. To model the example God wants our sons to see. And for sons to recognize the real challenges and dangers that await them in our culture, and how important it is to be well trained for the life that awaits them as adults. *Fathers and Sons* will help to do that in a powerful way.

The philosopher Francis Bacon said, "Some books are to be tasted, others to be swallowed, and some few to be chewed and digested." This is of the last version, for father and son to chew and digest together. It is what learning and leading is all about.

In a fresh way, Douglas Bond covers the waterfront of issues that young men must consider as they ponder the challenges of Christian manhood. Featuring the heroic lives of great thinkers, theologians, and warriors, Bond ultimately points young men to the Bible, the source of truth. *Fathers and Sons* will encourage you to focus on practical applications, to reject the pressures to compromise and conform to the culture around us, and to clean out the sin in your life and avoid immorality, and then to live lives that are pleasing and honoring to God.

Douglas Bond's engaging study will help us as men know how to think about our world and our responsibilities as sons and fathers and leaders. I would encourage dads and sons to read it together, to discuss it, to pray over what you've learned, and to memorize the key Scripture verses together.

Christian fathers need to be great leaders and Christian sons need to study leadership and see leadership modeled for them by their fathers. Douglas Bond has given us a book that will help us do that. My prayer is that in chewing and digesting this book, you'll see God's great plan for all of us as fathers and sons and have the wisdom and courage to follow our great leader, Jesus Christ, in all areas of our lives.

Bentley B. Rayburn
Major General, USAF (Retired)
Colorado Springs, Colorado

YOUNG MEN: THEIR WAY

1

THE WAY AND
THE WORD

Psalm 119:9–16

Life's No Joke

Your life as a teenage young man is an exciting and vigorous one, full of possibilities, hopes, dreams, and ambitions. You have many things you want to see and do, places you want to visit, things you want to know, things you want to own. In fact, you want to have it all. It's in your nature. All of this requires you to make many decisions, to make daily choices about what you are going to do, what you are going to become, where you are going to go. Some of these are big and some seem small, even inconsequential.

Which brings to mind Bill Watterson, creator of monster-in-miniature Calvin. I wonder if Watterson may not be the quintessential philosopher humorist alive today—perhaps in any day. He so memorably tickles the funny bone in our house that my sons and I frequently compare things going on around us with some crack-up episode from Calvin and Hobbes.

Watterson's hilarious, to be sure, but it's hilarity with a purpose. His periodic flashes of insight are skillfully packaged in witty perceptions about the relationship between sons and parents and about the human condition. After Watterson has made his fans bust up laughing, however, he gently prods thoughtful readers to pause and consider the enduring things.

In one such place Watterson has Calvin muse, in witty lines of verse, "I made a big decision a little while ago," but poor Calvin then admits that he's a bit unclear about just what it was that made the decision so important. As the poem progresses, Watterson perceptively observes that even the simple choices, the seemingly inconsequential ones, at the last, may "prove to be essential"; they may make all the difference in a young man's life.

If Watterson's Calvin is right, then young men need to be far more careful about the decisions they're making. Big or small, decisions have consequences.

Who Are You?

You're young. You're probably healthy, strong, active, fascinated by many things around you, eager to take on the world, to seize the day, to live life to the fullest, to have fun. Some of you love sports, the squeak of tennis-shoe rubber on the gym floor, the blood and sweat of the gridiron, the crack of the bat on the ball, the thrill of victory. You're so into sports, you're intoxicated by the smell of the guys' locker room. Some of you love fast cars, the mall, pop music, designer clothing. Others of you like the outdoors, guns and shooting, stalking game, pickup trucks, and country music. Others of you fall somewhere between all of these, or in a category all your own. In fact, some of you just love being an individual. You say and do and wear things, at least in part, simply because others do not.

Most of you also claim to be Christians. Many of you have grown up in the church and in Christian homes. All of you are growing up with various degrees of exposure to popular culture. It may seem to some of you like there's a tug-of-war going on between your father and the pop culture that surrounds you. It probably seems this way to your father, too.

My guess is that there are times when your parents' beliefs and the things of God come into clearer focus, when all that they have taught you makes sense and, at some level, you believe it. I am equally certain that there are other times, perhaps many of these, when you are swept away in the tidal wave of enticing experiences offered you by the world, by your own flesh, and by the devil.

How do you find your way through all this? How do you navigate the winding, twisting, enticing way of life? How do you answer the great questions of life? How do you make the big decisions of your life?

Young man, you stand before a great divide, and it is absolutely essential that you take your heart in your hands, that you "make a big decision," as Watterson's Calvin put it, or as Joshua of old put it, that you "choose for yourselves this day whom you will serve" (Josh. 24:15).

The Real Question

In Psalm 119, the psalmist asks an important question about young men and their way. Teenage men are bombarded with choices about sports, jobs, money, girls, school, and ambitions. You are faced with consequential questions about how you will spend your time, with whom you will spend that time, what you will choose to think about, and who and what you will become.

All these questions and choices lie before you, but the psalmist cuts through them all to the real question: "How can a young man keep his way pure?" (Ps. 119:9a). The young man who gets so distracted by the tyranny of the immediate questions that he fails to ask this fundamental question, and keep asking it throughout his days, will not keep his way pure. He will be put to shame; will be cursed, not blessed; will not walk in God's ways; and will make decisions that lead him astray—decisions likely to bring a measure of grief and sorrow to his life now, but immeasurable grief and sorrow in eternity.

On the other hand, the young man who genuinely desires to know how to keep his way pure will hear the psalmist's answer, "By living according to [God's] word" (Ps. 119:9b). The young man who lives according to the Bible will walk in God's ways, will never be put to shame, and will be blessed in all he does. Because of God's grace and forgiveness, he will find happiness and contentment even when his way is strewn with sorrows and difficulties.

But many will try to tell you that you don't need the Bible to guide you in your way. Follow your heart, they'll tell you. After all, critics of the Bible insist that it's no different from other old books, that it doesn't give inspired information about your way, that it's full of inconsistencies and errors, and that it is thus not a reliable road map for your way in this world. Whomever you listen to, what you believe about the Bible will profoundly affect your way in this world—and in the next.

Throwing Rocks

Imagine one dry, hot afternoon in 1947. A teenage herder named Muhammad, napping on the shady side of a boulder, woke with a start. He may have detected a slight change in the rustling, bleating, and munching sounds that his herd of goats made as they foraged in the desert wastes near the northwestern foothills of the Dead Sea.

Hastily counting the scruffy backs of his goats, he frowned, and counted again. One of them was missing. It wasn't the first time. And he knew which one it was. Shuddering at the thought of explaining to his father that he'd lost one of the family goats, Muhammad cleared the drowsiness from his brain with a shake of his head. He sprang to his feet, calling for the goat.

20

His voice echoed off the rocky cliff that jutted into the cloudless blue sky above. *Stupid goat*, he thought as he scanned the cliffside. Two small, dark shadows caught his eye. He studied what looked like cavernous eye sockets on a sun-bleached skull high on the cliff face. Snatching up a stone, Muhammad cocked his arm and took careful aim at the bigger of the two voids.

Bedouin goatherds needed to be good at hurling stones. With a well-thrown rock Muhammad had often driven off wild dogs who stalked his herd for strays. With a heave, he released the stone and watched and listened as it flew toward the dark opening. He smiled as the rock soundlessly disappeared into the cave. Then came an odd sound—not the expected stone-on-rock collision. This was a hollow, shattering sound, the sound of breaking pottery.

Later, Muhammad scrambled up the cliff face, the dense blue waters of the Dead Sea stretching far below. Deep into the cave he crawled, feeling his way with his hands. Suddenly he felt before him the rounded shape of a tall clay jar. As his eyes adjusted to the dim light, he saw ten or more jars. He lifted the bowl-shaped lid of the nearest one. Hoping it wasn't home to scorpions, he cautiously pawed at the mysterious contents. Then he caught his breath. It was filled with scrolls.

Muhammad edh-Dhib, teenage goatherd, had stumbled across the most important archaeological discovery of the twentieth century: the Dead Sea Scrolls.

Pure in All Ages

Searching in eleven nearby caves, archaeologists unearthed 870 scrolls, meticulous copies of almost the entire Old Testament. Jewish and Catholic scholars, however, decided to keep the scrolls to themselves, barring Protestant scholars from studying them.

Until 1991. My friend and mountaineering partner, Hebrew scholar Martin Abegg (a.k.a. "Smarty Marty"), while working on his Ph.D. at the Hebrew University in Jerusalem, had come across a concordance on the Dead Sea Scrolls. Arduously, he had lifted every Hebrew "jot and tittle" of the scrolls out of the concordance, eventually making a copy of the scrolls available to all scholars.

Skeptics lined up, sifting through the scrolls, hoping to find substantial discrepancies and expose what they were certain would prove to be the fallacy of biblical inerrancy. Surely Christians, who claim that their Bible is the Word of God, would be silenced by this modern discovery.

To grasp just how significant this discovery was, it is helpful to consider certain facts about biblical manuscripts. Most English Bibles were translated from the Masoretic Text, a multigenerational copy of a copy of the originals, dating about nine hundred years after Christ. The Dead Sea Scrolls, however, were copied over a thousand years before the text used for most modern Bibles. How could versions of the Bible copied more than a thousand years apart possibly agree?

Three hundred years before the Dead Sea Scrolls were discovered, the Westminster divines had affirmed the Bible as "immediately inspired by God, and by his singular care and providence kept pure in all ages," thus concluding that the Hebrew and Greek manuscripts from which the English Bible comes "are therefore authentic."

But surely, wouldn't Muhammad's accidental discovery of these scrolls prove that those seventeenth-century Puritan preachers were a bit naive to have had such confidence in the Bible?

With all the dust having settled on the Dead Sea Scrolls, however, scholars generally agree that there is only 1 percent inconsistency between manuscripts of the Old Testament copied a thousand years apart. Moreover, the inconsistency has no material bearing on the historicity of the Bible or the Christian gospel. In fact, the much older Dead Sea Scroll version of Psalm 22 actually clarified ambiguities in verse 16, rendering it "they have pierced my hands and my feet," a still clearer prophetic reference to Christ's Roman crucifixion than that found in the Masoretic Text.

Fit Witness

All of this serves to confirm confidence in the authority, accuracy, inerrancy, and infallibility of the Bible. But if the archaeological jury is in, why do unbelievers still refuse to live according to God's Word? Why do they not care to keep their way pure?

Men remain in unbelief because God, as he reveals himself in his Word, is known and embraced by faith. If Muhammad had never stumbled upon the Dead Sea Scrolls, living according to God's Word would still remain the way to keep your way pure. Other discoveries will come and go. God's Word is self-authenticating and, therefore, not more true or less true because of new discoveries.

"God alone," wrote John Calvin, "is a fit witness of himself in his Word." Your confidence in the power, the trustworthiness, the absolute authority of God's Word does not derive from the confirming evidence found in the Dead Sea Scrolls. It's by faith that we understand that the world was framed by the word of God (Heb. 11:3). Thus, you may be absolutely certain that if you, by faith, heed the Word of God, you will keep your way pure.

What happened to Muhammad's goat that lost its way? I have no idea. But young men who are careless of their way, who neglect the Word of God and go their own way, will most certainly lose their footing and be forever lost.

Slippery Road to Hell

"There is not such an icy, slippery way betwixt you and heaven as youth," wrote Samuel Rutherford, one of the Westminster divines. His caution appears in a letter written June 16, 1637, to Earlston the Younger, a Scottish gentleman, probably a teenager.

Thousands of young men like Earlston would take up claymore and musket against the enemies of Christ and against the tyrannical persecutions of the Stuart kings. Many who fought also shed their blood for the "Crown rights of the Redeemer in his Kirk." Rutherford knew, however, that a young man could be on the right side, full of righteous indignation, defending the defenseless, fighting for the cause of truth, and yet slip into evil motives such as pride and revenge.

Ice is slippery stuff, as I learned while commuting on my bicycle one winter morning. As I banked into a left turn across traffic, my tire suddenly hit a patch of ice. Next thing I knew, I felt a bone-jarring blow on my left hip. Hopelessly tangled in my bike and book bag, I skidded across the pavement.

Moments before, I had felt the cold breeze on my face, had exhilarated in healthy morning exercise, and had probably even entertained some deluded sense of my own strength. But as I careered toward the grille of an oncoming school bus, all of that was gone. Everything was out of control. There was nothing I could do to stop things.

Similarly, patches of ice lie on every side of your way. But if you slip and fall on this road, the extent of the damage is far greater than a bunged-up hip. Physical hurts generally heal, especially when you are young and healthy. But mangle your immortal soul, and you'll regret it for eternity. You must beware.

Slippery temptations that Rutherford could never have imagined line your way. If his observation about youth and young men was true four hundred years ago, how much more ought you to be careful how you walk today, how much more must you diligently and daily take heed of the words of God.

Byways to Hell

Young man, you're on the road that has more byways to hell than any other stretch of highway you'll encounter throughout your days on this earth. With every breath you draw, you are developing the habits of mind, heart, and body that will shape who you will become in your adult life and that will shape your eternal destiny.

And everything in the world is against you. The road is lined with worldly enticements that "drip honey" and that are designed to allure you with words "smoother than oil" (Prov. 5:3). Around the next bend in the way, powerful giants, armed with weapons specifically designed to destroy you, lie in wait for your life. To top all, your greatest enemy is within the gates. Your own flesh is eager to sell all to the world and the devil.

Rutherford was right. You are on a slippery road. The more honest you are with yourself about this, the more skillful you will become in maintaining your footing, in standing fast. But you must beware.

Look Down the Road

Moreover, you should not delude yourself; what you are now as a teenager is in all likelihood what you will be throughout your life. Bill Watterson's Calvin didn't remember whether he turned left or right when he left his house, but he was certain that whichever it was, "I never veered: I walked in that direction." So it is with you, young man. Start down a pathway in your youth, and like it or not, you will probably be on the same path in your adulthood. How can a young man keep his way pure? Start on the right pathway today. Take heed of God's Word. Read it; study it; delight in it; obey it.

None of this comes naturally to you. Young men are fallen and so prefer pursuing pleasure today, having a good time right now, and enjoying all the excitement of immediate gratification. Young men, more than any others, are prone to presumption, to living thoughtless, careless lives, so long as they have their enjoyments right now. This is a critical part of the slipperiness of the way you are on.

"Young man," wrote nineteenth-century English pastor J. C. Ryle, "do not be deceived. Do not think you can willfully serve your self and your pleasures in the beginning of your life, and then go and serve God with ease at the end."

Wise young men know this, so they plan ahead; they look down the road. How shall a young man keep his way pure? Stand fast on God's Word; know your great need of him, and seek him with all your heart; hide God's Word in your heart; praise him; learn from him; speak to yourself about all the wonderful things God has done for you;

25

rejoice in obedience more than in gaining wealth; meditate on and delight in God's law—and do it now. Keep your way pure. Know that seemingly simple choices make big differences in where you will find yourself as an adult.

Watterson's Calvin is bewildered by where he finds himself today, and he's compelled to admit at the last, "I've wandered far astray." Don't wander astray. Make the big decision, and say with the other Calvin, John Calvin the Reformer, "My heart I offer Thee, Lord, promptly and sincerely."

Resolves

- To pray regularly together as father and son
- To make decisions, even seemingly inconsequential ones, with a greater sense of the long-term effects of those choices
- To cultivate a more heartfelt desire for a pure life
- To live according to God's Word, every step of the way

Scripture Memory

"How can a young man keep his way pure? By living according to your word."

Psalm 119:9

For Discussion

1. What does the word *pure* mean?
2. What is the role of the Bible in your day-to-day life right now?
3. Discuss changes you need to make to live "according to [God's] word."

"Join All the Glorious Names"

Thou art my Counselor,
My pattern, and my Guide,
And thou my Shepherd art;
O keep me near thy side;
Nor let my feet e'er turn astray
To wander in the crooked way.

Isaac Watts, 1707

For Further Study

Psalm 1; Proverbs 2:12–15; 4:23–27; 16:17

2

THE WAY TO THINK

Proverbs 4:26

The Absence of Thinking

"Think no more, lad; laugh, be jolly," wrote poet A. E. Housman, an imperative not unlike commanding a fish to swim. "Use your head!" for many young men means heading the soccer ball, hammering that black-and-white checkered animal skin right where you want it. But when it comes to using your head for skillful thinking, that's another matter.

No young man keeps his way pure, however, unless he learns to ponder the path of his feet (Prov. 4:26). Thinking demands concentration and effort; laughing and being jolly are so much easier. Hence, many young men do precious little thinking.

Consequently, it doesn't take much to find examples of men doing laughably stupid things because they failed to think before doing them. Consider the night security guard at a private airport who found his siphon hose stuck while attempting to siphon gas from a plane. Frustrated, he tried to get a closer look at the problem—by lighting a match. The plane exploded into flames. The thief suffered severe burns but survived.

Or how about the nineteen-year-old Ohio college student Robert Ricketts, who nearly lost his head when he was struck by a Conrail train? Unaccountably, he survived, and when questioned, he told police that he'd been trying to see how close to the moving train he could place his head without getting hit.

There are, of course, levels of foolish thinking (or lack thereof). The college kid's folly ranks higher because on some level—albeit a moronic one—he was thinking about what he was doing. On the other hand, the American tourist visiting London, distracted by the sights, who looks left instead of right, steps off the pavement, and is struck in the head by a speeding cab evokes more pity than a guy like Robert. Either way, however, serious consequences ensue from lack of thought.

"Believe me," wrote Bishop of Liverpool J. C. Ryle, "this world is not a world in which we can do well without thinking, and least of all do well in the matter of our souls. 'Don't think,' whispers Satan." To their peril, many young men heed the devil and "think no more."

Thinking Kept in Awe

Had the ancient Greeks known a guy who, just for kicks, would see how close he could get his head to a moving train, they may have thought twice about dubbing man *homo sapiens*, or "thinking man." Nevertheless, they were in part correct. Thinking makes the man—or breaks him. This is why Jesus said that lustful thoughts that originate in man's heart are a violation of the seventh commandment forbidding adultery. Or the man who entertains hateful thoughts about his brother, as Cain must have done, has violated the sixth commandment forbidding murder. "If you love Me, keep My commandments," Jesus

29

said (John 14:15 NKJV). Keeping and breaking God's commandments begins in your thoughts. Thus, how you think matters.

Warning a young Scottish laird against "the hot fiery lusts and passions of youth," Samuel Rutherford in a letter urged the young man to cultivate "sanctified thoughts, thoughts made conscious of, and called in, and kept in awe." Here Rutherford commends the habit of thinking about what you're thinking about. Worthwhile thinking is a conscious act. It doesn't just happen. Thinking about thinking is an essential skill that young men who would be wise must master.

As the Spirit of God enlightens your thought life, he enables you to detect flaws early, before they fester into intractable transgressions. When the first hint of uncharitable thought toward a weaker brother begins to take shape in your thoughts, you must call in those thoughts. Likewise, the instant your mind edges toward lustful thoughts—brace yourself, like a man—yank the chain.

I once asked a fifteen-year-old student what Rutherford meant by thoughts "called in." He mused for a moment and then perceptively replied, "Thoughts on a leash." You must keep your thoughts in check, on a leash, ready to yank them back to proper thoughts of God, yourself, and your neighbor.

Think of your thoughts as a one-year-old hunting dog in training. Just like an adolescent Labrador, you are easily distracted. Your thoughts, like the dog's, are easily drawn to this smell, or that stray cat, or that kid on a bicycle—or that mail carrier coming into the yard. Life easily becomes a flurry of slavering, out-of-control impulses, the result of unstudied thoughts that lead to a frantic, mindless—often short—existence. "Brothers, stop thinking like children," Paul urged. "In your thinking be adults" (1 Cor. 14:20).

The source of all our sinning is not our deeds or words but our thoughts. This is why Scripture calls wicked men to first forsake their thoughts (Isa. 55:7) and then their words and deeds. If you are to be godly, you must put off ungodly thoughts and put on godly thoughts. If you are to be courageous, you must first think courageous thoughts; if you are to be honest, you must think honest thoughts. If you are to be a man, by the grace of God and the power of his Holy Spirit, you must "put childish ways behind" (1 Cor. 13:11), and think like a man.

Keeping your thinking in awe of Christ is the surest way to rein in those reckless, foolish impulses, devoid of real thought. Keep your thoughts in awe of the grace and splendor of Christ, and there will be no room for foolish impulses, those crippling flights of fancy that land you in disaster.

Thinking and War

"There are no moral absolutes," insisted Nigel, a biology student from the University of York with whom I carried on an e-mail conversation for some months. The gist of this otherwise clever young English student's argument was that my Christianity was wrong and his naturalism was right. All the while, he insisted that what was wrong with my Christian worldview was that I believed in moral absolutes, whereas his enlightened naturalism knew that absolutely nothing was right or wrong, absolutely true or false—absolutely!

Gently, I tried to help Nigel see how absurd his argument was. If his worldview was correct, then why was he bothering to insist that my view—or any other view—was wrong? In the amoral world he was attempting to construct for himself, there would be no right or wrong ideas, so why would it ever occur to anyone to argue about anything? Though manifestly illogical, Nigel's naturalism held him fast, his mind remaining passionately devoted to its thoughtless dogma.

The apostle Paul wrote, "The weapons we fight with are not the weapons of the world. On the contrary, they have divine power to demolish strongholds. We demolish arguments and every pretension that sets itself up against the knowledge of God, and we take captive every thought to make it obedient to Christ" (2 Cor. 10:4–5).

Paul doesn't shy away from using violent language here. This is all-or-nothing war metaphor. Why? Because the stakes are high. There are no noncombatants in this conflict. If you don't demolish strongholds and take your thoughts captive to Christ, you yourself will be taken captive, made a slave, a prisoner of war, or worse. Put bluntly, when it comes to your thinking, Paul seems to be saying, "Kill or be killed."

Thinking and Logic

Perhaps it was Isaac Watts who best codified taking "captive every thought to make it obedient to Christ." Watts wrote, "*Veritas in puteo*, Truth lies in a well . . . [and] logic suppl[ies] us with steps whereby we may go down to reach the water." A Christian young man will be far better equipped to unmask bad thinking, to see the devil's schemes before they hit, if he studies logic. Watts argued that studying logic helps a man expose the "disguise and false colors in which many things appear to us in this present imperfect state."

Satan is in the business of deception, so his strategy is that "knavery puts on the face of justice; deceit and evil are often clothed in the shapes and appearances of truth and goodness." Watts saw logic as a way of aiding men in unmasking the deception: "Logic helps us strip off the outward disguise of things, and to behold and judge them in their own nature."

Watts was right; "knavery puts on the face of justice." Nowhere is this knavery seen more clearly today than when the gurus of political correctness, at war with moral absolutes, show themselves to be equally at war with logic and clear thinking. Today, more than ever, young men must learn to "strip off the outward disguise" of what passes for thinking.

The media, liberal politicians, and educational elites, ironically, claim the moral high ground for their programs. Yet how silly is it to insist that your ideas are morally right when you've denied the very absolutes necessary to make such claims? Consider, for example, *New York Times* columnist Anthony Lewis's declarative conclusions about people, such as Christians, who think they're certain about things: "Certainty is the enemy of decency and humanity."

Notice the basic problem with his moral conclusions. Anthony Lewis, like my naturalist friend Nigel, is certain he is right about the evils of certainty! He has just made an absolutist statement condemning people for being absolutists. *Homo sapiens* are compelled to ask, "Are you absolutely certain that certainty is so bad?"

Thinking and Amusement

Hollywood, predictably, is intoxicated with the cloudy brew that masquerades as intelligent thought. George Lucas, in *Star Wars, Episode III*, has young Obi-Wan Kenobi declare absolutely that "only a Sith lord deals in absolutes." Apparently the absurdity of making an absolutist statement decrying absolutes eluded Hollywood film editors.

This shouldn't surprise us. Hollywood is in the business of amusement. But how is a Christian young man supposed to think about his amusements when amusement means not thinking? How does a young man think about not thinking? "Better be wise in time," J. C. Ryle urges young men. "Better write 'poison' on all earthly pleasures. The most lawful of them must be used with moderation. All of them are soul-destroying if you give them your heart."

There's the rub. Most young men have given their hearts to amusement. The average American student graduating from high school has viewed sixteen thousand hours of television, not including vast hours spent playing video games. Ours is a society in which nearly everything is measured by its entertainment value. "Our politics, religion, news, athletics, education, and commerce have been transformed into congenial adjuncts of show business," wrote Neil Postman. "The result is that we are a people on the verge of amusing ourselves to death."

The Christian young man must be aware of this cultural crisis threatening on his horizon—and then stand with determination against it. "Do not conform any longer to the pattern of this world, but be transformed by the renewing of your mind. Then you will be able to test and approve what God's will is—his good, pleasing and perfect will" (Rom. 12:2). With your back against the world and a discerning mind, Paul urges you to "think . . . with sober judgment" (12:3), the very opposite of what amusement is designed to make you do.

Ryle urges young men to "guard your thoughts, and there is little fear about your deeds." But I suggest to you that a great deal of image-based media technology is calculated to make you drop your guard on your thoughts. Little wonder that a culture so entirely saturated with image media loses more and more of the ability "to test and approve what God's will is."

Fail to guard your thoughts, and the world's thinking will seem less absurd to you. Gorge yourself on what Hollywood shovels into the trough and kiss logic goodbye. A thoughtful young man will guard his precious ability to think by shutting down his computer games, turning off the television, and becoming much more restrained and selective about the DVDs he watches.

Then fill the vast amounts of available time by reading good books. Cautiously get your current news from honest print media, journalists who tell you up front that they select and interpret the events they report according to a worldview. Then learn to "demolish arguments and every pretension that sets itself up against the knowledge of God." With a clear mind, uncluttered by worldly deception, "take captive every thought to make it obedient to Christ" (2 Cor. 10:5).

Thinking and Worship

Nowhere do we need Christ to transform our thinking and renew our minds more than in worship. In worship, the devil wants your mind wandering—not wondering. Whether in family, private, or corporate worship, he prefers that you sleep and not think. He thinks ahead about this. Saturday night, for instance, he wants you to plunk in another movie—and another; he wants you to go to bed at 2 AM; he wants you to drag out of the sack ten minutes before church. Heed the devil Saturday night, and there's little fear of your thinking God's thoughts after him Sunday morning.

Thinking about worship requires preplanning—as does everything else worthwhile in life. Because Satan knows that you were made for worship, and that nothing is more important, he plans ahead and starts his sinister work Saturday night. So must you.

Think ahead about what you want to be thinking about during the worship service. Offer your heart to God, your inner thoughts and desires. In worship, love the Lord with all your mind and take every thought captive to Christ.

As you commune at the Lord's Table, think about what you are doing. Fill your mind with awe at the incarnation of Christ, his self-sacrificial death, his substitution for your sins, his lifeblood poured out, his body broken for you. While you breathe, pray for sanctified thinking.

Lutheran Christian Johannes Kepler, discoverer of the elliptical orbits of planets, when asked why he did science, is credited with replying that in scientific research he could "think God's thoughts after him." Thinking God's thoughts after him *is* worship. Likewise, taking every thought captive to the obedience of Christ *is* worship. Worshiping with your mind and heart wide awake to the wonder of redeeming love is the only way for a boy to grow up into a true man of God.

Thinking and the Bible

Thinking God's thoughts after him is not a vague, subjective activity. You don't need to assume the Socratic thinker posture, and sit around waiting to see what might come to mind. Nor do you need to conjure up vague sensations of what some tell you that worship should feel like.

There is only one way to have your mind renewed, your thinking sanctified, and your thought life reined in and kept in awe of God. Saturate yourself with the Word of God. Be deeply devoted to the Bible. Read it, meditate upon it, memorize it, live each moment of your life by its sacred truths. If necessary, die for it.

In short, think God's thoughts after him by reading and heeding the Bible. Young Scots preacher Robert Murray M'Cheyne, in a letter urging a young man to regularly read his Bible, suggested that readers "turn the Bible into prayer. Thus, if you were reading the 1st Psalm, spread the Bible on the chair before you, and kneel and pray, 'O Lord, give me the blessedness of the man. Let me not stand in the counsel of the ungodly.' This is the best way of knowing the meaning of the Bible, and of learning to pray."

Finally, if you want to know the truth and have your mind renewed and your thinking set free by God's Word, read with your ear to the ground for Christ the Redeemer. Read with your heart and mind burning within you for God to open the Scriptures to you. Be like the disciples on the road to Emmaus whose "eyes were opened and they recognized [Jesus]" (Luke 24:31).

Don't be foolish in your thinking and slow of heart. Look for Jesus as you read. He will open your eyes as he did theirs: "And beginning with Moses and all the Prophets, he explained to them what was said in all the Scriptures concerning himself" (Luke 24:27). Read looking for Christ, and you will find him.

"The quintessence of the Word of God," wrote C. H. Spurgeon, "is Christ. He is the constant theme of its sacred pages; from first to last they testify of him. Scripture is the royal chariot in which Jesus rides. We should always read Scripture in this light."

How will you know whether you are thinking God's thoughts after him? How will you know whether you have a renewed mind? How will you know whether your thoughts are captive to the obedience of Christ?

The sure way to know that your thinking is becoming sanctified is that worldly things will look smaller and less alluring. And then, as the things of earth grow strangely dim, wonder at Christ will fill your mind, his Word will enthrall your thoughts, his law will be your guide, and his way will be your delight.

Resolves

- To think about what I'm thinking about
- To call in and keep in awe my thoughts
- To sanctify my thinking by writing thoughts in a journal

Scripture Memory

"Do not think of yourself more highly than you ought, but rather think of yourself with sober judgment."

Romans 12:3

For Discussion

1. To prepare for thoughtful worship on Sunday, what changes in thinking and activity should a young man make on Saturday evening?
2. Discuss other examples of illogical thinking from the media and from your own words.

"Stricken, Smitten, and Afflicted"

Ye who think of sin but lightly
Nor suppose the evil great
Here may view its nature rightly,
Here its guilt may estimate.
Mark the sacrifice appointed,
See who bears the awful load;
'Tis the Word, the Lord's Anointed,
Son of Man and Son of God.

Thomas Kelly, 1804

For Further Study

Proverbs 23:7; Isaiah 55:7; Philippians 4:8; 2 Peter 3:1

3

THE WAY TO SEEK

2 Chronicles 26:1–5

Witness at Point-blank Range

Uzziah became king of Judah when he was only sixteen years old—about your age. Imagine everyone bowing and calling you "Your Majesty." Riches, the best food, clothes, houses—what a life! At first, Uzziah's heart was uncorrupted by it all. The inspired historian records that Uzziah "did what was right in the eyes of the LORD" (2 Chron. 26:4). Under the tutelage of Zechariah, he sought the Lord early and learned to fear God.

Not every young man, however, has a Zechariah to teach him the fear of the Lord, to guide him in seeking the Lord in his youth. The results can be devastating.

Cliff spent the first eighteen years of his life following his father from one motorcycle chain-gang rendezvous to the next. From his father, sergeant-at-arms of the Hell's Angels, Cliff learned to drink and do drugs, and he learned how easy it was to get what he wanted at gunpoint.

Cliff climbed the drug-dealing ranks until he eventually became a central kingpin in the western United States. One afternoon while he and his cronies divided up a shipment of cocaine worth millions on the street, a knock came at the door.

Drawing his weapon, he eased the door open a crack. There stood a young man with a grin on his face and Bible under his arm. Cliff threw the door open and grabbed the man by the throat, dragging him into the apartment.

"Who are you?" Cliff demanded, grinding the barrel of his .45-caliber into the man's temple. "What are you doing, hanging around my door?"

"I'm a Christian," gasped the young man. "I came to tell you how Christ's blood can wash you clean from all this."

Cliff was astonished. Was this a new vice-squad strategy, sending in a religious freak like this? He considered shooting the man then and there but decided that it all might be amusing.

Shoving him onto the couch, Cliff straddled a chair and trained his gun on the man's chest.

"Start talking," he ordered.

The young man did. He explained about the wages of Cliff's sinful life being death, about the mercy of God for sinners, even ones as bad as Cliff. Gaining confidence as he spoke, he opened his Bible and read, "Ye shall know the truth, and the truth shall make you free" (John 8:32 KJV).

"Shut up!" one of Cliff's dealers cut in. "Just kill him!"

Inexplicably, however, Cliff let the man go. It was the last he saw of the faithful soul-winner, but the man's words were never far from his mind. Months later, a drug deal went sour. Cliff shot and killed a man. He was arrested, tried, convicted, and sentenced to life in prison.

While in prison, Cliff met my friend Ken, a regular at the prison ministry. Ken confronted Cliff about his sin and need of Christ. Cliff retold the story of the fearless young man and his words, "Ye shall know the truth, and the truth shall make you free." Surrounded by bars and barbed wire, and confined on McNeil Island by the frigid waters of Puget Sound, Cliff found that those words meant more to him than ever. At last, he professed faith in Christ, and Ken began the long process of discipling him. Cliff had the time.

At first Cliff devoured every book Ken gave him, some of them heavy-duty theology. Cliff loved it. Like the seed in the parable of the sower, Cliff sprang up and flourished. Ken became his advocate for parole. Finally, after twenty-two years, Cliff was released. He often joked that his goal was to get back into that prison—with the gospel.

He got married, got a job, was active in giving his testimony, even preached. But all the habits of his youth were against him.

Habits and Trees

"Habits like trees," wrote J. C. Ryle, "are strengthened by age. A boy may bend an oak when it is a sapling, a hundred men cannot root it up when it is a full-grown tree. So it is with habits: the older they are the stronger they grow." And so it has proved to be for Cliff. Lies were the stock and store of his youth, and they are so entrenched in his life that no one is more deceived by his dishonesty than himself.

Why is this? "Habit is the nurse of sin," continued Ryle. "Every fresh act of sin lessens fear and remorse, hardens our hearts, blunts the edge of our conscience, and increases our evil inclination." Even unbelieving child psychologists tell us that the values formed in the earliest years of childhood profoundly shape the beliefs and practices—the habits—of adulthood.

Ask any honest Christian who grew up in unbelief. Though God in Christ graciously casts the guilt and penalty of his sin into the deepest sea, the consequences of sin are painfully real. A wise young man knows that God's grace does not sweep away the evil inclinations of his past. He will not be a fool and think that he can indulge in sin without damage. Nor will he imagine that it's God's business to forgive the sins of his youth. A wise young man expects lifelong punishment for the sins of his youth, and so seeks the Lord early and learns the fear of the Lord.

"If persons live long in sin," preached Jonathan Edwards in a sermon to young people, "though they be converted at last, yet they still have the ill habits that they contracted while they lived in sin. Those sins were so riveted onto them that grace doesn't perfectly root them out, and they will be a great disadvantage and hindrance."

The Bible and common sense are clear about the lasting and devastating consequences of youthful sinning. So why are young men so cavalier about it? It's because the deceiver is so good at deception. He's had thousands of years to practice. And he's had hosts of patsies to practice on. It's hard to argue with success: his tactics have worked so well with so many.

Deception Exposed

J. C. Ryle exposed the devil's strategy: The devil "will paint, and mask, and dress up sin, in order to make you fall in love with it. He will exalt the pleasure of wickedness, but he will keep out of sight the sting." This is what pop culture does best. Movies make fornication look so satisfying. Fashion gurus make immodesty look so enticing. Music makes recklessness seem so right; after all, "it can't be wrong if it feels so right."

And whom do the crafters of pop culture have in their crosshairs? Impressionable teenagers. As Edwards wrote, "Satan's great strife is to have the young people for his own." And today one of his chief allies in doing this is to dress up sin with the ubiquitous glitter of pop culture.

Unmasking the flip side of the deceiver's strategy, J. C. Ryle continued: "[Satan] will deform, and misrepresent, and caricature true religion, in order to make you take a dislike to it."

You sit through a sermon on holiness and the serpent hisses in your ear. "Believe all that," he seems to say, "and you'll waste away your fun years. It's too bad, really. I have so many good times in store for you. But all I have for you will never be as fun as it will be now—when you're young."

You've felt this. Being cool, in step with all that's young and fun, is so important to having a good time. Satan plays on this assumption. He desperately wants you to forget that being a Christian means not being with it, not conforming to the world, the flesh, and the devil. Being a Christian means saying no to the deceiver, and it means doing it now, when you are young.

Timing Is Everything

"Be wise in time," wrote Ryle. "What youth sows, old age must reap." But when sin rises enticingly before your eyes, you have a hard time remembering all of this. You forget the reality of sowing and reaping. Hanging out and having fun quickly descends into reckless foolishness, sin and folly that will yield a harvest of sorrow in your adult life—if you live that long.

Jonathan Edwards makes the point with sobering clarity: "The first minutes of your feeling hell's torments will make you thoroughly sensible of how vastly mistaken you were in thinking so lightly of the sins of your youth." You say that you're a Christian. But talk is cheap. Take sin lightly, and your profession notwithstanding, you may have all eternity to bemoan the sins of your youth. Too late you will see things clearly then, and you will wish that you had learned the fear of the Lord when you were young.

Timing is everything. Take a jump shot on the basketball court, for example. You plant your foot. You leap. You feel your momentum rising, and at just the right instant, as you hover at the apex of your spring, with a flick of your wrist, you release the ball and *Swish!*

So with life, timing is everything. You must learn the fear of the Lord at precisely the right time—in your youth. Wait until youth has passed, and it's off the rim, no good. The sins of your youth harden into the habits of your old age, and then you die. "Hell itself is truth known too late," wrote J. C. Ryle. A wise young man knows that timing is everything and so seeks the Lord early.

Puritan or Pleasure?

Satan is hell-bent on getting you to delay. One way is by drawing a caricature of the Christian life. He wants you to believe that you won't have any fun if you're a Christian, that fearing the Lord and walking in his ways is grindingly dull.

One way he does this is by giving you a distaste for the Puritans, the black-clad, killjoy buckle-heads of days gone by. Thanks to twentieth-century journalist and political commentator H. L. Mencken, modern man loves believing that "a Puritan is someone who is deathly afraid that someone, somewhere, is having fun."

And you want to have fun. Your mind sees the Joseph Badger painting of Puritan Jonathan Edwards: severe, joyless, a man who looks like he just swallowed a large prune, pit and all. You desperately don't want to be like that. But it's all part of Satan's lie.

Jonathan Edwards, the consummate Puritan—who in fact preferred swallowing chocolate to prunes, loved to go outside during thunderstorms, and enjoyed going for long horseback rides, and found great pleasure in the wife of his youth—argued that "if you become pious while young, it will tend to make your youth more abundantly pleasant."

Contrary to Satan's lie, youthful sinning doesn't produce pleasure. Ask any lifer serving out eternity in hell. Edwards taught that Christians should expect joy in a life lived in the fear of God. Moreover, he insisted that since God made the world and gave his law to govern it, living in the fear of God and in obedience to his Word "won't spoil the pleasure of your youth; it will increase it."

A righteous life increases pleasure? Where did Puritan Edwards get such a notion? From the Bible. Mencken and modern man's beef is not really with Puritans. It's with the Bible. The ways of wisdom and obedience to God "are pleasant ways, and all [wisdom's] paths are peace" (Prov. 3:17).

...ll for Satan's caricature of Puritans and the Christian life, a
...t C. S. Lewis considered one of the deceiver's "really solid
...e last hundred years." Know that the path of pleasure for
...ung man lies in the King's Highway—and nowhere else.

The Stakes Are High

But don't young men need to "sow their wild oats"? "Boys will
be boys," many say indulgently. Many Christian fathers are criticized
for expecting too high a standard for their sons. "I'll bet you did that
sort of thing when you were a teen," they say with a wink. "Lighten
up or you'll drive your children away." Edwards heard much the same
from indulgent parents in eighteenth-century New England. "We
must not expect gray hairs on green shoulders," they would chide their
minister.

How different this sounds from the Bible's urgent commands to
fathers and sons: "Make level paths for your feet and take only ways
that are firm" (Prov. 4:26). Why are sons throughout Proverbs urged to
heed their fathers' instruction? Why are you told, "Hold on to instruction, do not let it go; guard it well" (Prov. 4:13)? Because the stakes
are high. Heeding biblical instruction, walking in the path of God's
wisdom, is so important for young men because what's at stake is your
life.

Still, young men excuse their sin as if it had nothing to do with
the rest of their life. As Edwards observed, "Many seem to be bold in
wickedness when in their youth because they think it is excusable by
reason of their age; they seem to think youth is a proper time to be
wicked in." But he insisted that "God doesn't excuse them because they
were in their youth."

Beware of indulging this notion in your heart: "I'll turn from sin
when I am old. I'll time things so that I can have the world and salvation." Stop trifling with sin. You can't have it both ways, nor can you
turn real repentance on and off when you please. Because our hearts are
desperately wicked, the farther down the path of sin we allow ourselves

to travel, the more habitual sinning becomes, and the more difficult it becomes to discern whether repentance is genuine.

J. C. Ryle memorably put it like this: "I grant you that true repentance is never too late, but I warn you at the same time, late repentance is seldom true. I grant you, one penitent thief was converted in his last hours, that no man might despair; but I warn you, only one was converted, that no man might presume."

If you are calculating on repentance delayed until after you've had your fun, you are being presumptuous. If you are deferring seeking the Lord until you've tasted the world's counterfeit pleasures, heed the warning.

"You may be careless about your soul," wrote J. C. Ryle; "[Satan] is not." You must seek the Lord now and with all your heart because that is precisely what the devil is doing: seeking after your soul. Seek the Lord early or be sought out and devoured by the deceiver. He never misses a day of work. Neither can you. In matters of your soul, every day counts. Draw near to God now, or be sucked into the devil's clutches—perhaps forever.

Satan's Leftovers

Seek Christ early like the venerable martyr Polycarp, who in A.D. 155, moments before being stabbed and burned for refusing to worship Emperor Antoninus Pius, declared, "Eighty and six years have I served [Christ], and He never did me injury. How can I blaspheme my King and Savior?" Eighty-six years! By God's sovereign grace, Polycarp lived his entire life seeking God. Why? Because he sought the Lord at the very headwaters of his life.

Drug-dealing, murdering Cliff did not. God alone knows the true state of Cliff's soul. But all the habits of his youth were against him. He failed a court-ordered drug test. He got his wish. He went back to prison, but not as an evangelist. In disgrace and humiliation, he returned as a prisoner. His wife divorced him. His testimony of faith in Christ was besmeared by the sinful habits of his youth.

Cliff didn't have Polycarp's godly parents and their covenantal nurture, nor did he have the apostle John's instruction. He didn't have the incalculable blessing that Uzziah had of Zechariah's teaching him to fear the Lord early. Nor did Cliff have your privileges and spiritual advantages.

Remember, however, that "to whom much is given, from him much will be required" (Luke 12:48 NKJV). Don't be a fool and squander all you have been given in the vain pursuit of worldly pleasure. How foolish, as Edwards put it, "to spend all the best of life in the service of Satan, and in slavery to lust, and then to come in our old age and offer to God an old, decayed body and mind that have been almost worn out in the service of sin, so that there shall be nothing left for God but Satan's leftovers."

Do you want your life to be a feast of service to God and man, or last week's macaroni and cheese coagulating in the back of the refrigerator? Take youthful sin seriously. Don't be duped by the deceiver. Seek the Lord early.

Resolves

- To take the sins of my youth seriously
- To daily seek the Lord in the Word and prayer
- To beware of entertainments that make me satisfied with youthful sinning

Scripture Memory

"Seek the LORD while he may be found; call on him while he is near."

Isaiah 55:6

For Discussion

1. What things distract you from seeking the Lord?
2. What does it mean to fear the Lord?
3. Discuss the ways in which Satan's twofold strategy appears in your life.

"Have You Not Known, Have You Not Heard"

Mere human pow'r shall fast decay,
And youthful vigor cease;
But they who wait upon the Lord
In strength shall still increase.

Isaac Watts, 1707

For Further Study

Luke 23:39–43; 2 Timothy 2:22

4

THE WAY TO FALL

2 Chronicles 26:5, 16

Uzziah's Downfall

"As long as he sought the LORD, God gave him success," the inspired historian records of young Uzziah (2 Chron. 26:5b). And was he ever successful! A warrior king almost on a par with King David, Uzziah defeated the mighty Philistines, demolished the walls of their principal cities, and waged successful campaigns against the Arabs and the Ammonites. No other king could boast of so disciplined an army and of such deadly war machines—catapults and mechanized equipment for firing arrows. For his army and weaponry, even for advances in farming, Uzziah was the envy of other ancient kings.

But something was not right: "As long as he sought the LORD . . . ." With those words in verse 5, the chronicler hints that Uzziah is not going to stand fast. This young king had humbly sought help from the Lord and "was greatly helped." But here's the rub: "after

Uzziah became powerful, his pride led to his downfall" (2 Chron. 26:15b–16a).

So it will be with you if you do not persevere in seeking after God. On the heels of urging you to seek the Lord early, I wonder if some young men jump to the conclusion that seeking the Lord is a youthful activity, that if you do enough of it in your youth, you can live off the interest in your adult life. No way. Seeking the Lord is a continuum. It is daily rising up and calling him blessed. It is hourly vigilance over besetting sin. It is daily diligence in the Word and prayer. It is humble worship, seeking the Lord in his house on the Sabbath day. Genuine seeking is always in the present perfect tense—continuing, pressing on, straining every spiritual muscle after Christ—all things that Uzziah stopped doing.

Continue doing these things and you will have success. God does not make idle promises. You will succeed in mortifying sin, in effectual prayer, in heartfelt worship, in humble service, and at the last you will have the celestial success of Satan conquered and heaven won. Forget riches and fame—there's no greater success.

But many men—young and old—are brought low, like Uzziah, because when they gain a measure of success they become proud; they fail to give God credit for his work in them, his gifts given to them, his successes.

Sports and Pride

Moments before the 500-meter U.S. sprint kayak nationals final, I asked one of my sons what his race strategy was. "I win, they lose," he said with a grin. He's a big Ronald Reagan fan and likes quoting Reagan's Cold War strategy. Two days earlier he'd lost the 1,000-meter sprint to a Hungarian-born paddler by 48/100ths of a second and was absolutely determined not to cut things so close again. He did win the 500, and by a bigger margin. Winning is great—but then the monster pride has a chance to rear his ugly head.

Competitive sports, young men, and pride are a union forged in hell. If you are an athlete—or the father of one—you must particularly beware of pride. Why? Because, as C. S. Lewis put it:

> Pride is essentially competitive—is competitive by its very nature. Pride gets no pleasure out of having something, only out of having more of it than the next man. We say that people are proud of being rich, or clever, or good-looking, but they are not. They are proud of being richer, or cleverer, or better-looking than others. It is the comparison that makes you proud: the pleasure of being above the rest. It is Pride—the wish to be richer than some other rich man, and (still more) the wish for power. For, of course, power is what Pride really enjoys.

Most young men love competition. Men thrive on it. And we love power. We love being strong and being in control of people and situations. Many great things have been accomplished by powerful men straining to be the best. Consider General Bradley's quip as George Patton led the Third Army in victory after victory, ever deeper into German-held territory, in World War II: "Give George another headline and he'll be good for another thirty miles." It's embarrassing, but we're inclined to do more if we're getting lots of credit for doing it. Feed our pride, and we'll conquer the world.

Unlike war, where pride might motivate a young man to do great deeds that benefit others, in sports young men are easily consumed with shameless self-interest. Listen to the boasting of professional athletes. Watch the swagger of the varsity basketball jock. See the jutted chin and hauteur of the All-American quarterback. Gaze in disgust at the unabashed self-conceit of the running back as he struts and preens in the end zone. Listen to your teammates. Hear your own words. Look into your own heart. If you are a competitive athlete, beware of pride.

"If sports are supposed to build character," wrote Brad Wolverton in the *Chronicle of Higher Education*, "recent evidence suggests that college athletics is falling down on the job." He cites a study of the moral reasoning of seventy thousand college students conducted over two decades. The result? "Athletes have significantly lower moral-reasoning skills than the general student population." Moral reasoning—what the ancients called virtue—leads you to use your strength and skill in the interest of others. Competitive sports can flip things around. So impressed with your own athletic prowess, you sneer in disdain at others. Gradually, you begin to think of yourself as a worthy object of the most devout—and disgusting—self-worship.

Once you're on your knees before yourself, the absurdity of it all never occurs to you. How ridiculous for you to be puffed up over strengths and skills that God gave you! But seeing your pride for what it is requires a changed heart.

Only a grateful heart will keep the nonsense of your pride in check. Just when you're swelling up at your victory, offer thanksgiving that God gave you a healthy body, that he gave you the opportunity to develop your skill and, if you're really good at it, the particular talent that sets your performance above the pack. Remind yourself that this is God's doing.

Then brace yourself like a man. The devil slithers near. "Yes, but you've worked hard—harder than the rest," he hisses in your ear. "You're first on the water and last off every workout." Stop your ears. The devil woos with "honest trifles." Believe him and, as Shakespeare put it, he will "betray you in deepest consequence."

Insanity from Hell

C. S. Lewis has little good to say about pride. "It comes direct from Hell," he wrote. "Pride is spiritual cancer; it eats up the very possibility of love, or contentment, or even common sense." He's just getting warmed up. "The essential vice, the utmost evil, is Pride. There is no fault which makes a man more unpopular, and no fault which we are more unconscious of in ourselves." He argues that all other sins "are mere fleabites in comparison: it was through Pride that the devil became the devil: Pride leads to every other vice; it is the complete anti-God state of mind."

51

In one of the Bible's classic passages on pride, the prophet Daniel records the history of how pride ate up the common sense of another great king of the ancient world. Nebuchadnezzar designed and built the magnificent hanging gardens of Babylon, one of the seven wonders of the world. It was a splendid sight, and Nebuchadnezzar was intensely proud of it. Like Uzziah, Nebuchadnezzar grew so proud that he gave himself credit for the splendor of his entire empire. Seizing glory that belonged to God, and setting himself up as God, he personified pride, "the complete anti-God state of mind." For this, Nebuchadnezzar became a madman, more like a wolf than a human.

With a just God, the punishment always fits the crime. No punishment could have been more fitting for this proud man. Pride dehumanizes a man. You are most human when you are closest to God, when you acknowledge his ways, when you bow before his sovereignty, when you say that God does what he pleases, that his kingdom is an eternal kingdom, when you say, "Heaven rules!" But pride makes you see things upside down and inside out. Pride, like insanity, grossly distorts reality.

Nebuchadnezzar's self-conceit made him believe the utter nonsense that he had made himself, his strength, his intellect, his very life. Believing the ridiculous notion that you have accomplished anything by your own mighty power, for "the glory of [your own] majesty," is nothing short of insanity.

Thus, God punished Nebuchadnezzar by letting the full impact of his pride come down on his head. Chained to a stump, eating grass like a beast, Nebuchadnezzar finally learned that "those who walk in pride [God] is able to humble" (Dan. 4:37). Finally, he learned that "Heaven rules" (4:26).

Nebuchadnezzar's son Belshazzar, however, didn't get this. Fathers train sons, alas, more persuasively by our vices than by our virtues. Son Belshazzar lost his entire kingdom to the Medes and the Persians—and his very life—because he "set [him]self up against the Lord of heaven," and because he "did not honor the God who holds in his hand [his] life and all [his] ways" (Dan. 5:23).

Walk in pride, and you lose your common sense. Persist in pr and you become a madman. Press on in pride, and you end up wher pride began: hell. God resists the proud. He gives grace to the humble. Walk in humility—or prepare to eat grass.

Know It All

Anglican bishop J. C. Ryle called pride "the oldest sin in the world. Satan and his angels fell by pride. Thus pride stocked hell with its first inhabitants." Ryle warns that, next only to Satan and his angels, "pride never reigns anywhere so powerfully as in the heart of a young man," and it puts young men in particularly dangerous positions. "Pride makes us rest satisfied with ourselves, thinking we are good enough as we are." And when you think you are good enough as you are, you are in deep weeds. You fail to be teachable. Why bother learning when you're smug and satisfied with yourself?

Lewis in the opening letter of *The Screwtape Letters* gives demonic lesson one in tempting a young man into hell: "Best of all, give him the grand general idea that he knows it all." This is an easy sell for him. It's a strategy that has worked exceptionally well for the devil over the millennia, and it continues to work on your soul. But it's a temptation entirely dependent on your pride. We love believing this lie.

Similarly, Ryle argues that pride "closes our ears against all advice." How many times have you resented your father's advice this week? You feel as though you already know what's best for you, so why listen to his advice? I remember feeling this resentment at the words of my own father. You've got to get over this, and Ryle offers particularly valuable advice to curb this foolish expression of your pride; don't close your ears to it:

> Do not be too confident in your own judgment. Cease to be sure that you are always right, and others always wrong. Be distrustful of your own opinion when you find it contrary to that of older men than yourself, and especially to that of your own parents. Age gives experience and therefore deserves respect. Never be ashamed of being a learner. The wisest men would tell

always learners, and are humbled to find after all how little
ow.

atched and listened to a twenty-two-year-old fool
n a man of fifty at a regatta where everyone was sup-
pºsed to be having fun. It was shameful. But you would never do that.
Not out loud, maybe. But how often have you responded to advice
with internalized smart-mouthed, know-it-all comments? True, it's
better manners not to speak disrespectfully, but the pride is still there
deeply rooted in your heart. Being a Christian man is about rooting it
out.

Pride and Gunpowder

"To be proud," continued Ryle, "is to be more like the devil and
fallen Adam, than like Christ." But you're called to be like Christ, who
was born in a barn, became friends with sinners and sick people, washed
his disciples' feet, and was despised and rejected by the big shots of his
day, finally submitting to the most ignominious suffering and death
for our salvation. If anyone had a right to be proud, it was the second
member of the eternal Godhead—but Christ was not proud.

Neither was his follower John Newton. When Newton took up
his ministerial duties and moved into the Old Vicarage in Olney, in
1764, he rearranged his garret study. Instead of looking out on the
lovely river valley and the fourteenth-century Gothic church, he looked
on the rows of tenement houses where the needy of his parish lived and
worked. Soon the upper crust in Olney resented Newton: he was too
busy with the poor to attend them when they held court at their fine
dinners and balls. They despised a minister who refused to fawn on
them like Jane Austen's ministerial caricature Mr. Collins, who made
himself a laughingstock by constant gushing over his venerable patron-
ess, Lady Catherine de Bourgh.

In Newton's day, the ministry was a way to schmooze with the
rich and famous. Newton never did so, but he knew many ministers

who did, and gave this advice to a young pastor: "It is easy for me to advise you to be humble, but while human nature remains in its present state, there will be almost the same connection between popularity and pride, as between fire and gunpowder: they cannot meet without an explosion, at least not unless the gunpowder is kept very damp."

How do you keep your pride damp? By having the same mind as Jesus. He came "not to be served, but to serve, and to give his life as a ransom for many" (Matt. 20:28). Be honest about your powers. Christ's are infinite and original; yours are derived and pathetically finite. He is God; you are not. Yet Christ was humble, and he calls you—who have no right to be proud—to humbly follow in his steps.

Be Little

Irrational as it is, many Christian young men swagger on in their pride. They speak condescendingly to parents and teachers. They are rude. They are so "wise in [their] own eyes" (Prov. 26:12) that they strut as if they knew it all.

But maybe you are bright, gifted, talented, strong, and highly capable. Compared with the rest of teenage young men on the planet, most of you are highly privileged. Some of you believe it when your grandparents gush at how gifted you are. Maybe you really are gifted. So how do you avoid pride?

Listen to humble, gifted tinker John Bunyan in *Grace Abounding to the Chief of Sinners* as he addresses the gifted young man's sin: "Gifts being alone [are] dangerous because of the evils that attend those that have them—pride, desire for vainglory, self-conceit." He warns that if a young man rests in his gifts and not in the grace of God, he will "fall short of the grace of God." A wise young man "has cause also to walk humbly with God and be little in his own eyes, and to remember that his gifts are not his own, but the church's, and that by them he is made a servant to the church." There's that word again—*servant*.

Avoid pride by humbly using your gifts, great or small, to serve others in Christ's name. And for the rest of us who may not be so gifted, Bunyan memorably concludes, "Great grace and small gifts are better than great gifts and no grace."

Talented, gifted as you are, you are not nearly as great as the devil wants you to believe. The devil loves pride because pride makes you an idol worshiper—with you as idol. He'll do anything to keep you from worshiping the living God, giver of all gifts.

Swollen with pride at his success, Uzziah forgot all this. "His pride led to his downfall" (2 Chron. 26:16). Not content merely to be king, Uzziah usurped the priestly role, was struck with leprosy, and was "excluded from the temple of the LORD" (26:21). Young men, walk humbly with your God. Gratefully appreciate your gifts and the gifts of others as the true gifts of God that they are. Then humbly "serve the LORD with gladness" (Ps. 100:2a NKJV).

Resolves

- To pray regularly together as father and son
- To humbly express gratitude to God and others for my privileges and gifts
- To use my gifts and strength to serve others

Scripture Memory

"Do not think of yourself more highly than you ought, but rather think of yourself with sober judgment."

Romans 12:3

For Discussion

1. What is the difference between pride and boasting?
2. Is it possible to overcome boasting and still be proud?
3. In what ways does pride create trouble in your relationship with your father?

"O for a Closer Walk with God"

The dearest idol I have known,
Whate'er that idol be,
Help me to tear it from Thy throne,
And worship only Thee.

William Cowper, 1779

For Further Study

Proverbs 26:12; 1 Corinthians 8:2; Colossians 3:12; 1 Peter 5:5

5

THE WAY TO SELF-DESTRUCTION

1 Peter 2:1–10

Lonnie Arnold is one of those men who walk into a room and everybody sits up; he begins speaking and they sit up even straighter. Lonnie is a cop; he keeps bad guys at bay in a tough inner-city neighborhood, probably why he was a featured officer on the television series Cops. *Some might mistakenly conclude that kids sit up and listen when Lonnie enters the room because he is tall, has a booming voice, and packs a no-nonsense Glock .40 at the hip, but I don't think so. Lonnie, a PCA ruling elder and gifted teacher, knows what young men are thinking; he's seen it all; he knows the street; he knows the temptations and pitfalls of youth better than most. What's more, Lonnie has a wonderful wife and seven really happy children. So when Lonnie starts talking, men listen.*

Shotgun Despair

Steering my patrol car back toward the precinct, I tensed as emergency-call tones suddenly broke the silence on my police radio. The dispatcher said, "I need units to respond to a man with a gun."

Instantly I began a mental conversation with myself. *What kind of man with a gun? Did he just rob someone? A gang conflict? Family fight?* "*Man with a gun,*" I mused. Law-enforcement officers learn that any call can be lethal, but all the more so when a bad guy is known to be wielding a firearm. I needed hard facts.

Accelerating my patrol car toward the call, my mind raced down a path of bad memories. *Ron, a fellow officer, had been killed in the line of duty a year ago, shot with his own gun while struggling with a suspect. Another officer in my department had been killed only weeks ago. Bullets kill the good guys, too. In the United States, dozens of officers are killed every year—and the count keeps going up.* "Man with a gun." I had to have more facts.

The dispatcher's voice broke in again. "The suspect is a white male in his late teens, about 5'7", brown hair. He ran his friends out of the apartment, closed himself inside. Says he has a gun to his own head. His friends said they couldn't reason with him."

"Copy," I replied. I took a deep breath and switched on my lights and siren. "Lord, keep us safe," I prayed as I steered my squad car onto the street.

As I sped toward the apartment complex, my heart beat faster as adrenaline raced through my veins. I reminded myself: *This is how officers get killed. Get ready. Keep safe. No unnecessary risks. Cover the man next to me. Keep something between myself and the suspect—something that can stop bullets.*

I radioed the three other units responding to the call. "John 3, take the north side of the apartment. John 4, take the east side with me, and John 5, take the west side."

As we arrived, we turned off our emergency lights and parked out of sight. If the suspect changed his mind and started shooting at us, I didn't want to give him an easy target. Drawing my Glock .40-caliber handgun, I got out of my squad car. Crouching low, I took up a position behind a large dumpster from which I had a clear line of sight to the apartment. For several seconds I waited. There was no sign of life, and the windows and door were closed.

"Where are the friends?" I heard John 3 ask the dispatcher in a measured whisper. "Maybe they can tell us what's going on."

The friends were at the far side of the parking lot—two white females and another white male. Staying low in the shadows, I saw John 3 move toward them. Moments later, he gave us an update on the radio.

"The suspect's name is David. His friends came over to cheer him up. They say he's had a rough time lately. He was worse than usual this time. While they were talking, he left the room and returned wielding a shotgun. Then he crammed a round into the chamber and started yelling. He told them to get out if they didn't want to see him blow his head off. They said he looked like he'd really do it this time, so they ran out."

I radioed the dispatcher. "Telephone inside and see if you can get him to come to the door—without the shotgun." A few minutes went by—probably a good sign. Maybe the dispatcher was talking some sense into the guy.

"He's coming to the door," the dispatcher announced over the radio.

"The gun?" I called back.

"I'm not sure if he's put down the gun," came the reply.

A moment later the door slowly began to open. I eased off the safety and leveled my gun at the doorway.

Don't you do the suicide-by-cop routine, I thought. Suicide by cop happens when a suspect loses the nerve to pull the trigger on himself, so he brandishes his weapon at the police and forces us to do it for him. *Turn that shotgun toward me, or any of my men—I shoot.*

As David opened the door, he held the shotgun at his side. For the moment, the business end was toward the floor.

"David, this is the police," I called. "I know you're going through difficult times. We want to help. But you have to put the gun down first."

He looked down at the gun. *Don't do it,* I thought. Next he squinted into the darkness—in my direction. "Just set the gun down," I said in as soothing a tone as I could muster.

After one last look at it, David bent over and laid the gun down in the doorway.

"That's right," I said. "Now step slowly toward my voice."

His shoulders drooped as he shuffled closer, and his face was strained with emotion. When he got to us, we patted him down to ensure that he had no other weapons and put him in the back of my car.

"I Was Afraid"

Relieved, I sat down in the front seat of my car and took a deep breath. I turned around and looked at David, noticing that he was well dressed and looked healthy and intelligent. "Why didn't you pull the trigger and shoot yourself?" I asked.

"I was afraid," he said.

"What's going to keep you from pulling it next time?"

He sat quietly for a moment, as if he were searching his mind for an answer, and then said in a whisper, "I don't know."

"You need something to live for—a purpose bigger than yourself. Everyone goes through hard times, but you need to understand the purpose of your life so that you don't give up when it gets tough. David, God can help you deal with the difficulties of life."

He eyed me in the dim light.

"I wasn't even scheduled to work tonight," I continued, "but it seems as if God wanted you and me to have a talk. Did you go to church when you were growing up?"

"Yes, my family went to church regularly."

I smiled and said, "So you're a prodigal son."

He looked up quickly. "How'd you know?"

"You're one of many," I said. "But bad as things may be, there's hope. You need to start by going back home—to the Lord. He will receive you with the love of a father. He'll help you become the man you are called to be. Then start attending a good church, and ask the Lord to show you the purpose of your life. Will you think about doing that?"

He said, "Yes, I will."

I learned more of his story as we talked. Too soon David was taken to the hospital. Siren shrieking and emergency lights flashing, an ambulance hastened David into the night. Meanwhile, I prayed that God would use this event in his life to draw him back to Christ.

Where David Went Astray

Life had become difficult for David, so difficult that he was ready to end it all. The only solution to his problems seemed to be suicide. Lots of kids in America come to the same conclusion; suicide is the third leading cause of death among young people. What's more, seven times more young men attempt to solve their problems by suicide than young women.

Enticed by his own sinful desires and by the world, David took what he thought were only small steps away from God and his ways and toward the world and all it promised him. First, he started admiring the freedom of his friends. According to him, "their parents didn't have so many rules or guidelines to follow." He used this difference as a reason to justify his ingratitude and bitterness toward his parents. He resented their rules and questioned their love, focusing instead on "his rights." That attitude led to open disobedience. Instead of obeying his parents and esteeming their godly wisdom, David often found ways to break the rules. He stopped applying himself in school. He went to church only occasionally. He started dating a non-Christian girl, and he took up drinking—lots of drinking.

Sin enticed David with the false promise of carefree fun, only to lead him from one disappointment to another. Soon he discovered that he couldn't get a good job because he didn't have any skills. His girlfriend dumped him for another guy. His drinking depressed him,

but it was a distraction he couldn't seem to do witho
all, his mind was so clouded with sin that his memo
ing love for his children had been smothered by
his sinning.

David is not unique. Can you see sin's ability to deceive
you down the wrong path? I'm sure that David didn't plan for his li.
to come to this, but it did. How did a young man from a Christian
home eventually find himself in the back of a police car? One thing is
certain: it didn't happen all at once. By his own admission, it resulted
from small sins, minor transgressions, petty concessions to worldliness.
And it could happen to you.

Although David had attended church for years and received sound
biblical teaching from the Word of God, he forgot what God promised
him in Christ. He forgot who he was and the life of faith he was called
to live.

On a Path of Self-Destruction

In today's Scripture reading, the apostle Peter reminds us that
every Christian is a spiritual rags-to-riches story. Each story, including
yours, begins in darkness because we are sinful by nature and born with
our backs turned against God. Left in this condition, we are self-centered, self-indulgent, self-important, and on a path of self-destruction.
Our natural love for our own pleasure disregards the commandments
of God. We dismiss any obligation to honor him. We blow off any
threat of judgment, as if ignoring it or denying it will make it go away.
We don't take God seriously. Many foolish men have lightly said, "So
what if I go to hell; at least I'll be there with all my friends."

Young man, understand this: there is no greater danger than being
in spiritual darkness. And here is what ought to make you tremble. No
man can free himself from it. The darkness he loves blinds his mind
to the truth, so that even when truth is right in front of him, he can't
grasp it. This same darkness enslaves the affections and will to do evil,

instead of repenting, a man will cling to the sin that is dragging him toward eternal punishment. These are the rags.

Peter goes on to describe how God, of his own initiative, chose to lift us out of our dark rebellion and bring us into the marvelous light of salvation. In his great mercy, he stripped away our spiritual blindness, revealing the wickedness of our sin and the loveliness of Jesus, the Savior of sinners. In his compassionate mercy, God cast our sin into his vast ocean of forgiveness, not treating us according to our sins. In his unfailing mercy, He changed our love for darkness into a love for his light. In his abundant mercy, he transformed us from spiritual nobodies into his own precious possessions. In his enduring mercy, he hears our prayers, sympathetically helps us in our weakness, and assures us that he will never leave or forsake us. In his immeasurable mercy, God has elevated us to be his royal priests and holy nation to declare the goodness of the Giver of eternal life. These are the riches.

Strain toward What Is Ahead

Scripture is filled with stories of men transformed by the mercy of God. And it sets them before us as examples to be followed. These men defied the world, subdued the flesh, and resisted the devil for the sake of Christ. The world tried to call them back to their old life of spiritual rags, but they would not return to it. The riches of God's mercy and the gift of being the people of God were too valuable to cast aside.

Therefore, Moses "refused to be known as the son of Pharaoh's daughter. He chose to be mistreated along with the people of God rather than to enjoy the pleasures of sin for a short time. He regarded disgrace for the sake of Christ as of greater value than the treasures of Egypt" (Heb. 11:24–26).

Similarly, the apostle Paul wrote, "But whatever was to my profit I now consider loss for the sake of Christ. What is more, I consider everything a loss compared to the surpassing greatness of knowing Christ Jesus my Lord, for whose sake I have lost all things" (Phil. 3:7–8). He went on to say, "But one thing I do: Forgetting what is behind and straining toward what is ahead, I press on toward the goal to win the prize for which God has called me heavenward in Christ Jesus" (3:13b–14).

No doubt Moses and Paul struggled with temptation, but they would not go back to the sinful life from which they had been delivered. Because God had given far more than they had given up, these men pressed and strained forward in the Christian life. And so must you.

Learn from David's fall, and count the mercy of God more valuable than the glitter of the world. Press toward heaven and strain toward the prize. And when the world tries to call you back to a life of sin, say to yourself, "Rags are not worthy of my time, for I am a child of God."

Resolves

- To put off things, people, or circumstances that entice me to sin
- To fill my time with edifying activities and people who will help me love Christ and not the world
- To meet with my youth pastor or an elder in my church and make myself accountable to him

Scripture Memory

"For the grace of God that brings salvation has appeared to all men. It teaches us to say 'No' to ungodliness and worldly passions, and to live self-controlled, upright and godly lives in this present age."

Titus 2:11–12

For Discussion

1. Discuss how David's thinking grew into sinful behavior. What caused him to develop a sinful attitude toward his parents? How did he view his parents? What type of rebellious behavior was the result of his attitude?

2. Discuss the deceitfulness of sin. What was David originally enticed by? How did he expect his life to improve? Did sin deliver what David expected?

3. What kinds of things entice you to sin? What false promises are you are tempted to believe? Pick a sin and figure out consequences that are likely to result from your disobedience.

"Sun of My Soul, Thou Savior Dear"

If some poor wand'ring child of thine
Have spurned today the voice divine,
Now, Lord, the gracious work begin;
Let him no more lie down in sin.

John Keble, 1820

For Further Study

1 Corinthians 10:13; Hebrews 4:14–16; James 1:13–15

YOUNG MEN: THEIR IDOLS

6

RUNNING THE WRONG RACE

1 Corinthians 9:24–27; 1 Timothy 4:7–8

Super Bowl Sunday

Someone once observed, "Men worship their work, work at their play, and play at their worship." Not only is this progression of flip-flopping nouns to verbs syntactically clever, one need only observe the average male, young or old, to see how profoundly true this observation is.

Men get their priorities turned around all the time, and most of the motivation behind the reversal is play. We are selfish, and we love to play. Men worship what they love, and we love sports and games so much that we make idols out of our games. Men almost constantly give themselves—body and soul—to the wrong things.

I recently heard a humorous story about the Super Bowl that underscores the importance of maintaining right priorities. After one football fan had found his seat in the sold-out stadium, he looked in astonishment at the empty seat by the man next to him. The game started, but nobody came to take the seat. At last the fellow said to the stranger next to him: "I can't believe that seat didn't sell!"

"It did," replied the man, his eyes riveted on the field. "It was for my wife."

"So where is she?" asked the man.

"She died."

"Oh, I'm sorry," said the man awkwardly. "Still, I can't understand why one of your friends or family didn't want the seat."

"Me either. But they all insisted on going to the funeral."

What a brute. What kind of guy cares more about football and the Super Bowl than about grieving for his lost wife? A man who does this sort of thing, no doubt, rationalizes his behavior on the grounds of frugality and stewardship. After all, cheap seats the week of the Super Bowl sell for just shy of three thousand dollars a pop, with most seats selling for seven to eight thousand dollars each. Respect for the dead notwithstanding, it wouldn't be prudent to waste that kind of cash, now, would it?

Is there something wrong here?

What's more, Super Bowl worship happens to take place on Sunday when real Christian men will be worshiping God in church. On the lowest church-attendance Sunday of the year, many churches capitulate to the cult of sports and entertainment by modifying or canceling services; some pastors wear their favorite football jersey in the pulpit. It's only once a year, some say, a concession that leads many men permanently out of the pew and into the bleachers—or the more sinister posture of slouching on the couch with a six-pack, bloodshot eyes glued to the television.

Sports and Worship

I've heard grown men wrench Paul's sports metaphor out of shape and hastily conclude that there's no danger from sports. Which only serves to prove my point: males are desperate to flip priorities around so that they can play and have their fun. Yet no one who actually reads one of Paul's sports-analogy passages can honestly maintain this stance. Remember, Paul is writing to Greek Corinthians, who loved their sports and games, and he capitalizes on their priorities, on what they worshiped: the games. I wonder what Paul would home in on for us.

Worshiping and sports is no new thing. One morning in August, I strolled through rows of ancient pillars once part of the Temple of Zeus at the original site of the Olympic Games in Greece. My imagination went to work as I gazed on the ancient athletics fields laid out around that temple. I imagined the press of bodies and muscle, the lithe young men stretching, their eyes on the prize, and then the instant of silence as the athletes crouched to their mark, and the heart-pounding excitement as they were off, every muscle straining toward the goal, their sweaty bodies glistening in the Ionian sunlight—and with a final lunge, the victor crossing the finish line, the cries of triumph, the priest of Zeus placing the laurel crown on the brow of the single victorious athlete.

Strict Training

Paul may have seen Greek athletes training for the games; as a male, he may have found it thrilling in a way. But make no mistake here. Paul is not giving an argument for (or against) athletics. He is in earnest about your soul. "Do you not know that in a race all the runners run, but only one gets the prize? Run in such a way as to get the prize" (1 Cor. 9:24). He's appealing to your love of athletic competition, of being the best. In a race there are lots of runners, but all of them lose except one. Tradition has it that Koroibos, a cook from a small town near Olympia, won the first Olympics running race in 776 B.C. In the only race that matters, Paul says, be like Koroibos.

But how does one runner leave the others behind and break the tape? Strict training. My two oldest sons are six-time national-champion sprint kayak racers; they've been on the podium many times in national competitions. How did they get there? Prodigious quantities of food, and strict training. In winter, they paddle in frigid temperatures, in driving snow and rain; they paddle when it's so cold that the chase boat has to break ice ahead of them in the harbor. Winning takes strict training, self-control, determination—beating their bodies and making them their slaves.

But Paul is not talking about sprint kayaking any more than he is talking about running. "[Athletes] do it to get a crown that will not last; but we do it to get a crown that will last forever" (1 Cor. 9:25b). And if strict training is required to win a temporal crown, how much more so to win an eternal crown at the end of the race. There are priorities here: "I beat my body and make it my slave," Paul says, "to get a crown that will last forever" (9:27, 25). No race comes close in importance to winning this crown.

To be a Christian man who wins the race, you must enter into strict spiritual training. You must bring your body under the control of the Spirit of God. You must not be mastered by your body and its fleshly desires. You must beat it and make it your slave, bringing every spiritual muscle under the discipline of holiness. There's no room for passive holiness in this race, no room to "let go and let God." There's nothing passive about Paul's language.

Self-Control

But there is a wrong way to train. "I do not run like a man running aimlessly; I do not fight like a man beating the air" (1 Cor. 9:26). The athlete who approaches his training "aimlessly," striving away at nothing, wins nothing. All the more true in the self-discipline of your life of faith. The guy who beats at the air, who trains without direction, is lacking in self-control. Sprinter Michael Johnson, five-time Olympic gold medalist, one of the fastest men on earth, said, "The first thing an athlete has to realize is that you are always in control. And you need to maintain that control."

Better runner than theologian, still, Johnson gets near the point. God controls all things, and as his son and image-bearer, you are called to control many things, especially your body. The first time my boys attempted to paddle an Olympic-class sprint kayak, they flipped over in a matter of seconds. These sleek, twenty-six-pound, carbon-fiber torpedoes are extremely fast—when you finally learn to control them. Till then, they're only fast at dumping you into the water.

If self-control is essential to success in sports, it is all the more so in life. But most men leave their self-control on the playing field and are ninety-eight-pound neophytes when it comes to spiritual and moral self-control. The game's the thing, and life sort of aimlessly happens.

A Game—or Life?

Paul clarifies the problem of sports and life priorities for men in 1 Timothy 4:7–8: "Train yourself to be godly. For physical training is of some value, but godliness has value for all things, holding promise for both the present life and the life to come."

There it is: athletics has some value. But the key word is *some*. Paul's point is that a young man ought to be consumed—not with sports, but with training himself "to be godly." Why? Because godliness is far more important than sports; eternity is far more important than now.

My sons have entered strict training in hopes of going to the Olympics one day. They love it and work hard at it. But all their physical training is worth nothing if they are not disciplining themselves for the purpose of godliness. If sports stops being a game and becomes life for them, what should have "some value" instead becomes an idol and loses all value. I do not want my sons to switch their priorities and become idolaters.

I know an athletics coach who grew up in a Christian home but has switched religions. He now worships the games; he eats, drinks, and sleeps athletics. He has entered into strict discipline, but it holds no promise for the future. If he continues the race as he is now, his prize will not be "a crown that will last forever" (1 Cor. 9:25). No one is exempt. Nothing is easier for young men than to get priorities turned completely around.

My sons' coach told the story of a young man whose father thought sprint kayak racing was a waste of time and ordered his son to quit. His son weighed things out and made his choice. He rejected his father's advice, left home, and pursued racing and the Olympics. His father disowned him. The story was supposed to be an illustration of the level of dedication required to excel—an example of someone who had his priorities straight. In fact, it tragically demonstrates someone pursuing "a crown that will not last" (1 Cor. 9:25). If you're serious about the only race that matters on the judgment day, be extremely cautious about which crown you strain after.

Games for the Fat and Lazy

Our high-tech age has developed new and improved ways for men to get their priorities convoluted. Paul wrote that physical exercise is of "some value," but I wonder whether he would find any value whatsoever in virtual game-playing on the video screen.

According to a Michigan State University survey, boys spend twice as much time playing video games as girls: twenty-three hours a week glued to the computer monitor playing virtual games, and about the same in front of the television. Some think that's okay. I wonder.

I fear that easy-thrills video games may lead to the death of manhood. An entire generation of males, no longer capable of being men, are being enervated by addiction to virtual adventure, virtual exploits, exhilaration created by high-tech special effects flashing madly on the screen before them. Young men intoxicated with artificial sports are in a bad way. For them, there just isn't time or interest left for living life to the hilt.

Life for many young men has become the video game, a life that's easy, without demand, without relationship, with instant gratification transmitted through the thumbs. Studies have found a direct link between "the obesity epidemic among American youth" and adolescent addiction to video games. When young men exercise only their thumbs, they get fat, lazy, and sedentary, unfit to rise up and be real men.

Game Junkies

Young men are hooked, and the creators and retailers of video games are ecstatic. Video games are a multibillion-dollar annual industry in America, with designers developing games for children as young as two years old. Hook you early and they've got you for life, maybe for eternity. Most agree that addiction to these games damages a young man's brain development, but worse still, it may be damaging his conscience.

A study conducted by the National Institute on Media and the Family found "groundbreaking discoveries in brain science" strongly suggesting that during brain growth spurts, "teenagers are wiring the circuits for self control, responsibility and relationships that they will carry with them into adulthood. The latest brain research shows that violent [video] games activate the anger center of the teenage brain while dampening the brain's 'conscience.' " The study concludes that the worst effect of many video games "is the culture of disrespect they create."

One elated reviewer described a popular video game as "a game with everything but morals." Many video games celebrate gang culture, or brutality, or crudity, or make violence toward women seem normal. Ninety-eight percent of pediatricians surveyed believe that entertainment violence experienced in video games harms a child's development. Nevertheless, many Christian young men are nothing short of addicts, and their manhood will be shipwrecked as a result.

But a young man serious about winning the prize, about gaining a crown that lasts forever, will have nothing but contempt for habits that weaken his self-control and sense of responsibility, and that damage his mind and his moral conscience.

Young men need special restraints to avoid slavery to technological fighting, shooting, car-theft, fantasy role-playing, and action-adventure games. These games were designed to place a large ring in your nose and lead you, unresisting, back to the computer-game trough, hour after hour, day after day—a lifetime wasted away, heart pumping with artificially induced excitement as you blow away the latest cyber bad guys.

But it's everyone else who's addicted, not you, right? Don't kid yourself. At the birthday party of one of my sons, one young man could not stop talking about video games and his latest cyber exploits. When he finally paused for breath, I suggested that he resolve to spend less time playing and thinking and talking about these games. "Like, I don't really play 'em very much," he replied. "Like, I don't play as much as my older brother. He plays the coolest game, and the other day, it was like, he racked up so many points . . . ." Back again to the lodestone. Addiction is like that. You're always sure it's the other guy who suffers with it.

Run the Real Race

God didn't make young men for an artificial race. He made you for strict training for the race of life, to win the prize of the upward call of God through Christ Jesus. He didn't make you to waste twenty-three hours, or even three hours, a week playing a mind-numbing video game. And you know it. Become a video-game junkie, waste your wonder juices on what is fake, and the transcendent thrills will no longer look real, will no longer thrill. Give your wonder to the wrong race, and you will have no wonder left for the things of God and eternity, no enthusiasm for doing right in a world that has gone desperately wrong, no energy to develop your mind and body for excellence and service, no trembling excitement for the worship of Jesus Christ.

Stop in your tracks. Stop working at your play; stop worshiping your play. Make a clean break. Go into "strict training." Start to live again. Begin by taking a baseball bat to your video games—to your computer, if you must. Cut off the right arm of video games; gouge out the right eye of those cheap thrills. Do it now. Make no mistake. It may be the difference between a pathetic existence and a life that's full and rich, between a crown that doesn't last and one that lasts forever.

Real men run the real race and win the real crown.

Resolves

- To put my greatest energy into things that last forever
- To keep my love of sports and play under control
- To think of my life as a race and heaven and eternal life the finish line

Scripture Memory

"I press on to take hold of that for which Christ Jesus took hold of me."

Philippians 3:12b

For Discussion

1. Why do you think men are prone to confuse their priorities when it comes to sports and games?
2. What role does pride play in your priorities?
3. What did Paul mean in 1 Corinthians 9:27 when he wrote, "so that . . . I myself will not be disqualified for the prize"?
4. What is at stake in the race of life? Why is it so important that you keep your priorities in order, that you run the right race?

"Fight the Good Fight"

Run the straight race through God's good grace,
Lift up thine eyes, and seek his face;
Life with its way before us lies,
Christ is the path, and Christ the prize.

John S. B. Monsell, 1863

For Further Study

Proverbs 6:6–11; Philippians 3:12–4:1

7

CLIMBING THE WRONG MOUNTAIN

Luke 4:1–12

Sharp End of the Rope

Loose rock slid down the glacial moraine, sounding like dinner plates shattering on a kitchen floor, as Peruvian guides unceremoniously dragged a rigid form off the ice and onto the skree. My lungs gasping for oxygen, I jammed my ice axe into the glacier and leaned on it for support. A knot formed in the pit of my stomach, and every nerve in my body tingled in protest. Slowly I made sense of what I was seeing.

Wrapped in flour sacks and multicolored climbing rope, that rigid form was the corpse of a climber, one of seven who would die that summer on the mountain. Above the grim scene loomed the defiant west face of 22,207-foot Huascarán, the second-highest mountain in the

Andes. For months I had trained to meet the challenge of this summit. Just then, however, I felt too weak to take another step.

I had long prided myself on being a hard-core climber: careful, but always eager to take the sharp end of the rope, always eager for a more difficult mountaineering challenge. But for the first time I was gripped with fear and asked myself, *That guy died climbing this mountain. It could happen to me. Is it really worth it?*

Extreme Sports

In his Ph.D. research, Eric Brymer developed a definition for *extreme sports*: "a leisure or recreation activity where the most likely outcome of a mismanaged accident or mistake [is] death." Brymer found that extreme sports particularly appeal to young men, and are often accompanied by the trappings of youth culture, including extreme clothing, and reckless music that conjures up the feelings of invincibility needed for the high-risk activities. The more cavalier participants like referring to what they do as "deathsports."

Extreme sports have been around for a long time, though there are new variations and the risk factor has escalated considerably in recent years. In the 1960s and '70s, stunt biker Evel Knievel fractured nearly forty bones, including breaking his back seven different times. For all his daredevilry, he is considered the grandfather of extreme sports.

Crippled and in excruciating pain from arthritis, Knievel has undergone a liver transplant and a hip replacement, and doctors finally installed a morphine drug pump in his abdomen in an effort to control pain. Hundreds of spine-jarring, daredevil motorcycle jumps have fused the bones in his back. He was once in a coma for weeks after crash-landing while attempting to jump the fountain at Caesar's Palace. He has made failed jump attempts over rattlesnake pits, shark tanks, river canyons, and double-decker buses. For his pains, he made, and squandered, millions as the quintessential daredevil.

The glory days long past, Knievel still boasts, "I was the first one to ever do a wheelie on a motorcycle while standing on the seat—ever."

Pretty impressive stuff. I wonder how that boast will serve him on the judgment day. Nearing the end of his life, he sits in an easy chair, mind dulled with pain medication that never quite alleviates the bone-throbbing arthritis pain. Flanked by oxygen tanks and tubes necessary to keep his hardening lungs pumping, he wheezes, "I have no regrets."

What does daredevil Evel Knievel have to do with my mountaineering? A great deal more than—in my climbing days—I cared to admit. I've finally become convinced that my version of mountaineering was an extreme sport—not unlike his. High on that big mountain in Peru and on many others I've climbed, "the most likely outcome of a mismanaged accident or mistake was death." My climbing was a "deathsport."

Extreme Sports Defended

That night, high in the Andes Mountains of Peru, they laid out the dead climber's body next to my tent. Separated by two thin layers of tent nylon and the garish flour sack that shrouded the climber's body, I began a slow, often reluctant reevaluation of my rationale justifying an obsession with climbing mountains. Here's what I used to say about climbing and my faith:

God created mountains. So when I climb high on their summits I see his handiwork and draw closer to him. I can praise and worship God from a mountaintop just as well as (I was tempted to say "even better than") at church. I remember singing Isaac Watts at the top of my voice from the summit of the Eiger, so thrilled was I by the majesty of the Swiss Alps, and so thrilled, I thought, with the God who made them. What's wrong, you ask, with singing Watts on the summit of a mountain? Perhaps nothing. Until you consider that the Eiger has killed more climbers than any other European mountain, and at its base is a large cemetery.

One could make the necessary changes for bungee jumping, more extreme forms of skating, skydiving, motorcycle racing, and whatever other radical activities future generations of young men invent.

Or how about this one: What healthier activity could there be for men than to be working in common cause overcoming obstacles together? I liked using John Bunyan's metaphor of the Christian life as an uphill journey to justify climbing higher and more difficult peaks, peaks conquered in partnership with others:

> The hill, though high, I covet to ascend,
> The difficulty will not me offend,
> For I perceive the way to life lies here.
> Come, pluck up heart, let's neither faint nor fear:
> Better, though difficult, the right way to go,
> Than wrong, though easy, where the end is woe.

Or there is the often-abused rationale that goes something like this: "As a climber I'll be uniquely positioned to witness to a stratum of society with which Christians (the ordinary ones) largely have no contact," the old, sanctimonious, fence-straddling, foot-in-both-worlds argument.

Surmounting Sin

Lame arguments justifying pet activities are usually convincing only to the already convinced. It shouldn't be a surprise that several problems emerge with this kind of rationale.

Sure, the heavens declare the glory of God, and I can worship God anywhere. But this begs the question. God called Israel to worship him in a particular place, time, and way. And Christians are called to gather as a body with fellow believers, making worship a priority before which other activities bow, and all the more so as the day of Christ approaches. My climbing frequently took precedence over corporate worship on the Lord's Day. Know for certain that any activity, extreme or otherwise, that regularly replaces church, the God-ordained means of Christian maturity, must necessarily lead us away from the King's Highway, the straight and narrow path to heaven.

The climbing metaphor used to justify literal mountaineering, in the end, doesn't wash. Ironically, the higher I climbed, literally, the less energy I put into surmounting sin in my life, and the further I strayed from the uphill path of Christian manhood. Be honest with yourself. I'm not alone in this.

What's more, my desperate rationale for worshiping God in nature failed to reckon with Scripture, which tells us how readily we worship the creation and ourselves rather than the Creator.

One of my past climbing heroes is a case in point. Nobody has climbed as many of the world's highest and most difficult mountains as Reinhold Messner—often alone and without oxygen. Of his extreme mountaineering exploits, Messner said, "There's no more human rulers if I'm out there. There's no religion which is controlling me and telling me how I have to behave. There's just pure nature . . . the nature in myself, and the nature outside." Declaring that when climbing there are moments when all doubt and questioning are gone, he explained, "Myself living—I am the answer."

Not only may we be setting ourselves up to worship nature by total commitment to extreme mountaineering or any other deathsport, but such commitment may become a setup for shameless self-deification.

Healthy Pride?

But what's wrong with the argument that mountaineering is a healthy, wild-at-heart-male activity? Heaps! Are there any voluntary activities that regularly remove men from family, church, and work responsibilities that can have real benefit for anyone, including the selfish male participant? A climbing partner of mine, the father of four and an elder in his church, took five vacation days away from his family to climb the classic east face of Mt. Whitney—with me. He's now divorced and no longer in leadership.

Whatever benefit I gained from camaraderie was overshadowed by the ill effects of my primary motive: pride. Standard climber lingo proves that I'm not alone here: "What route? No way, that's a walk-up! How fast? Did you lead the crux? Like, who needs a rope on that route?" I wonder how effective a witness I could have been when I was so clearly motivated by pride.

Never daunted, my shameless sense of invincibility was invigorated each time I reached the summit of some mountain. Of course, I hoped others were as impressed with me as I was with myself. It's embarrassing to admit all this. When you stop and think about it, though, hard-core climbing and male pride and irresponsibility are a perfect match—but it's a marriage made in hell, not in heaven.

After Messner's 1978 climb of the world's highest mountain without oxygen, he said, "After Everest, I was feeling I could do anything." Later, at a celebration in honor of Messner and the first successful climb of an 8,000-meter peak without oxygen, Messner dismissed criticism for not taking his nation's flag to the summit: "I went up for myself."

Manly as scaling high mountains appears on the surface, hardcore climbing and other extreme sports actually emasculate men by encouraging us to use up precious time, strength, and skill on activities that serve no one—we may even be proud to say—but ourselves.

Biblical manhood, on the other hand, calls young men to use their strength and skill for others. For the young man, this means willingly helping your younger siblings, your mother, classmates, and others who need your strengths. For the adult, it means especially caring for wives and children—responsibilities for which there is little time when mountains or motorcycles beckon.

Pride Wounds

That same self-serving pride led me to foolish risk-taking. Though mine don't rival Evel Knievel's, I still have scars and permanent aches and pains directly caused by excessive risk-taking to feed my monster pride.

A climbing partner and I were both air-lifted with broken bones after a near-disastrous fall from the northwest buttress of Dragontail Peak in the Washington Cascade Mountains. He spent weeks in the hospital after reconstructive surgery. I saw him recently. In the last twenty years he'd undergone four more surgeries, the last one less than two years ago. He will never fully recover. So much for a healthy activity.

I know of a pastor who became intrigued by mountaineering and was eventually killed after a fall in Colorado. He left behind his wife and four children. I know of Christian men in their thirties, some with wives and children, who were killed when a violent storm struck during a winter ascent of Mt. Hood.

Every young man and his father must grapple with where lines are crossed from healthy outdoor challenges enjoyed together and to the glory of God to those activities with risks too great and costs too high for the involvement of responsible Christian men. The Word of God and my own experiences have compelled me to conclude that big-mountain climbing, extreme rock-climbing, and most winter ascents fall into that category of extreme activities simply too dangerous for a Christian who takes the sanctity of life seriously.

From a vast array of high-risk extreme sports, young men can collect pride wounds that they, like Evel Knievel, will have to live with—or, worse, that will kill them. A wise young man will soberly and prayerfully weigh the worth of activities that he gives himself to, and that could cost him his life.

Prayer Covers All?

Before setting out on a dangerous climb, I often prayed for safety. It bothered me to learn that, after a fashion, so did Evel Knievel. "Help me make a good jump," he claims to have prayed. Prayers of this kind, prayers for success in high-risk recreational activities, trivialize praying. How can I, with any integrity, pray earnestly for persecuted Christians who daily risk their lives for Christ, and for men laying their lives on the line in combat—and also pray that God would keep me safe while I indulge in daredevil thrill-seeking? Something is wrong with my praying here.

It's a presumptuous prayer that asks God to give his angels charge over my pursuit of risky personal thrills and prideful ambitions. In Luke 4:9–12, Satan tempted our Lord to throw himself down from the pinnacle of the temple, even quoting a proof text from Scripture to get him to do it. Christ replied, "Do not put the Lord your God to the test" (4:12, quoting Deut. 6:16). I fear that I often did.

During most of my climbing years, I was young, single, and immature. No real justification, but when I see a Christian man with family and church responsibilities get that look in his eyes, and then begin talking excitedly about getting involved in some extreme activity, I try to reason with him. But a man with a deluded sense of invincibility rarely listens.

If what I am saying does not move you, read C. Everett Koop's little book *Sometimes Mountains Move*. My praying mother begged me to read it. I wept as Dr. Koop described the tragic death of his twenty-year-old son in the White Mountains. I was sobered by the deep emptiness felt by a father grieving over his son. I could easily have been that son.

The world's greatest mountaineer, Reinhold Messner, exposed himself to high-risk dangers in the mountains because, as he said, after you survived these hazards, "You are reborn." Yet he was forced to admit, "In my generation, half of the leading climbers died in the mountains."

Unlike the seven who died on the mountain that summer in Peru, I came home from that climb, thanks to my mother's real prayers. Two years later, however, a climbing partner of mine, married just five months, left eager to climb Huascarán. He didn't come home, and all that the Peruvian guides recovered for his young widow were bits and pieces of his climbing gear, strewn about the ice fall.

God or Idols

We shouldn't need all these anecdotes to see our way clearly here. The Bible acknowledges the allure of mountains and, by extension, all the other high-risk, tough-guy distractions that you and I are so good at finding, but the Lord calls you and me to look beyond our selfish ambitions and joyfully shoulder our duty to serve others for Christ's sake.

I used to quote only the first verse of Psalm 121, "I will lift up mine eyes unto the hills, from whence cometh my help," and twist it into another proof text justifying my climbing habit. Read on. The next verse clears up any confusion: "My help cometh from the LORD, which made heaven and earth" (KJV).

Extreme sports such as big-mountain high-risk climbing demand everything of those who participate. They're like a religion. They have their own language, their own heroes, their own guidebooks, their own clothes, even their own rituals. Commitment to them is like religion, too: it's all or nothing.

Of course mountains aren't evil. Fathers and sons can and ought to have many God-glorifying episodes trekking, skiing, and camping together in the wilderness. But wise fathers and sons will know the potent allure of the conquest. Real men will take seriously just how easy it is to cross the line, scorn the sanctity of life, and become self-worshiping idolaters.

Just as the Bible nowhere says that mountains are evil, neither is there any express command in Scripture against carbon fiber, climbing rope, crampons, skates, parachutes, or even the component parts that make up a motorcycle. But this begs the question. The Bible warns us against many kinds of sinning that are far more subtle than saying "yes" when the answer is "no," or stealing our neighbor's donkey.

For example, gold in and of itself is not evil. Neither is a cute newborn calf. But combine the two and you've got trouble. Make a golden calf, bow down and worship the thing—and you've got idolatry. Of course, there's nothing evil about snowboards and ice axes. But combine them with pride and total commitment to extreme mountain sports, and you've got another idolater. I know. I've never yet seen a man be totally committed to hard-core climbing or any other extreme sport and to Christ. I'm convinced that it can't be done.

In my case, because I lifted my eyes to mountains instead of to the Lord, my preoccupation with climbing became my idol. Climbing was my religion, and I was very devout. Obsessed with it, I never really took on the important challenges of conquering my own sinful desires. Much ground remains to be ascended, but at least now I'm on the right mountain.

Young man, look to the Lord. Following Christ already demands high-risk, extreme commitment. Lay aside anything that rivals true religion. Risk your life for things that matter for eternity. Stop looking to mountains, motorcycles, or parachutes. Look to Christ.

Resolves

- To pray regularly together as father and son
- To allow no rival to my total commitment to following Christ
- To practice self-control when I find my interest awakened by the thrill of some extreme sport
- To ask myself whether an activity I want to pursue will encourage pride or humility, distraction or self-control

Scripture Memory

"The highway of the upright avoids evil; he who guards his way guards his soul."

Proverbs 16:17

For Discussion

1. How did Jesus respond when Satan tempted him to throw himself down from the pinnacle of the temple?
2. Evaluate the arguments you have heard others use to defend their liberty to engage in extreme sports.
3. Discuss how a Christian young man would decide what activities are helpful to his Christian walk and what ones demand too much of him.

"Pilgrim Hymn"

Who would true valour see,
Let him come hither;
One here will constant be,
Come wind, come weather.
There's no discouragement
Shall make him once relent
His first avowed intent
To be a pilgrim.

John Bunyan, 1678

For Further Study

Psalm 121; 1 Corinthians 7:3; Hebrews 12

8

WORSHIPING THE WRONG GOD

Matthew 19:16–30

Big Bucks!

Seven-time Cy Young Award winner Roger Clemens has pitched for twenty-two seasons in the major leagues. To date, he has also received the richest contract in the history of baseball: $18 million—for a single year of playing the game.

What would you do with that much money? With it Clemens could start up thirty-six Subway sandwich shops. Or he could advertise to eighty-eight million sports fans during the Super Bowl. At $2.5 million for a whopping thirty seconds, he could buy about three and a half minutes of airtime. Or, at $250,000 each, he could buy seventy-two Ferrari 612 Scaglietti sports cars. Or he could buy a Starbucks latte every day for the next fourteen thousand years—assuming they don't raise the price.

When my son recently showed me a picture of the Ferrari and let the price slip, I nearly choked. "It's a pretty good deal, for what you get," he said. "We could sell the house."

This is the same son who likes to stop at the sports-car dealership and take digital pictures of himself grinning beside absurdly expensive little autos. The other day I succumbed to his urgings. After parking our "people carrier," as a friend of mine calls our Suburban, the entire family walked through the door.

Shiny red and black cars with foreign-sounding names glittered enticingly in the showroom. The salesman looked dubious, as if mentally tallying up the numbers, multiplying by cost of living per capita, and sizing me up for "ability to purchase." Judging from his expression, the arithmetic wasn't working.

After wiping my toddler's nose, I asked, "Do you have anything in an eight-passenger model?"

Money and Men

Real men protect and provide for their wives and children, and a wise young man prepares early for a life of faithful and productive work—work that is rewarded with money, with which he, in turn, provides for his family, supports the church, and gives to the needy. So God has ordained it.

Combine men and money, however, and things get distorted. Throughout time the need to earn money has led many men to worship it. Thus, it is said, "men worship their work, work at their play, and play at their worship." They worship their work, in part, because it's the source of money. Men are creative at rationalizing their obsession with money, insisting that they are doing it for the children, or for the church building fund, or for foreign missions. In the Middle Ages the standard rationale for worshiping gold was to fund a crusade to the Holy Land.

We'll take up laziness and poverty in another place, but it seems fair to say that if poverty has slain its thousands, prosperity has slain its tens of thousands. Consider the last fifty years in America. Columnist Paul Johnson observed that today in every stratum of the social ladder people have more material wealth than they did half a century ago. Even America's poor drive Cadillacs and wear designer tennis shoes. But in the same period, he observed a disturbing decline in religious morality. Thus, while the standard of living has soared, it has left "Christianity much weaker," suggesting the troubling conclusion that when men have to decide between money and morality, money almost always wins.

Money and Young Men

The rich young man who approached Jesus that day in Judea seemed genuinely interested in getting eternal life; he came to the right man with his question, and he called Jesus "good" (Matt. 19:16). Like you, he was at least superficially moral. When Jesus told him to obey the commandments if he wanted to enter life, he said, "All these I have kept" (19:20). Significantly, Jesus had not listed the first two commandments, that he was to worship God alone and not an idol. Jesus understood this young man's heart: his wealth was his god.

So when Jesus told him to "sell your possessions and give to the poor" (19:21), the young man made his choice. He preferred keeping his earthly treasures over storing up treasures in heaven. He preferred to follow after his earthly wealth rather than to follow Jesus. To be sure, it wasn't an easy choice; he went away sad. Nevertheless, he chose money over Jesus and eternal life because money had become his god.

Salvation is a free gift of sovereign grace, pitched on poor, lost sinners, doomed for destruction, and no man, rich or not, can get eternal life by doing anything. But it is harder for a rich man to realize how poor and lost he is. His riches give him an artificial sense of his worth, of his own "ability to purchase" what is not for sale at any temporal price. The debt is too great, his earthly currency too paltry, next to the surpassing worth of Christ and eternal life. A rich man by seeking after riches blinds himself to these realities. And young men are easily drawn into the illusion.

Like Barry Minkow, who learned to love money when he was a teen. As a shrewd sixteen-year-old, he started a business in his parents' garage to "impress girls." But this was no ordinary business. Barry came up with an elaborate money-fraud scam, using loans secured by organized crime. "I learned that money brought respect," he says today, "and it was like a narcotic. I couldn't live without it." Worth over $300 million before it vaporized, his money scam became one of the biggest frauds in U.S. history. *Time* magazine reported that while in prison Barry had become a Christian and, after serving his time, had become a preacher—and an FBI employee. Because he knows how men think about money, he has uncovered fraud scams worth over $1 billion.

Pearls and Problems

No matter how many generations conclude that money can't buy happiness, every generation seems painfully destined to learn the lesson over again. The need for food, clothing, and shelter quickly explodes into the need for disposable money for a million other things. Before we know it, we're trapped. Money becomes essential to our existence, and then it takes over and becomes the very soul of our existence.

In John Steinbeck's *The Pearl*, the poor but contented pearl-diver Kino, distressed at his baby's illness, sets out to find "the pearl of the world" so that he can afford medical care for his son. He finds the pearl but quickly becomes its slave. "The pearl has become my soul," he realizes too late. "If I give it up I shall lose my soul." Perversely, his inability to give it up destroys his livelihood, the tender relationship with his wife, and his son's life. Finally, when his pursuit of temporal gain to solve his troubles has utterly failed, he listens to his wife. "This thing is evil. This pearl is like a sin! It will destroy us." And together they throw it back into the sea.

I know what you're thinking: surely there was some way to keep the wealth from the pearl and not lose everything else. After all, pearls are neutral; pearls aren't evil in themselves, and think how much good could be done with all that money. The same argument could be used about the rich young man's wealth—and Jesus told him to get rid of it. Martyr Jim Elliot put it this way: "He is no fool who gives what he cannot keep to gain what he cannot lose." Still, you're inclined to believe the devil's lie that wealth solves problems, and that you alone of all people in the cosmos won't be corrupted by it. That's what Kino thought.

Money Trap

That's also what Jack Whittaker and his wife thought in 2003 when they won the then largest undivided lottery jackpot in the history of state-sponsored gambling in the United States. Two years after winning $113 million, his wife, Jewel, lamented their good fortune: "I wish I would have torn the ticket up." Arrested twice for drunk driving and once for assault, her husband is now in court-ordered rehabilitation, and joins the ranks of thousands of other lottery winners whose lives have been shipwrecked on the shoals of easy money.

Mounds of green paper, silver, gold—they're not the real problem. Kino's pearl wasn't the problem. A pearl is the product of a piece of sand that irritated the blobby existence of some oyster, which proceeded to surround the irritation with disgusting mucus until a pearl was formed. No, pearls aren't the problem.

The apostle Paul exposes the real problem in 1 Timothy 6:5–10: financial gain does not bring contentment. Godliness brings contentment. "People who want to get rich fall into temptation and a trap and into many foolish and harmful desires that plunge men into ruin and destruction. For the love of money is a root of all kinds of evil" (6:9–10a). Money is just glorified dirt; wanting it is what destroys you.

Still, young men want it. They refuse to believe what Paul wrote and persist in believing that money will bring them happiness and power. Young men who think this way just fall into the trap. Get this straight when you're young. It gets worse when you're older as you fall under the unchallenged assumptions of your adult peers, most of whom will believe the lie about riches. Put your hope in money and you are destined for ruin and destruction, and some have even "wandered from the faith" (1 Tim. 6:10). Heed the caution—or else.

Money, Get Away!

In 1973, psychedelic Cambridge band Pink Floyd created a hit that included a paraphrase of Paul's condemnation of money, "Money, so they say, Is the root of all evil today." Accompanied by cash-register sound effects chink-chinking ominously, song writer Roger Waters leads off with the line, "Money, get away." Pink Floyd's hit song seems to be an attempt to grapple with the superficiality of modern man's love of money.

Ironically, "Money" sold over forty million copies. I suspect Pink Floyd grabbed the cash in both fists and substantially added to their own stash. Many have probably crooned along but missed the implied criticism—and the irony. Most young men probably think the stuff money can buy, catalogued in the song, sounds pretty good. Maybe not the caviar, but a new car? How about a Ferrari—that would be nice. Beware. According to Paul, the only certain thing money gets you is ruin.

Less encumbered by hypocrisy, and a better poet, George Herbert was a young man in the fast lane in seventeenth-century English intellectual life. A distinguished scholar at Cambridge, he was eventually made the public orator for one of the most prestigious universities in the world. Wealth and fame lay at his feet. Then in 1630 he left it all and became the pastor of a tiny backwater parish outside of Salisbury. Here he lived in obscurity, preaching the gospel and writing poetry. Herbert's sonnet, "Money," written nearly four hundred years ago, suggests that loving money is not just modern man's problem:

> Money, thou bane of bliss and source of woe,
> Whence com'st thou, that thou art so fresh and fine?
> I know thy parentage is base and low:
> Man found thee poor and dirty in a mine.

Surely thou didst so little contribute
To this great kingdom which thou now has got,
That he was fain, when thou wert destitute,
To dig thee out of thy dark cave and grot:
Thus forcing thee, by fire he made thee bright:
Nay, thou hast got the face of man; for we
Have with our stamp and seal transferred our right:
Thou are the man, and man but dross to thee.
   Man calleth thee his wealth, who made thee rich,
   And while he digs thee out, falls in the ditch.

Herbert cleverly exposes the absurdity of a man's giving himself to something poor and dirty that he dug out of a hole in the ground, to which he transferred his image, gave up his rights, became willing slave—then he plunges headlong into the ditch that he has dug with his own hands, never to rise again. Herbert's imaginative description makes giving yourself to money look pretty stupid. Yet when the image he has drawn fades in our mind, we eagerly edge back toward the ditch.

Money and Church

In a Massachusetts Institute of Technology study, economist Jonathan Gruber reported that people who go to church become wealthier. Similarly, a Harvard study found a specific correlation between belief in life after death and economic prosperity. Some Christians find these discoveries exciting: think how much good we can do with the cash.

The Bible does indicate that Christian virtues, such as hard work, diligence, and excellence, often yield temporal rewards. But the young man who sets out to be rich, instead of setting out to be righteous, is destined for ruin. "Whoever trusts in his riches will fall, but the righteous will thrive like a green leaf" (Prov. 11:28). It is the lie of the devil that makes you think that riches will make you thrive. Riches don't make you thrive. Righteousness makes you thrive.

I know a few wealthy people, and I can think of several quintessentially generous people among them. But all the wealthy people I know made their fortunes before they were Christians. I wonder, if they were currently seeking after riches as they claim to be seeking after heaven, which of these they would achieve. They wouldn't achieve both, and neither will you.

Someday if your wealth increases as a result of work and diligence, be sure that it happens while you're seeking first Christ and his kingdom and righteousness, but beware. Don't set your heart on it. If you know that you're prone to the love of money—and what wise young man doesn't know this?—then pray like wise Agur that God would not give you riches; "otherwise, I may have too much and disown you" (Prov. 30:8–9).

Money or Christ

How different things might have been in the American colonies if more young men in Massachusetts had prayed like Agur. Piety and the Puritan work ethic produced in one generation a prosperity from which we have never recovered. Colonial minister Cotton Mather lamented, "Religion begat prosperity and the daughter devoured the mother." Poor men who remained in the old country and suffered for Christ will fare better on the judgment day.

John Neilson of Corsock made his choice. After the Restoration in 1660, Neilson refused to bow to the adulterer King Charles II, the usurper of the "crown rights of the Redeemer in his Kirk." For Neilson's stand, the king's dragoons forced him from his ancestral castle in Glenkens, Scotland. Destitute, with his wife and children, he "took to the heather." Hunted by the scourge of the Covenanters, James Turner, captain of the king's garrison in Dumfries, Neilson not only lost all his lands and wealth for his loyalty to Christ's Crown and Covenant, but his wife died of exposure in their flight. Finally taken at Rullion Green, Neilson was marched to the Grassmarket in Edinburgh on December 14, 1666. Before his voice was drowned out by the ominous drum roll, he spoke boldly before the king's henchmen: "If I had many worlds I would lay them all down, as now I do my life for Christ and his cause."

This clear-sighted Scots laird was no fool. He gave what he could not keep to win what enriches for all eternity. Young man, be like this saintly man. Start by knowing your heart when it comes to money, and stop daydreaming about it.

Far from envying Roger Clemens, a wise young man should pity him. He can have his $18 million a year. Most likely it will be his ruin. Don't try to serve two masters. It's Christ or money, not both. Know that Christ and the Word of God are infinitely more valuable than money. Know that "the ordinances of the LORD are sure and altogether righteous. They are more precious than gold, than much pure gold" (Ps. 19:9b–10a).

Resolves

- To cut off daydreaming about being rich
- To regularly pray that God would not make me rich
- To tithe at least 10 percent of all I earn
- To look for ways to use some of my money to help those who have less
- To develop the lifelong habit of prayerfully setting my affections on things above with every paycheck I receive

Scripture Memory

"No servant can serve two masters. Either he will hate the one and love the other, or he will be devoted to the one and despise the other. You cannot serve both God and Money."

Luke 16:13

For Discussion

1. Discuss how to be a good provider but not a lover of money.
2. What profession or vocation do you want to pursue? Discuss your motives.
3. What is the difference between being an owner of your money and a steward?

4. In what specific ways can you discipline yourself so that you will not become a lover of money?

"Jesus, Priceless Treasure"

Hence with earthly treasure!
Thou art all my pleasure,
Jesus, all my choice.
Hence, thou empty glory!
Naught to me thy story,
Told with tempting voice.
Pain or loss
Or shame or cross
Shall not from my Savior move me,
Since he deigns to love me.

Johann Franck, 1655

For Further Reading

Proverbs 30:2–9; Revelation 3:14–22

9

WORSHIPING
LIKE A MAN

2 Kings 16:10; 17:7–41

Playing at Worship

One pundit suggests that American Christians "play at their worship." I suspect that most Christians would object. Entertainment-evangelism "worship," for them, is the best thing that's happened to church; the worship center is full, and look how happy everybody is.

But the numbers are skewed. According to the Barna Research Group, though five out of six males consider themselves Christians, only two out of six regularly go to church. They may be full, but American churches are two-thirds female and one-third male.

There are many reasons for this, but changes in music take center stage. Yet the debate over worship music, ironically, isn't about worship. Few proponents of contemporary music ask what music is appropriate for the worship of God. Instead, "they [imitated] the nations around them" (2 Kings 17:15), in order to evangelize them.

A leading church-growth guru candidly admits to this. "What kind of music do you listen to?" he asked the folks in his community. "I didn't have one person who said, 'I listen to organ music.' Not one. It was 96–97 percent adult contemporary, middle-of-the-road pop. So, we made a strategic decision that we are unapologetically a contemporary music church."

Well-intentioned Christians have reinvented what goes on at church by shifting the question. Seeker-friendly church leaders generally ask: "What does the world like to listen to?" rather than "What music pleases God?" Thus, church growth becomes the all-excusing rationale for what people sing in church. And they tell us it's working. "Right after we made that decision and stopped trying to please everybody," claimed one growth guru, his church "exploded with growth." End of discussion.

Or is it? Roman emperors packed out arenas by giving entertainment-crazed citizens what they liked. People showed up in droves. We, too, are a culture that values amusement. We like to feel good. We like to sway and clap. We like rapid images passing before us. We like celebrity. And we'll pay for it. Church-growth proponents argue that cashing in on the postmodern infatuation with entertaining music will fill churches. So give them what they want.

The late Neil Postman, in his book *Amusing Ourselves to Death*, cites the executive director of the National Religious Broadcasters, who seems to agree with the church-growth philosophy: "You can get your share of the audience only by offering people something they want."

Postman, though no Christian, made the perceptive observation: "This is an unusual religious credo. There is no great religious leader— from the Buddha to Moses to Jesus to Mohammed to Luther—who offered people what they want. Only what they need."

When the church fashions worship to entertain the world, to give people what they want, it inevitably creates, as one journalist termed it, "a Christian ghetto watering down the gospel." Moreover, when the

101

goal is to make Christian worship appealing to a feminized culture, we inevitably alter the message and make it less offensive—and less Christian.

Whenever the people of Israel imitated the pagan worship of the nations around them, God became angry and judged them. Thus, John Calvin urged that "all human inventions in worship be removed and driven from us, which God himself justly abominates." Far from aping the world, Christian men ought to stand against the impulse to reinvent worship so that it looks and sounds like the world.

Loud, Loud, Loud!

In *The Screwtape Letters*, C. S. Lewis describes heaven as a region of music and silence. The demon Screwtape is frustrated by this reality: "Music and silence—how I detest them both!" He boasts that in hell:

> No moment of infernal time has been surrendered to either of those abominable forces, but all has been occupied by Noise—Noise, the great dynamism, the audible expression of all that is exultant, ruthless, and virile—Noise which alone defends us from silly qualms, despairing scruples, and impossible desires. We will make the whole universe a noise in the end. We have already made great strides in this direction as regards earth. The melodies and silence of Heaven will be shouted down in the end. But I admit we are not yet loud enough, or anything like it.

Contemporary church-growth enthusiasts, however, don't seem to agree. "We are loud," says one megachurch pastor. "We are really, really loud. I say, 'We're not gonna turn it down.' "

Conversely, Lewis sees music and silence as complementary features of heaven. He gets this, of course, from biblical passages in which God calls us to "be still, and know that I am God" (Ps. 46:10), and to "sing for joy" (Ps. 149:5).

But does high-volume rock 'n' roll fit with the music and silence that Lewis describes, or does it sound more like the noise and loudness that Screwtape and many church-growth leaders prefer? This isn't as hard a question as we've made it. Nevertheless, church-growth advocates and most musicians agree with pop-music expert Don Butler: "Every style and form of music can become gospel, whether it's jazz, pop, rock 'n' roll, or rap" (*Inhouse Music*, March/April 1991).

J. R. R. Tolkien readers will immediately think of Boromir, who urged the Fellowship, rather than destroying the Ring, to use its power—for good ends. Like the postconservative church, Boromir, too, was certain that he would not be corrupted by that power. He was wrong.

Beware. If entertainment-evangelism advocates can convince you that music is amoral, merely a matter of taste, then the discussion ends—and so does discernment. Wise young men, however, will be suspicious of conclusions that sweep away moral judgment.

Moral or Amoral?

In the preface to the *Genevan Psalter* of 1545, Calvin wrote of music that "there is hardly anything in the world with more power to turn the morals of men." Yet Christians today insist that "music is amoral." As if to say, "Just use the Ring!"

But historically, nobody has thought music was amoral. Even agnostic Ralph Vaughan Williams in his preface to *The English Hymnal* wrote, "Good music for worship is a moral issue. The eternal gospel cannot be commended with disposable, fashionable music styles, otherwise there is the implication that the gospel itself is somehow disposable and temporary." Tragically, well-intentioned Christians, confused by the amoral argument, may be undermining the gospel by making it appear throwaway to the watching world.

Paste in whatever words you want; loud entertainment music already conveys its own message. Certainly it makes people clap and feel exhilarated, but it's not conducive to careful thinking about the whole counsel of God. Entertainment music creates a feel-good atmosphere, but it doesn't work well to make men feel bad. It does excitement and infatuation well but is bankrupt on conviction and repentance—essentials of biblical evangelism.

Traditionally, music in church was employed to commend the objective message, to play second fiddle to the words. But entertainment evangelism switches this around. Eager to "imitate . . . the nations around them" (2 Kings 17:15), musicians force the high objective truths of the Bible into the background. Thus, praise songs repeatedly state adoration but with almost no doctrinal reasons given to biblically support and adorn those statements. And increasingly the object of adoration is vague.

Gene Edward Veith, writing for *World* magazine, concluded his review of a wide range of popular Christian materials: "So much of this Christian material says nothing about Jesus Christ."

How ironic! I thought evangelism was the reason for using pop music. So why remove much of the explicit Christian content from the lyrics? Though the Bible is clear that Christ is "a stone of stumbling and a rock of offense" (1 Peter 2:8 NKJV, quoting Isa. 8:14), we're still afraid to offend the world. The Spirit of God removes the offense only through the objective truths of the Word of God—the very thing that postconservative Christians are watering down in their music. Little wonder, then, that the church looks and sounds and acts like the world—instead of the reverse.

Look at Me!

Visiting a church one Sunday morning, I cautiously led my family through a minefield of microphone wires and amp cords to our seats—just beneath a speaker the size of a piano. My kids stared wide-eyed at the bongo drums, the Starbucks coffee in nearly every hand, the female worship leaders and effeminate males on stage in their Hawaiian shirts. One of my young sons leaned over and whispered, "Is this an entertainment show?"

One thing is indisputable: seeker-friendly services are shaped by the entertainment industry. Of course, they're using entertainment as a means to an end: evangelism. Many church leaders want to get seekers in the door by entertaining them with pop music. But is this compatible with the spirit of celebrity seen throughout the entertainment world?

Michael Bloodgood, heavy-metal bassist and Calvary Chapel pastor, thinks it is. "We're like Billy Graham with guitars. Rock and roll is neutral. It depends on the spirit."

Check out the album covers on the latest ads from your Christian bookstore if you want to discern the spirit. You'll discover shameless aping of secular musicians: provocative females, touchy-feely males, piercings and tattoos, and armed-crossing hauteur. Plunk in the CD and you will hear desperate mainstream-wannabes screaming to be noticed by secular record labels.

Late rock musician Keith Green saw all this coming. "It isn't the beat that offends me, nor the volume—it's the spirit. It's the 'look at me!' attitude I have seen at concert after concert, and the 'Can't you see we are as good as the world!' syndrome I have heard on record after record." And that was decades ago. Things have not improved.

British pastor John Blanchard, in his little book *Pop Goes the Gospel*, says this worldly exhibitionism sets up Christians to act like "stars instead of servants." He argues that the entertainment model inevitably leads to a groping for celebrity status and is why entertainment evangelism "so easily encourages worldliness."

The church seems desperate to imitate what historian Paul Johnson observed about culture in general: "Entertainment [has] displaced traditional culture as the focus of attention, and celebrity has ejected quality as the measure of value."

I Don't Listen to the Words

Getting the musical cart before the objective-content horse is not simply a contemporary issue. Calvin faced it in the sixteenth century: "We must beware lest our ears be more intent on the music than our minds on the spiritual meaning of the words. Songs composed merely to tickle and delight the ear are unbecoming to the majesty of the church and cannot but be most displeasing to God."

Long before Calvin, Augustine wrote approvingly of church singing, but added strong caution: "Nevertheless, when it happens that I am more moved by the song than the thing which is sung, I confess that I sin in a manner deserving punishment."

What would these saints say about Christian worship today? Their concerns predated the development of instruments and amplification technology designed to create psychological euphoria with loud musical noise. A thoughtful young man, a future leader in the church, must ask: "Does contemporary entertainment music draw attention to itself and to the performers, or does it aid in making understandable the objective meaning of the words being sung?" The jury is in. Most Christians, however, refuse to hear the verdict.

What is the universal response when parents ask kids why they listen to secular music with trashy lyrics? "I don't listen to the words." Amusement music is produced to effect an emotional response from the music itself rather than an intellectual response to the meaning of the words. Which compels the conclusion that entertainment music is a poor choice to renew the minds of unbelievers. I wonder how many music-loving megachurchgoers "don't listen to the words."

Whose Evangelism?

J. I. Packer wrote, "When evangelism is not fed, fertilized and controlled by theology it becomes a stylized performance seeking its effect through manipulative skills rather than the power of vision and the force of truth." John Blanchard exposes the problem of depending on music to do what only the Spirit and Word of God can do: "Musical conditioning is not the same as the Holy Spirit challenging the mind to think, the spirit to be still, and the heart to be humbled in the presence of God." In this they are stating only what the church has thought and practiced for centuries—until now.

Martin Luther made a clear distinction between worthy and unworthy music: "We know that the devil's music is distasteful and insufferable." But many Christians roll their eyes when someone says,

WORSHIPING LIKE A MAN

"Rock has always been the devil's music." Yet it was rocker David Bowie who said this. He went on: "You can't convince me that it isn't. I believe that rock 'n' roll is dangerous." Still, the church imagines that by using music styles conceived in the sexual revolution, it is plundering the Egyptians. The reverse, however, may prove true.

Burk Parsons, managing editor of *Tabletalk* and founding member of the Backstreet Boys, quit rock 'n' roll. Why? "The world of show business is the world of man-centered entertainment. The foundational philosophy of man-centered entertainment is to do whatever it takes in order to attract millions of fans and to make millions of dollars." This requires the "entertainment gurus" to track all the latest cultural fads and follow the "whims and fancies" of the music-listening public, as church-growth experts candidly admit to doing. Parsons continues, "This has become the philosophy of many evangelicals [who] have exchanged God-centered worship for man-centered entertainment that is founded upon the ever-changing principles of the culture rather than upon the unchanging principles of the Word of God." He calls us to worship according to the Word of God, "which transcends the current trends of modern culture."

Entertainment church-growth experts claim, however, that no church will grow if it does not change over to contemporary music. These experts may be correct about the power of loud pop music to change people. Decades before, rocker Jimi Hendrix understood this: "Music is a spiritual thing of its own. You can hypnotize people with the music and when you get them at their weakest point you can preach into the subconscious what you want to say."

London preacher Martyn Lloyd-Jones wrote concerning music's power, "We can become drunk on music. Music can have the effect of creating an emotional state in which the mind is no longer functioning as it should be, and no longer discriminating."

I wonder whether Christians now, blinded by a flawed theology of salvation, expect music to do what only the Holy Spirit can do: woo sinners by changing their minds and wills, not by first altering their emotions, but by drawing them by the power of the Word to repentance and faith in Christ.

Worship Like a Man

Examination of contemporary church music exposes a number of problems: overfamiliarity and sentimentalism; the tendency to bring God down to man's understanding; lyrics written by young people who are musicians first, rather than hymn poetry written by experienced, gifted Christians with theological training; the tendency to sing about what we're singing about; simplistic repetitiveness; lack of biblical progression of thought; in short, the dumbing-down of the message in order to fit it into the entertainment medium.

But let me speak man-to-man with you about the feminization of Christian worship. This has happened in many pernicious ways, but perhaps nowhere more uncomfortably for Christian young men than in singing.

In contemporary worship, the girls stand caressing the air with their hands, swaying with the pounding rhythm of the music, their voices hushed and breathy, eyes pinched closed, crooning along with the worship leaders.

What are most guys doing? Shuffling their feet uncomfortably. Embarrassed by the public display of emotions, and embarrassed—or allured—by the provocative outfits and yearning posture of the female worship leaders or soloists.

Christine Rosen in the *Wall Street Journal* connected plummeting male church attendance with the growing number of women taking leadership roles in the church. And in his recent book, Steve Farrar decries the "feminization of our boys" in contemporary worship. "Am I in a church or a spa?" he asks. "At a deal like that, you don't bring your Bible, you bring your moisturizer."

In his book *Why Men Hate Going to Church*, David Murrow argues that because contemporary worship is "tilted toward the feminine heart, created for sensitive women and soft-hearted men to meet

Jesus," a masculine man feels emasculated, "like he has to check his testosterone at the sanctuary door."

In the canon of classic hymns, however (see "A Young Man's Hymnal" at the back of this book), men through the centuries have sung of battles and fighting, of conquest and triumph—in short, of the manly Christian themes found in the Psalms.

"But today's praise songs are mainly love songs to Jesus," wrote Murrow, offering the example: "Hold me close, let your love surround me . . . I'm desperate without you . . . Jesus, I'm so in love with you." Another song that a student gave me begins, "Your love is extravagant; your friendship—mmmm—intimate." These "Jesus-is-my-girlfriend" songs represent a genre choked with songs that no Christ-honoring, self-respecting young man can sing.

A serious Christian man is stumped. Women worship leaders and effeminate men make you feel unspiritual if you don't sing and behave like women. What are you to do? Know for starters that "you don't have to be a girlie man to be a godly man."

This is war—culture war. It's time to break ranks with feminized worship and restore biblical manhood to the church. It begins with you and your generation. Prepare yourself to step up with manly leadership. Worship God in the splendor of his holiness. Cultivate a deep appreciation for what men in the church have sung through the centuries. Then "Rise up, [young] men of God! Have done with lesser things."

Resolves

- To be psalmlike in my worship
- To winsomely shoulder leadership responsibility
- To seek out manly Christian role models

Scripture Memory

"Worship the LORD in the splendor of his holiness. Tremble before him, all the earth!"

1 Chronicles 16:29b–30a

For Discussion

1. Read five praise-song lyrics; then compare them with five of the hymn texts at the end of this book.
2. Why is it important to give and adorn the reasons for praising God rather than repeatedly stating the praise?
3. Is it legitimate to replace or alter hymns because they are too difficult?
4. Is worship difficult? What other important things in life are difficult?

"The Church's One Foundation"

Though with a scornful wonder
Men see her sore oppressed,
By schisms rent asunder,
By heresies distressed,
Yet saints their watch are keeping,
Their cry goes up, "How long?"
And soon the night of weeping
Shall be the morn of song.

Samuel J. Stone, 1866

For Further Study

Psalm 100; *Give Praise to God*, edited by Philip Graham Ryken; *The Accidental Voyage*, by Douglas Bond

YOUNG MEN: THEIR RELATIONSHIPS

10

SELF-CONTROL AND WOMEN

Proverbs 6:20–29

Honor Father *and* Mother

"Give me a good Presbyterian mother," someone has said, "and any old thing will do for a father." Not most men's favorite axiom, but where is the kernel of truth here? If you paused for a moment and listed all the things your mother has done for you in the last twenty-four hours, the list would be considerably longer than most of you think.

Try these for starters: She made breakfast, made lunches, did the dishes (several times in twenty-four hours), did laundry, tidied up after you in the living room, cleaned the toilets, bought large quantities of food at the grocery store, homeschooled your siblings, changed diapers, wiped noses, read stories to your little sister (who threw up in the night—three times, at precisely forty-five-minute intervals), cleared

113

out junk from the basement, sold it on eBay, planned a birthday party, baked a cake for it, got gas in the car, vacuumed graham-cracker crumbs off the seats, shuttled kids to and from the library—the YMCA—the dentist—the thrift store, prepared a nice dinner, all the while praying without ceasing for her family and dozens of hurting people in your church, in your neighborhood, and throughout the world. Do you get the idea? I'm sure I've left out many things. Consult Proverbs 31 for the more complete list.

Aside from the fact that you wouldn't exist without your mother, let's face it: without her, your life would be empty. Little wonder that the Bible commands you to honor and obey her. Equally, your father's life would be empty without his wife, your mother. Thus, the Bible commands your father to love her, to treat her with gentleness and understanding, to be considerate of her weaknesses (1 Peter 3:7).

The Fall

As you observe your mother and develop that list, you might begin to wonder why the Bible ever had to command such things to men about loving and respecting wives and mothers. Wouldn't young men just naturally honor and obey their mothers? Wouldn't husbands naturally love and be good to their wives?

Let me pause and remind you of an event called the fall. Men have been busy ever since blaming our wives for our sins, finding fault with them, and teaching our sons to dishonor and disobey them by our self-centered, irresponsible attitude toward women.

On the other hand, your mother may not actually do many of the things listed above. She may be a mom who has sold her soul to the postmodern notion that "the best moms think about themselves first." I know a young man whose mother is so busy thinking about her own needs and wants and desires that it never occurs to her to do any of the things listed above for her son, and he suffers. Nevertheless, the Bible commands him to honor his mother. But few of you are in his place—and yet the Bible has to command you to honor and obey your mother?

A boy who hopes to be a man someday will begin honoring and obeying his mother now. And a father who wants his son to be a real man will know that his son is minutely scrutinizing how he treats his wife and other women. I suspect that nothing more significantly shapes a son's behavior toward women than watching how his father speaks to and about his wife.

Like Father, Like Son

Once a father realizes that his manner toward his wife profoundly shapes his sons' attitudes toward women in general, that father will leave no stone unturned as he minutely scrutinizes his speech and actions toward his wife.

Several things need to be mortified, to be put to death, between husbands and their wives. For starters, a wise, loving husband will never belittle his wife in front of his son. As head of his household, he may from time to time need to rebuke his wife—some wives will require more rebuking than others—but a wise husband will make certain that his son could never construe his rebuking as an insult to her honorable role as matron of the household.

A father who shoves his wife off that cliff loses the right to be dismayed when his son blows off his mother and speaks disrespectfully to and about her. Nor should that father be surprised if his son grows up to mistreat women. A father may think that a verbal rebuke in front of the kids is appropriate; his son will think this means that he can flagrantly show disrespect to his mother, and it will most likely spill over into how he treats all women.

The Bible commands husbands to nurture and instruct their wives and for wives to "learn in quietness and full submission" (1 Tim. 2:11–15), but nowhere on the many pages of the Bible that teach male headship is there anything that remotely gives a man the right to bully, insult, or belittle his wife. Male leadership must always be seasoned with self-sacrificial love or it ceases to be biblical leadership. Biblical leadership calls husbands to love their wives "as Christ loved the church

115

and gave himself up for her" (Eph. 5:25). And this love will replace all unkind speech with complimentary words, lovingly and frequently delivered.

If a son grows up hearing his father criticize instead of compliment his mother, he will be a fool: "A foolish man despises his mother" (Prov. 15:20b). Behind every son who grows up to be a foolish son is likely to be a foolish father who cherished his deeply flawed notion of headship more than he loved his wife.

Ravens and Vultures

I remember when each of my oldest sons passed up their mother's height mark penciled on the kitchen doorjamb. What elation! What triumph! Life was now good. Things were finally as they ought to have been all along. So their glowing features seemed to convey.

"The glory of young men is their strength" (Prov. 20:29a), as anyone who has spent much time with teenage young men has observed. As sons flex in front of the bathroom mirror, or mangle themselves on a parking meter while admiring their physique reflected in the shop windows, a sinister thing can occur. They may begin to resent that slight woman who dominates their life, who tells them what they can and cannot do.

Young men are stronger than they will be after entropy has wreaked its havoc on their muscles. I'm reminded of this every time I attempt to have a push-up contest with my teenage sons. When will I learn to sit by in my gray-headed splendor and let the young bucks go at it?

Gray hair is "the splendor of the old" (Prov. 20:29b) because wise old men ought to know just how fleeting and deceptive strength is. Old men should know that the young man who waits on himself and his own strength instead of waiting on the Lord and finding his strength in God will "utterly fall" (Isa. 40:30 KJV). He may look as though he stands, as though he is strong and invincible, but if he hopes in his own strength, he will be disappointed. If he leans on his own strength and understanding, his paths will not be straight; they will wind aimlessly through a misspent and miserable life—miserable for the young man himself, as well as for everyone whose life he touches.

And all because he turned up his nose at the instruction of his parents and thought he knew better than his frail little mother. No wonder Solomon reserves some of his most graphic rebukes for sons who have nothing but scorn for their mothers: "The eye that mocks a father, that scorns obedience to a mother, will be pecked out by the ravens of the valley, will be eaten by the vultures" (Prov. 30:17).

It Gets Worse

Things grow infinitely worse here if a father foolishly rebukes his wife in front of the family. Fathers who do this undermine every other good instruction they give their sons. The monster so created has long arms.

Sons who see their father belittle their mother by rebuking her in front of them will join in with an unrestrained will. These sons will speak dishonorably of their mothers when they talk with their friends. They will bully and manipulate their mothers in order to get what they want. They will also do this with sisters and female peers.

Furthermore, no father should be surprised at sons who've listened to him insult his wife, who then grow up to manipulate women so that they can get what they want from them sexually. Teach them that male headship means belittling their mother and they will think of women as their slaves, playthings to do their bidding, toys that give pleasure for a little while and then are cast off for something better.

Moreover, lack of care in conversation about sex with sons can easily lower their sexual barriers. Wise fathers are careful not to turn candor about sex into titillation for their sons. There "must not be even a hint of sexual immorality" (Eph. 5:3) in conversation with sons, no casual or jesting conversation about sex. I remember hearing an otherwise upstanding Christian man crack a joke replete with sexual innuendo. Apparently he was in the habit of doing so in front of his two sons. One he later caught going to pornographic sites on the Web;

117

the other was eventually caught preying on girls for nonromantic, recreational sexual contact.

Death to Arguing

Another thing that sons should never see or hear their parents doing is arguing. Your mother and father don't always see eye to eye on things. There may be ongoing tensions, unresolved conflicts, disagreements that will never be fully sorted out this side of eternity. Husbands and wives who claim otherwise have added lying to their other sins.

Though it's a fallen world, by God's grace, joy and harmony, peace and love, can and ought to reign in imperfect households. It denies the gospel of grace to claim that only in homes where Mom and Dad's relationship is perfect can there be godly nurture and the fruits of the Spirit lived out and practiced in the home.

Nevertheless, I have the rich blessing of having no recollection of my parents' ever arguing. Does this mean that they never disagreed on anything? That total depravity was for others, not for them? Not at all. What it means is that they were wise enough to practice self-control when they disagreed. I never saw or heard arguing because they loved each other, their children, and Christ so much that they agreed never to argue about their disagreements in front of their children. The result was a peaceful, quiet home, though not a perfect home, one that was conducive to all kinds of spiritual, intellectual, and creative development. Emotional energy was not wasted on harsh words or unkind speech, and so we were taught to love one another by my father's example of never arguing with my mother.

This is a no-brainer: A father who argues with his wife will raise sons who argue with their mother. Other problems are likely to follow. As adults these sons will scorn the opinions of women, will disregard the Bible's commands to honor and respect women, to treat them with understanding, consideration, and deference to their uniquely feminine weaknesses. These sons will use their strength to show women who's boss, and will probably view women as objects that exist merely to fulfill male desires.

Tone of Voice

Discussing things with self-control and respect is another matter. We used to have family meetings when I was growing up. My father listened carefully to what everyone had to say, and then he would quietly make his decision. But in these family meetings, we lost the right to speak if we used a tone of voice that was insulting to anyone else. I usually silenced my voice by insulting my sister.

Tone of voice plays a huge role in turning thoughtful discussion into unkind argument. Fathers must carefully listen to the tone of voice they use with their wives and daughters. The same words can be said in a tone of voice that conveys scorn and disrespect for the one with whom you are disagreeing. Our tongues can set the course of our lives on fire, and the tone of voice does so as much as the words spoken.

Sons have selective hearing, but it becomes precise and acute when it comes to the nuances of their father's tone of voice. They know, for example, when a father is being sarcastic with his wife by the tone in his voice. They know by the tone of voice when the father doesn't really feel what he is saying. They know the lift in the voice that means "You're an idiot!" The words themselves may never be spoken, but the tone of voice eloquently conveys the idea.

A son so trained will not only use the tone, but also use the father's unspoken words. If only it could be exactly "like father, like son," fathers passing on their sins without augmentation, so that sons were at least no worse than their fathers. But it doesn't work that way. Sons will ordinarily be like their fathers—but worse. Fathers, therefore, must put to death unkind speech and all nuances of unkindness in tones of voice—or else.

Fighting

My father was intolerant of fighting. "Never hit girls" was an inviolable creed. If I fought with my sister, verbally or otherwise, I had to kiss her and make up—on the lips! We rarely fought. But there was one kind of fighting that my father not only allowed but encouraged.

119

I didn't get it at the time, but when my sister got into the eighth grade she became attractive to older boys. I recall one summer evening while playing our favorite neighborhood outdoor game, ninth-grade Marty and eleventh-grade Leroy began behaving inappropriately toward my sister. I was a scrawny sixth grader, but I flew at them, fists blazing. Though they beat me to a pulp, I was happy: they were too busy pounding on me to pester my sister. My dad did not punish me for this kind of fighting; in fact, he praised me. I wore the cuts and bruises, black eyes, and cockeyed glasses with pride.

This didn't happen by accident. My dear mother didn't really understand it. It's no fault in her; she's never been a boy. Her creed went like this: "No roughhousing!" Thankfully, my father gently overruled her, and we frequently rolled around on the floor and wrestled. Later this evolved into nail-driving and lumber-hefting contests while sweating side by side at work. I regularly roughhouse with my own sons; we spar with fencing foils, shoot shotguns at the trap range, compete at splitting firewood, and engage in lots of back-slapping and a not-too-gentle boxing about the torso. My youngest son loves facing off with fists or sticks, or just rolling around poking and punching with me and his brothers. This all requires boundaries, but fathers and sons need this outlet.

Recent studies conclusively show that boys who grew up roughhousing with their fathers were significantly less likely to do poorly in school, get involved in drugs, be sexually active before marriage, or be involved in other forms of violent and self-destructive behavior. A broken chair or lamp is chump change by comparison.

Noble Women

Women can't be faulted for not getting this concept. They're different from men. Husbands and fathers, however, must gently instruct them in what it's like being a boy—and find appropriate times and places for roughhousing. It's forgivable that mothers mistakenly think that well-behaved sons ought to behave like their sisters. Forgivable and correctable. Boys must be nurtured in what it means to be well-behaved and mannerly—for boys and men. Confusion here leaves boys emasculated, gnawing their lip and wringing their hands when their sisters and mothers are in peril.

My youngest daughter sits quietly on my lap and reads story-books, softly cooing and stroking the kitty in the pictures. Meanwhile, my youngest son bolts from the couch and wants to act out the story with swords and guns. Why is this? "God made them male and female" (Matt. 19:4, quoting Gen. 1:27), and an important part of being male is learning how to use your strength to protect and provide for women. Good fathers will help their sons rein in the pride and self-love that renders them unfit to protect and provide, and they will help their wives understand the difference between young men and women.

Finally, it is far from correct to conclude that "any old thing will do for a father." Sons need godly fathers. It is, however, impossible to fully tally the importance of a godly mother, though right-thinking fathers and sons should live out their days making the attempt. If Paul could claim to be the chief of sinners, every well-trained son is able to say of his mother, "Many women do noble things, but you surpass them all" (Prov. 31:29). He learns to say this from his father.

Resolves

- To pray regularly together as father and son
- To speak and act toward wives and mothers with gentleness and respect
- To never insult or belittle women

Scripture Memory

"The eye that mocks a father, that scorns obedience to a mother, will be pecked out by the ravens of the valley, will be eaten by the vultures."

Proverbs 30:17

For Discussion

1. If a young man views his strength as a means of gratifying his vanity, what effect does this attitude have on his mother, his sisters, and other women?
2. What activities help young men to honor their mothers and other women?
3. Has feminism made things better or worse for women? Discuss.

"The Son of God Goes Forth to War"

A noble army, men and boys,
The matron and the maid,
Around the Savior's throne rejoice,
In robes of light arrayed.

Reginald Heber, 1827

For Further Study

Proverbs 1:8–9; 10:1; 15:20; 19:26; 20:20; 23:22; 23:24–25; 28:24

11

SELF-CONTROL AND SEX

1 Thessalonians 2:4b, 10–12; 4:1–12

How Not to Please God

In my imagination, I can still remember sights, sounds, and smells of the bustling ancient Greek city of Thessaloníki from my visit there in the summer of 1982. One of my main objectives while there was to find a quiet spot and read on location Paul's two letters to the first-century Christians who had once lived there.

Amid the blaring horns of Thessaloníki cabdrivers and the bleating of goats, I read in Acts how Paul had preached there in a Jewish synagogue three Sabbaths running, reasoning from the Scriptures about Christ and the gospel. Many Jews and God-fearing Greeks and "not a few prominent women" (Acts 17:4) were converted to Christ and joined Paul, and the devil hated it. Soon, jealous men "rounded up some bad characters from the marketplace, formed a mob and started a riot" (17:5). Paul and Silas were swept away to nearby Berea and safety, where a few days later, not to be eluded, hotheads from Thessalonica followed, stirring the crowds into a frenzy of rioting there, too.

Men who lack self-control start riots. Thessalonica had plenty such men, and this would not be the last riot in that city. Recollecting my experience in bustling modern Thessaloníki, I'm reminded of a tragic event that took place in those same streets during the rule of Emperor Theodosius in A.D. 390. New imperial taxes had sparked riots against the emperor throughout the eastern part of the empire. In an atmosphere already seething with unrest, one of Theodosius's generals, Botheric, in a fit of jealousy, threw a popular chariot driver into prison for allegedly seducing his homosexual lover.

Chariot racing was pretty important to the riotous mob in Thessalonica, so angry fans of the chariot driver killed Botheric, parading his bloody corpse through the streets. Emperor Theodosius, a professing Christian, not to be outdone by a mob, plotted a treacherous retaliation. While jubilant Thessalonians cheered madly at the next chariot races, at Theodosius's orders, soldiers surrounded the circus and put to the sword some seven thousand people. Only a handful of these had murdered Botheric—a classic example of overkill. And a classic example of how not to please God.

When word reached saintly Bishop Ambrose, courageously, he and the church suspended Emperor Theodosius from the Lord's Supper until such time as he gave meaningful evidence of true repentance. The emperor eventually did repent and was restored to fellowship on December 25, 390, bringing to a close perhaps one of the most public and high-level cases of church discipline in the history of the church.

Father to Son

Paul wrote to the new Christians in this same city, to "brothers loved by God," whom God had chosen before the foundation of the world (1 Thess. 1:4–5). Their faith was real, and Paul wrote to commend them for it. By God's grace, they had become "imitators" of Paul and the other apostles, and had become a "model to all the believers in

Macedonia and Achaia" (1:6–7). Paul spares nothing in commending these saints: "Your faith in God has become known everywhere" (1:8).

Paul then gives a defense of his ministry among the Thessalonian church, how that against "strong opposition" (2:2) (remember the riots), he proclaimed the gospel to them, not "trying to please men but God" (2:4b). He proceeds to make an important analogy for them and for us. "For you know that we dealt with each of you as a father deals with his own [sons], encouraging, comforting and urging you to live lives worthy of God, who calls you into his kingdom and glory" (2:11–12).

Highest Standards

Put simply, Paul is assuming that fathers will be encouragers, comforters, and those who urge their sons.

You don't mind encouragement. You probably like it. And a good father will organize all his interaction with his son so as to inspire him with courage. The Roman world in Paul's day was a hostile world. So is yours. To live a faithful life then and now requires courage. So a good father wants to teach his son how to be courageous. To do this, a father must first model courage: he must show his son how to stand fast against the world, how to resist the urge to turn and run when the going gets tough. With zeal and passion, a good father wants to inspire courage in his son.

Things were definitely getting tough for Christians in the Roman world. This kind of encouragement wasn't about helping your son not cry over spilled goat milk. The goal of Paul's encouragement to his spiritual sons in Thessalonica was that they would "live lives worthy of God" (1 Thess. 2:12). On the flip side, back a page or so in my Bible, Paul tells fathers not to embitter their sons or they will become discouraged (Col. 3:21). Discouraging our sons is the opposite of inspiring courage, and good fathers avoid it.

But a good father also knows that his son is still being formed, that he is still young, that he is a work in progress. He knows that due to weakness his son messes up. So he is also ready to comfort his son when he stumbles, when he falls smack on his face, and when he is afraid. The goal of the comforting is also that his son might live a life worthy of God. We fathers can embitter our sons. We can forget that we did not mature overnight, that we stumbled and that we needed— and still need—encouragement and comforting if we are to please God with our lives.

But how can anyone live a life worthy of God? This is a high standard; some would say it's too high. But not Paul. He tells us that we are called to "be blameless and holy in the presence of our God and Father" (1 Thess. 3:13). Yes, it is a high standard—it's God's.

Fathering and the Blowtorch

In order to live up to such high standards, a young son needs lots of encouragement and lots of comfort. But he also needs lots of *urging*, a word that recurs throughout Paul's letter. Urging is what you do to a baseball, or a soccer ball, or a tennis ball. It is also what you do to a rusty bolt that refuses to break loose.

Many years ago, my dad and I rebuilt a rusty old 1961 Volkswagen Carmen Ghia. It was a big project, and it seemed like every nut and bolt was welded in place with rust. How did we break a really tough one loose? When half a can of WD-40, and reefing with all our strength, wouldn't budge it, we fired up the blowtorch and applied some heat to the pesky thing. If that didn't work, we got out the sledgehammer and gave it a few whacks. When even that wouldn't work, it was time for drastic measures.

Paul wants us to get the point, so he used the word *urge* often in his letters. *The American Heritage Dictionary* defines the verb *urge*: "1. To force or drive forward or onward; impel. 2. To entreat earnestly and often repeatedly; exhort." This is the part where sons begin to squirm. You're okay with encouraging and comforting, but it's the urging bit that chafes—I remember. The writer of Hebrews (12:7–11) compares God our heavenly Father with good earthly fathers who show that they love their sons by urging them, by exerting force upon them, by pushing or driving them forcefully, or (put another way) by disciplining them.

Celebrated London preacher Martyn Lloyd-Jones in a sermon preached in 1942 said that "there are times when we have 'to be cruel to be kind.' It is a difficult task for the [father], a task from which he shrinks. But if he has the real interest of [his son] at heart he just has to do it. It is always more pleasant to soothe or to comfort than to cause pain."

But a good father does not "soothe or comfort" when it is urging that his son needs. He knows that he has to do it, so he urges, he disciplines the son he loves, as Ambrose and the church elders did with Emperor Theodosius.

Tennis and the Backside

Though it happened more than thirty years ago, the nerve endings in my backside still twitch when I think about it. I was fourteen when my father gave me my last traditional urging—five of them. My dad had played tennis in college, and he had a killer forehand. And like a good tennis player, he had the uncanny ability to bring a hefty 1x6 down on precisely the same piece of flesh with every blow. I will never forget them, nor will I ever be able to thank my father enough for those urgings.

What had I done? I'd been disrespectful to my mother. Nothing raised the ire of my father more than a smart-mouth reply from a son to his mother. My words were the final straw, and he was determined to take drastic measures to stop those words and the attitude behind them.

"Do not withhold discipline from a child; if you punish him with the rod, he will not die. Punish him with the rod and save his soul from death" (Prov. 23:13–14). In that spirit, my father beat eternal death and hell out of me. It was a major turning point in my life. Moreover, I am deeply grateful that he did not apply encouraging or comforting in this instance. He had no doubt been doing these all along. But I was a know-it-all punk who needed driving forward forcibly. And, praise be to God, my father did it with every blow.

Encouraging, comforting, and urging—all three are important parts of good fathering. We fathers need to practice all of these, in love and with wisdom, applying the appropriate one at the appropriate time. Sons who know the high standard and who want to please God need to expect and welcome all three components, including the one you like least—the urging.

How to Live

Paul wraps it all up with final instructions on how you must "live in order to please God" (1 Thess. 4:1). He gives this critical instruction not on his own hook, but "by the authority of the Lord Jesus" (4:2). He urges the Thessalonians to heed it, warning them that "he who rejects this instruction does not reject man but God" (4:8). Sit up. What he has to say is important.

First he tells you that "this is the will of God, your sanctification" (4:3 NKJV). What is sanctification? It is increasing in holiness "more and more." Paul says, "We . . . urge you in the Lord Jesus to do this more and more" (4:1), and then he repeats this urging a few verses later (4:10). He doesn't want you to relax, to sleep in the Enchanted Ground, to grow complacent. So Paul urges you to pursue holiness, because without holiness no young man will see the Lord.

Paul is not one to waste words. He gets right to the issue. "It is God's will . . . that you should avoid sexual immorality" (4:3). Deep down, no honest young man thinks it odd that Paul puts his oar in here. You live in a sex-saturated world. Turn on the computer, pick up the newsmagazine, drive past the billboard, wait in line at the grocery store—everywhere you turn, sex stares you in the face. And is it ever enticing! Combine that with millions of raging sex hormones doing backflips in your glands, and Paul's urgings become intensely relevant. He hits the mark, and you know it.

At first blush, however, it might seem as though Paul is not using very strong language here. "Avoid" might give the impression of casual advice that you might just sort of kind of want to consider thinking about. But look again. He doesn't say, "Don't have sex before marriage." He says, "Avoid sexual immorality." This is significant. "Avoid" here means to halt long before sexual intercourse, to never take the minutest first step down a path that could lead to fornication. "Avoid" means that in your mind, words, and conduct, "there must not be even a hint of sexual immorality" (Eph. 5:3). They don't put "Caution: Road Washed Out" signs at the very brink of the washout. It's too late to stop the car then. They put those signs at spaced-out intervals, long before the danger.

What are the road signs, the hints, that must be avoided? They're in your mind, and they're called "lust." If you are serious about pleasing God, you must "avoid" the incremental sexual ideas that creep into your mind, that hold your eyes that split second longer on the magazine cover, or on the anatomy of a provocatively dressed girl. If you are serious about pleasing God, you must not allow "even a hint of sexual immorality" to pause for a split second on the radar screen of your mind and heart. If you do, you are not obeying Paul's instruction to "avoid sexual immorality."

It is all good and well to tell you to avoid sexual immorality. But how to do it? Paul's answer: "Learn to control [your] own body in a way that is holy and honorable" (1 Thess. 4:4). That's the opposite of indulging in "passionate lust like the heathen" (4:5), no doubt referring to the sex- and sports-crazed Thessalonians. The word *learn* implies a careful process with incremental steps, and it implies that you will need to gain skill in this, that you will need practice, that you will need to "do this more and more" (4:1).

Put another way, Paul is urging you to put on purity and put off impurity, to mortify sin, and to vivify holiness. There's that high standard again. You aren't at liberty to nod your head vaguely and dismiss it with the flimsy excuse, "I'm a kid. Kids are supposed to explore and get as close to the cliff edge as possible. Holy and honorable? That's a ridiculously high standard for sex."

Paul's Blowtorch

Paul doesn't want any confusion here. He is not merely offering free advice, take it or leave it. Not on your life. He says, "The Lord will punish men for all such sins" (4:6). If calling you to please God by sexual purity is not enough incentive, Paul reminds you that God will punish you for "all such" sexual sinning.

"Punishment is for the unsaved," you say. Not so fast. My father's urgings that day when I was fourteen were punishments of a type. The psalmist wrote, "You were to Israel a forgiving God, though you punished their misdeeds" (Ps. 99:8). Christian young man, if you treat God's Word with contempt by willfully blowing off Paul's instruction, make no mistake, you will be punished.

The grace of God notwithstanding, you will bear the inevitable consequences of your sexual disobedience in this life, anything from sexually transmitted diseases, to a lifetime of slavery to pornography, to broken relationships, to divorce, even to kids who don't want to be near you because they know what an out-of-control jerk their father really is. So much for consequences now.

Persist in "passionate lust like the heathen," get as close to fornication as you can, indulge in the lust of the eyes, and eventually the lusts of the flesh will destroy you. Ultimately, no persistent adulterer enters the kingdom of heaven. On the judgment day there will be some young men who claimed to be Christians who will hear—this ought to horrify you—"I never knew you. Away from me, you evildoers!" (Matt. 7:23). Learn self-control today so that you won't enter eternity with those words ringing everlastingly in your ears.

Paul is in earnest here. Don't trifle with self-control and sexual sins. And don't pass off your lusts and fantasies, your hidden emotional attachments and infatuations, as if Paul were not addressing you. He says that "all such" sexual sins must be avoided (4:6), and that includes the lust that has not yet become the act.

Live to please God, or expect to feel his lash, his blowtorch, his everlasting displeasure that produces "weeping and gnashing of teeth" (Matt. 13:42). Far too many young men are like riotous Thessalonians with little or no self-control, heaping up misery for themselves and leaving it in their wake. Know that you will get the same in eternity. Live to please God now, in honor and holiness, and pleasure beyond your wildest imagining awaits you at God's right hand and forevermore.

Resolves

- (Son) To honor my father as he works to be faithful by encouraging, comforting, and urging me
- (Father) To show my son how to please God with my own self-control, and to encourage, comfort, and urge him on in faith
- To cultivate self-control and avoid even a hint of sexual sinning
- To avoid all occasions and opportunities for lust and sexual sinning
- To put on brotherly love in place of lust and sexual sinning

Scripture Memory

"The evil deeds of a wicked man ensnare him; the cords of his sin hold him fast. He will die for lack of discipline, led astray by his own great folly."

Proverbs 5:22–23

For Discussion

1. In what situations do you find yourself most tempted to succumb to lustful and impure thoughts?
2. What changes in television viewing, movies, music,

131

magazines, and books do you need to make?

3. What friends or other influences make you more vulnerable to lust and sexual sinning?

4. What steps should you take to make yourself more accountable in these areas?

5. What changes do you need to make in thoughts and deeds to practice brotherly love toward others?

"Rise, My Soul, to Watch and Pray"

Watch against thyself, my soul, lest with grace thou trifle;
Let not self thy thoughts control nor God's mercy stifle.
Pride and sin lurk within all thy hopes to scatter;
Heed not when they flatter.

Johann B. Freystein, 1697

For Further Study

Read all or part of Proverbs 5:1–23; 6:20–35; 7:1–27

12

SELF-CONTROL
OUT OF CONTROL

Hebrews 13:1–4

Kissing

You're squirming in your seat. Kissing? Gross out! You remember thinking and speaking that way back when you were a hairless prepubescent. Be honest. Deep within you something has changed. What used to make you gag and moan about girls' germs now fascinates you. You find yourself thinking uncomfortably about being close to, talking with, touching the hand of, even kissing a beautiful young woman.

You may get angry with yourself when you find your mind revolving around the discovery that there are curious differences between boys and girls. You may even bend over backward to try to reassert your disgust at the notion of love and kissing. Yet none of it rings true anymore. Something has dramatically changed in your being. Go ahead, make Herculean efforts to expunge it, but deep down you know that sex lurks uncomfortably beneath many of your thoughts and secret desires.

My stirrings began in sixth grade. I had always been dutifully grossed out at girls, and if I accidentally touched a girl I had developed an entire cleansing ritual to rid myself of the contagion. But one day something changed. I recall being deeply puzzled by it all. I found myself suddenly noticing how different girls looked from boys, and try as I might, I couldn't help finding that difference interesting, even alluring. And then I found myself doing some of the stupidest things I'd ever done in my life to try to get the attention of certain girls in my class. You know, endearing things such as yanking on a ponytail, hiding a backpack, even attempting great feats of strength at recess to impress them with my manliness.

Those early stirrings grew into one of the most powerful desires known to man, and did I ever burn with that desire through my high school years. Virtually everything I did took sex into account. I found myself thinking constantly about girls, and then about a specific girl. It nearly ruined me.

If you're not there yet, beware; it's just around the corner. If you are there, brace up like a man and listen carefully. Heed what I am about to say, and pleasure and happiness await you. Ignore it, and get set for a life of misery and ruin.

It's Just a Kiss

In F. Scott Fitzgerald's classic Jazz Age novel *The Great Gatsby*, the title character launches an obsessive idealization of the alluring socialite Daisy Buchanan. There is nothing Jay Gatsby will not do to win her, including creating an elaborate fantasy of his own existence, if only he can have his true love. What began such a powerful attachment?

It all happened one hot summer evening when he kissed her. Fitzgerald described the instant like this:

His heart beat faster and faster as Daisy's white face came up to his own. He knew that when he kissed this girl, and forever wed his unutterable visions to her perishable breath, his mind would never romp again like the mind of God. At his lips' touch she blossomed for him like a flower and the incarnation was complete.

Put another way, when he kissed her he gave himself, body and soul, to her, and no impediment in his mind could keep them apart. Gatsby wed himself to a dream that turned out to be a delusion. Give yourself emotionally to a delusion and you, like Gatsby, will beget devastation and ruin.

You're probably thinking, "What's the big deal? It's just a kiss." So says the postmodern world you live in. Wiser minds through the centuries, however, have not agreed.

Renaissance scholar Desiderius Erasmus of Rotterdam (1469–1536), in his colloquy *The Wooer and the Maiden*, exposed the sexual impatience of a young man attempting to woo Maria, a chaste young woman who liked him but was wisely cautious.

His advances frustrated, the young man asked, "Shan't I have anything from you to take with me?"

Maria replied, "This scent ball, which may gladden your heart."

"Add a kiss at least," moaned the wooer.

Maria said, "I want to deliver to you a virginity whole and unimpaired."

The wooer scoffed. "Does a kiss rob you of your virginity?"

Maria cleverly replied, "Then do you want me to bestow my kisses on others too?"

The wooer was indignant. "Of course not. I want your kisses kept for me."

"I'll keep them for you," Maria replied, and for that reason, "I wouldn't dare give away kisses just now." She offered him a handshake instead and concluded, "Meanwhile, I'll pray Christ to bless and prosper us both in what we do."

Later in the same Renaissance, William Shakespeare probably borrowed from Erasmus in his wooing scene between Henry V and

135

Princess Katherine of France. When Henry declared that he would kiss Katherine's lips, she objected that ladies don't kiss that way before marriage. "Nice customs curtsy to great kings," Henry insisted. "Dear Kate, we are the makers of manners." And then he stole a kiss from her. "You have witchcraft in your lips, Kate," he concluded.

In both of these scenes the young women are wiser than the young men. Maria understood that a kiss was a big deal, that a piece of her irretrievable virginity was relinquished in a kiss. Henry V was a typical king who believed that he was above the customs built into society, in this case ones designed to protect the chastity of ladies before marriage.

But you may still be wondering what could possibly be wrong with holding hands, a friendly hug, or a kiss. Let me explain.

One Flesh and Hormones

God designed men and women differently. You've noticed. But there's far more to those differences than meets the eye. God designed women's bodies to respond powerfully to romantic touching by producing the hormone oxytocin; the more intimate the touching, the more oxytocin her body produces.

Jennifer Roback Morse, research fellow at Stanford's Hoover Institute, author of *Smart Sex: Finding Life-Long Love in a Hook-Up World*, explains how a woman's body works: "The flood of oxytocin increases her desire for further touch[ing]. Her body is literally changed." Because of this, Morse continues, "modern physiology is discovering that the attachments we feel toward our sexual partners are more than mere feelings, and more than cultural conditionings."

C. S. Lewis in *The Screwtape Letters* put it like this: "The truth is that wherever a man lies with a woman there, whether they like it or not, a transcendental relation is set up between them which must be eternally enjoyed or endured." Morse and Lewis are attempting to explain what the apostle Paul called being "united to [your] wife," or becoming "one flesh" (Eph. 5:31, quoting Gen. 2:24).

Thus, by holding hands, by sitting wedged tightly next to each other, by hugging and caressing, and by kissing, you and a young woman create far more than you may have bargained for. Morse observes that a woman's hormones help "create an involuntary chemical commitment, a powerful bond, between the partners."

Protest all you can, a romantic relationship with a girl that involves intimate touching before marriage "creates its own hormonal glue." Furthermore, Morse continues, "Neither our bodies nor our souls will allow us to completely undo the connections between sexual activity, devoted love for another adult, and babies." Morse, a scholar who makes no declaration of being a Christian that I am aware of, nevertheless seems consistent with the Bible when she observes that "our whole spiritual, emotional, and psychological being is bound up in the act [of making love]."

Perhaps modern sexual theory is finally catching up with the apostle Paul, who wrote that the man who commits fornication, unlike other sins, is sinning against his own body (1 Cor. 6:18). Since there is an organic binding of a man and a woman together as "bone of my bones and flesh of my flesh" in sexual intercourse (Gen. 2:23), the Bible describes sexual sinning as having irrevocable long-term consequences.

Clearly, sexual activity binds you forever in some mysterious way to another human being. But if this human being is not your wife, you are in eternal deep weeds. The point is, like it or not, there's no going back with sexual activity. You are stuck for life with the results.

Similarly, God designed your body to bond organically with a woman's in sexual intimacy. Nearly all physiologists agree that the predominantly male hormone vasopressin, the "monogamy molecule," is produced as men engage in levels of sexual activity with a woman, all of which contributes to the fathering impulse "to protect, provide, and take responsibility for others."

All of this is simply confirming evidence of what the Bible has always taught about love, sex, and total commitment for life. Toy with romance and sex outside of biblical boundaries and it degenerates into a distorted commingling of human anatomy that, when the instantaneous pleasure fades, produces the most lasting unhappiness for individuals and for the society adulterated by no-commitment sex.

"During my student days," Dr. Morse admits, "I more or less did the whole sexual revolution. I got to be an expert on what doesn't work. And it was not a jolly time. I hurt myself and other people. I was wrong. I am now sorry for the harm I caused myself and others, harm that I can never fully repair. The sexual revolution," concludes Morse, "has been profoundly anti-social."

Sadly, Morse had to learn all this the hard way. Your Bible, however, repeatedly warns you against lust and sexual sin so that you won't have to. But if you approach relationships with girls as recreational activities to gratify your sexual fantasies, even when you "don't go too far," at best you will regret it—with lifelong baggage in tow. At worst it will destroy your life and the lives of many others who will inevitably be affected by the folly of your choices.

Partaking of Someone's Soul

Though our culture says to go ahead and hold, hug, caress, and kiss, it is profoundly dishonest to detach these romantic forms of touching from making love. And there is no more romantic and intimate form of lovemaking leading to sexual intercourse than kissing.

I'm not talking about the lipstick besmeared smack that your great-aunt leaves on your cheek. Though it's hard to put into words, you know the difference. Like Erasmus, playwright Edmond Rostand finds words to define the difference.

Rostand created quintessentially chivalrous Cyrano de Bergerac, who, though secretly in love with Roxane, is afraid to declare his love because of his big nose and clownish appearance. Then along comes a handsome but bungling and inarticulate suitor who enlists Cyrano's assistance in giving him poetic words of passion and love to use in his wooing of Roxane. Cyrano finds himself in the painful position of employing his poetic skill in winning Roxane's hand in marriage—for his rival. Impatient with Cyrano's heartfelt eloquence, the rival wooer blurts out that he wants a kiss from Roxane. Cyrano attempts to repair the bluntness by defining a romantic kiss:

> A kiss! When all is said, what is a kiss? An oath of allegiance taken in closer proximity, a promise more precise, a seal on a confession, a rose-red dot upon the letter i in loving; a secret which elects the mouth for ear; an instant of eternity murmuring like a bee; balmy communion with a flavor of flowers; a fashion of inhaling each other's heart, and of tasting, on the brink of the lips, each other's soul.

There's nothing throwaway in this definition. There are no exit clauses, no withdrawal strategy, no as-long-as-our-love-shall-last nonsense. This definition employs total-commitment words: *allegiance, promise, seal, confession, eternity, communion, heart,* and *soul.*

Like Rostand, other perceptive individuals through the ages have understood that a kiss belongs with total commitment to your wife. It is not a consumer good, it is not for casual contact, for self-gratification; a kiss is the intimate sealing and promising of yourself to another with an undying confession wherein you willingly bind your very soul to the soul of another—forever.

After hearing all this, Rostand's impetuous wooer wonders whether kissing Roxane might not mean a bit more than he bargained for. "But now I feel as if I ought not!" he declares. Learn from his conclusion. Kissing is an intimate expression of lifelong commitment. It belongs only within the boundaries of marriage. Be wise like Erasmus's Maria, and keep your kisses and caresses for your wife.

A Hook-up World

You might be saying to yourself that this view of romance and kissing is too difficult. It would require you to be radically different from the world you live in. You're dead right. But isn't that what being a Christian means?

I live near the West Coast city of Seattle, Washington, known as the hookup capital of the USA, the place to go and have casual, no-commitment sexual contact, the one-night-stand capital of America. The fallout is devastating. Seattle has the second-highest homosexual population in the United States, an above-average divorce rate, the second-lowest church attendance in the United States, and many other ignominious distinctions proportionate to its promiscuity.

Tragically, the church in the region is not immune. I could tell of a church officer who, while directing a Christian ministry, slipped into an emotional attachment with an employee. Before he knew it, it had escalated into a romantic one. Providentially, he was caught before it plummeted into a sexual one.

I could tell of another church officer, a husband and father, who succumbed to the hookup region and began living a double life, consorting with prostitutes and utterly destroying his life and family.

I could tell of a highly effective church planter for the conservative denomination of which he was a part, with a lovely wife and four precious children, who, when his Seattle church began to grow, employed one of his recent converts to help in the office. Within months, still evangelizing and ministering, he was committing adultery with her.

Believe it: young men are not exempt. I could tell of one who began preying on younger teenage girls in his church. Picking his favorites, he enticed them to kiss and make out, all under the otherwise watchful eye of Christian parents, teachers, pastors, and elders—all to the devastation of his church and family when it finally became known.

Wherever you live, you are not exempt from sexual sin. Christians can get sucked into the vacuum of this hookup world, a world that winks at sin and views sexual intimacy as a consumer product. You are bombarded by this mind-set on every side, in music, movies, fashion. But casual Hollywood sex does not, and cannot, deliver. Though the film industry justifies its sexually explicit content on the basis of realism, in reality it's giving you cheap, distorted fantasyland.

Romance and Sex: Package Deal

If you date girls and look forward to the thrill of touching and kissing, you've been duped, and you're playing with fire—and you will get burned. Kissing is reserved for lovemaking with your wife; thus, outside of marriage it becomes part of fornication, pre-sex that robs you and another of irretrievable virginity.

Recreational romance and casual sexual contact is a setup for infidelity, brokenness, discontentment, unhappiness, and divorce. It trains you for unfaithfulness, for deriving sensual pleasure from another man's wife—which she is likely to be someday, and it will trouble you (and her) all your days. Give your emotions casually to a girl and you are trading the full measure of that delirious sexual pleasure that God has reserved for you to enjoy with your wife.

When your emotions are intoxicated by sexual arousal, you lose the ability to differentiate between short-term thrill and genuine love. Sure, it makes you feel ecstatic, like you're on top of the world, floating with the stars, transported into a mystical wonderland.

God designed sexual love that way, but he placed boundaries around it, made it sacred and wonderful, set apart, and pure, one of the most satisfying experiences of life. But it is a package deal based on total commitment for life: love, marriage, sexual intercourse, pregnancy, children, nurture—it is beyond wonder. But things of such wonder require maturity and self-control; they require love. Perceptively, Shakespeare defined the purity of a man's love for a woman by his willingness to "give and hazard all" for her—as Christ did for his bride (Eph. 5). Until you're ready to give and hazard all, you're not ready for kissing.

Erasmus's Maria argued that because love is blind and because romantically charged emotions are inherently unreliable—even less reliable when encumbered by the "hormonal glue" of touching and kissing—wise young people will welcome and seek out the guidance of godly parents. So must you.

There's one route to sexual purity: self-control based on total commitment to virginity—emotional and physical—a virginity of the soul. If you want Christ to bless you in all that you do, don't give the smallest amount of your soul away in superficial lovemaking.

Resolves

- To commit myself to not even a hint of sexual immorality
- To think of all levels of sexual contact as part of lovemaking
- To keep my way pure
- To talk honestly with my parents about sex

Scripture Memory

"Among you there must not be even a hint of sexual immorality, or of any kind of impurity, or of greed, because these are improper for God's holy people."

Ephesians 5:3

For Discussion

1. What is the difference between a girl who is a friend and a girlfriend?
2. How does a young man speak and behave around girls in a way that avoids romantic misunderstandings?
3. List words, deeds, and situations that a young man who takes sexual purity seriously will avoid.

"The Sands of Time Are Sinking"

O Christ, he is the fountain, the deep sweet well of love!
The streams on earth I've tasted more deep I'll drink above:
There to an ocean fulness his mercy doth expand,
And glory, glory dwelleth in Emmanuel's land.

Anne Cousin, 1857 (based on Samuel Rutherford)

For Further Study

Proverbs 5–7; 1 Corinthians 13; Ephesians 5:22–33; *Passion and Purity*, by Elisabeth Elliot

13

SELF-CONTROL INSIDE OUT

Hebrews 4:12–16

Something Rotten

My senior year of high school, I was elected student-body president. Looking back, I have some regrets. I wasn't a particularly good president. On the other hand, I wasn't a particularly bad one, either—just bland mediocre.

I was outwardly obedient to my parents and respectful to my teachers, outwardly conforming to the expectations laid out for me. I didn't swear, or drink, or smoke, or cheat on tests. I didn't even drive fast. In fact, my friends said that I drove like an old lady. I don't think anyone would have labeled me rebellious. In fact, I suspect that most adults in my life, including my parents, thought that I was a pretty good Christian kid.

But I knew better. I knew that I was proud, was often lazy, and had allowed myself an emotional attachment that was pushing the limits, that my heart was all too cold and indifferent toward Christ, that I preferred a good time over holiness and a circumspect life.

Still, I was involved in the Christian Service Club, and often went out Friday after school to witness on the street in the drug-dealing, hard-living, red-light district of town. But there was another fellow in student government whom I looked up to as the model of Christian maturity. Jerry was the student leader of the Christian Service Club, a role that seemed to suit him well. I remember feeling a bit uncomfortable about my spiritual deficiencies when around him, but I liked and respected him.

Time passed. We graduated and went our separate ways. Jerry went to Bible college and later became a youth pastor. He married a lovely young woman, and they had several children. All seemed well. Until one day his wife discovered a stray receipt in the car. It was from a pornographic video store. There had to be some mistake. There wasn't. She was devastated.

As the story unfolded, so did Jerry's secret life. In Bible college, he and his roommates had begun renting pornographic videos, just for kicks. He became a slave. So for years, while pastoring the youth at his church, reading Bible stories to his children, telling his wife he loved her, he had viewed pornographic videos by stealth.

And then he got caught.

Inner Life

We expect this from worldly high school kids. But how did it happen to someone like Jerry? As nearly as anyone can know, Jerry allowed sin a mere toehold at first. Perhaps it started as pride derived from his prowess on the basketball court. He was a brilliant athlete. He was handsome, well liked, popular with girls, a good student, polished and mannerly. But he allowed a toehold for the devil, a foothold that became a broad ledge, then a wide plain; at last it grew to an immovable continent of sinning. All because he failed to turn and flee at the first blush.

"Take heed of secret sins," wrote Puritan pastor Jeremiah Burroughs. "They undo thee if loved and maintained: one moth may spoil the garment; one leak drown the ship . . . so one sin may damn the soul."

Jerry's life, his wife's life, his children's lives will never be the same. Why? Because Jerry failed to practice self-control, because he failed to guard his heart against secret sins, and because he maintained and nurtured those sins. It has more or less ruined his earthly life. God alone knows whether it has damned his soul.

Secret sinning is easier today than it was before the Internet removed shame, the last defense against pornography. A man used to have to face another man across the counter or at the ticket booth when he went slinking after the cesspool of pornography, but not so in your world. A veritable quagmire of sexually explicit viewing is but a click of the mouse away, and all in the privacy of your own room. Shame is gone. Puritan divine John Owen put it this way: "Custom of sinning takes away the sense of it; the course of the world takes away the shame of it."

But then our depraved mind plays an old trick with this suggestion. Isn't it better that they remain secret sins? At least then we're not flagrantly living out and practicing our sins. After all, these are secret sins, small ones, that hurt no one. I've even heard the lame argument that pornography is healthy for men. Those who suggest this do so in defiance of all evidence: sociological, physiological, psychological, and, most importantly, theological.

Satan uses sin like fire. He urges you to start small and in secret. He tells you that such sins—if sins they be—are insignificant and inconsequential. But like sparks, small sins grow and spread until their fire engulfs the house and all in it. "It is Satan's custom," wrote Puritan Thomas Manton, "by small sins to draw us to greater, as little sticks set the great ones on fire, and a wisp of straw kindles a block of wood."

Kill or Be Killed

Young men must hold firmly to the faith, or they will stumble and fall. Christ was tempted in all ways as you are, yet he remained firm in faith without succumbing to temptation and sin. Therefore, put your confidence in Christ. When temptations rise, go to him. You can't hide your secret sins from him anyway.

"The eyes of the LORD are everywhere, keeping watch on the wicked and the good" (Prov. 15:3). Go ahead. Tell Christ all your struggles. Don't try to hide them. Lay your sins at Jesus' feet. Go to him and find grace to help in time of need. But do it now. Allow the devil not even a toehold in your heart for sin. Allow no spark of sin to smolder in your lap.

With sin, you must venture all on the first attempt. Don't think that you can take sin on by half measures. When facing an enemy in combat, I'm told, you don't wait to see what kind of firepower he will hurl at you. You unload the magazine when he first rears his ugly head. You don't dally around, wondering if he's not so bad after all, or entertain notions that he really wants to be friends. You take careful aim and squeeze the trigger, and you don't stop until he's dead. Ask Jerry. You must be ruthless with your secret sins, or they will be ruthless with you.

"Use sin as it will use you," wrote Richard Baxter. "Spare it not, for it will not spare you. It is your murderer. Use it, therefore, as a murderer should be used. Kill it before it kills you."

Crafty Satan

"There is great care about dress," wrote John Calvin, quoting Latin philosopher Cato, "but great carelessness about virtue." Why do we find it easy to be careless about virtue? Probably because virtue is internal and so we think it is hidden. Correspondingly, young men tend to expend greater energy on external things precisely because they are not hidden. Let's be honest; you tend to care more about how you appear to others on the outside than how you really are in your heart.

146

Hence, the outward appearance of having things all together spiritually is more important to many young men than actually making spiritual progress, taking ground from the devil, growing in grace, and triumphing over sin. It's so much easier to affect the appearance of these things. Remember, however, what Jesus said of the Pharisees: "On the outside you appear to people as righteous but on the inside you are full of hypocrisy and wickedness" (Matt. 23:28). Just as Jesus knew their hearts, he knows yours.

Satan wants you to conceal your sin—and die. He has a far easier time leading you to despair and to give in to temptation when he can induce you to conceal sin. Remember, however, that the wages of sin is death. The Lord, on the other hand, calls you to forsake sin—and live. "To forsake sin," wrote Puritan William Gurnall, "is to leave it without any thought reserved of returning to it again."

Satan is crafty. He wants you to conceal your secret sins because then you won't, once and for all, forsake them. You'll keep a candle burning and reserve a room in your heart for those sins. But when you own up to your temptations and sins, forsaking them without reservation, the work of repentance has begun. By the grace of God, it continues as you turn away in shame and leave the sin behind. Then, firm in faith, go forward with the help of your heavenly Father—and with the help of your earthly one.

Nothing Hidden

Much of our problem with temptation and secret sins comes from being worldly-minded. So distracted by things of sight, we fail to remember the eye of the Lord. We fail to believe that "nothing in all creation is hidden from God's sight. Everything is uncovered and laid bare before the eyes of him to whom we must give account" (Heb. 4:13).

Keep this truth before your mind, moment by moment, and the "secret" nature of inner sinning will not seem so secret to you. You avoid many sins because the public consequences would be too devastating to bear. For that reason, some young men delude themselves into thinking that secret sins are not so bad because nobody knows about them. Never forget, however, that "everything is uncovered and laid bare"—about your heart, about your thought life, about your deepest desires and urges. God sees all. And you will give an account of all.

Most young men have secrets they keep from their dad. They hope he never finds out about some of what they do and say when he is not there. They would never want him to find out some of their private thoughts and desires and some of the things they do in secret.

Ultimate Self-Love

Some young men, especially ones who have given in to pornography, have relinquished self-control and have become slaves to sexual self-manipulation or masturbation. Young men who do this emphatically do not want their fathers to know about it. Yet, enslaved as they are to the easy self-gratification of masturbation, they feel the need to rationalize their sin. Some argue that it's okay because it makes them less inclined to have sexual intercourse before marriage, or because it helps them avoid lust, or because nobody else is harmed by it. These arguments are like a boat made of chicken wire. Honest young men know that Paul's exhortation against "even a hint of sexual immorality, or of any kind of impurity" (Eph. 5:3), clearly has to include masturbation.

Throughout the pages of the Bible, lovemaking is always to be mutually enjoyed between a man and his wife. "Sex is for sharing," as Philip Graham Ryken puts it. Thus, biblical lovemaking can be thought of as an intimate microcosm of the Christian life; we gain pleasure only when we use our strength to give pleasure to others. Therefore, masturbation is a sin in the same root way that loving yourself and not your neighbor is a sin.

So a young man who gives in to masturbation is indulging in a grotesque self-intimacy that makes his own pleasure the most important thing. Don't kid yourself. Any sin that places you in the center will affect others. Give in to masturbation and you will be less fit for married love; you should expect it to burden future intimacy with your wife. It's no overstatement to say that the secret sin of masturbation is the ultimate expression of "self-love, idolizing avaricious self," as Samuel Rutherford described our soul-killing preoccupation with self-gratification.

But no sin, however secret we imagine it to be, is kept secret from our heavenly Father. Yet many young men think they just couldn't bear to have their dad know about some of those sins. More concerned with preserving a deeply flawed appearance of virtue than actually owning up to your vices and seeking help, you flounder on alone.

Attempting to hide temptation and sin, moreover, not only enables small sins to grow into bigger sins, but also weakens your fellowship with man and God. Concealing your struggles with lust, with pride, with anger, and with other sins creates a Berlin Wall where there needs to be a wide, well-traveled, two-way highway between you and both your heavenly and earthly fathers.

One of the means by which God gives you grace to help in time of need is by honest conversation about your secret sins with your father. Any father worth the name already knows what you are thinking and desiring in your heart. He already knows what you're tempted to jest about with your friends in the locker room. He already knows what you feel and long for about girls and sex. Talk to him about it; don't hide.

From the Heart

Many Christian young men practice external habits of conformity to parents and to the Lord, but inwardly they have developed the habit of carelessness—as I did in my youth. They live as if God had not said, "Above all else, guard your heart, for it is the wellspring of life" (Prov. 4:23). You can check the boxes of external conformity as Jerry did, but if you are not guarding your heart, your sin will find you out.

Amaziah, king of Judah, was probably like I was as a high school senior. "He did what was right in the eyes of the LORD, but not wholeheartedly" (2 Chron. 25:2). Eventually he forgot that "God has the power to help or to overthrow" (25:8), and he "sought the gods of Edom" (25:20). At last, he "would not listen" (25:20), and he "turned away from following the LORD" (25:27). Because Amaziah failed to kill the secret sins of his heart, Jerusalem was destroyed; his own people conspired against him, and slew him. All this happened because he did not do what was right before the face of God—with a whole heart.

You know what *wholehearted* means. You do sports wholeheartedly; you shoot wholeheartedly; you eat pizza wholeheartedly; you play video games wholeheartedly; you pursue girls wholeheartedly; you want a fast car wholeheartedly; you want independence wholeheartedly. But do you do what is right in the eyes of the Lord—wholeheartedly?

Look up the verses at the end of this chapter. Why does the Bible continually urge sons to this kind of heart religion? Why does the book of Proverbs repeatedly say things such as: "Listen, my son, to your father's instruction" (Prov. 1:8)? Because young men really don't like listening to and obeying others. With all their heart, they want to do what they want to do.

A young man, however, who doesn't want to ruin his life as Jerry ruined his must listen to instruction and obey—but it must be from the heart. There is no room for the begrudging, slouching "obedience" here. It must be from the heart. You may obey outwardly but with your heart grumbling and chafing, kicking against the goads, as it were. But this is not doing what is right in the eyes of the Lord, wholeheartedly.

A wise son guards his heart and expunges every hint of secret sinning. He talks to his heavenly Father and his earthly one about his struggles with sin. He knows that concealing sin brings death, but that confessing and forsaking sin brings forgiveness and victory. Wise men know that "it is good to find out our sins," as Puritan Thomas Watson put it, "lest they find us out."

Resolves

- To keep a closer watch on my inner life
- To pray regularly together as father and son
- To speak with my heavenly and earthly fathers about my temptations and secret sins
- To root out inward disobedience and contemptuous mental replies to my parents

Scripture Memory

"Above all else, guard your heart, for it is the wellspring of life."

Proverbs 4:23

For Discussion

1. In what company are you more inclined toward secret sinning?
2. What music, movies, or books predispose your heart to secret sinning?
3. Why is it hard to talk with your father about temptations you face?

"Rise, My Soul, to Watch and Pray"

Watch against the devil's snares, lest asleep he find thee;
For indeed no pains he spares to deceive and blind thee.
Satan's prey oft are they who secure are sleeping
And no watch are keeping.

Johann B. Freystein, 1697

For Further Study

1 Samuel 16:7b; Psalm 111:1; Proverbs 3:1–2; 4:1–2; 6:20–21; 7:1–3

14

SELF-CONTROL OUTSIDE IN

Psalm 98; Zephaniah 3:17

"Bad Guys!"

Martin Luther extolled the "perfect wisdom of God in his wonderful work of music." Hymn writer and musician Luther was also an irrepressible pugilist who was unafraid to denounce all who disagreed with him: "He who does not find [music] an inexpressible miracle of the Lord is truly a clod and is not worthy to be considered a man." Luther was right. If you want to be considered a man, you, too, must think rightly about music.

Recently my three-year-old helped my own thinking about music. Seemingly distracted with his toys while I followed the libretto and listened to Christopher Hogwood's rendition of Handel's *Messiah*, we weren't two bars into the hard-driving fierceness conveyed in the orchestral overture leading to the crucifixion when my son scrunched up his face, looked at me, and said, "Bad guys!"

How does instrumental music convey foreboding badness so clearly even to a child? I'd like to believe it's because he's a genius, but he's not. It's because once sounds are arranged into music, they are not neutral.

Once you put letters together and make words and sentences, those letters have lost whatever neutrality they may have otherwise had. So it is with isolated sounds. Arrange those sounds into an orchestral overture and they mean something. Generals know this: arrange bugle sounds one way and it means "charge"; arrange them another way and it means "retreat." Dentists know this, too. They don't play the Ring-wraith music from the soundtrack to *The Lord of the Rings* in their waiting rooms. Why? Because music is not neutral.

My toddler's conclusion about music was articulated more expansively by Dr. Howard Hanson, one-time director of Eastman School of Music at the University of Rochester: "Music can be soothing or invigorating, ennobling or vulgarizing, philosophical or orgiastic. It has powers for evil as well as for good."

Neutrality Debunked

Studies on the effects of music and learning have gained worldwide attention with the "Mozart effect." Codiscoverer of the "Mozart effect," Dr. Gordon Shaw, claims that "music can enhance how we think, reason and create." Since the original findings in 1993, the "Mozart effect" has repeatedly shown that students who listen to classical music and take music lessons do significantly better in school. The conclusions are not a close call.

Researchers at the inner-city 95th Street School in Los Angeles have discovered that underprivileged schoolchildren who listened to Mozart's Sonata for Two Pianos in D Major, and who took music lessons, in just four months scored 27 percent higher on their math tests than students who didn't listen to classical music.

Another study compared nineteen schoolchildren who were taught using classical music with fourteen classmates who studied without classical music. In eight months, the students who learned without classical music improved in spatial IQs by 6 percent, but the nineteen who were taught using Mozart logged a 46 percent increase in spatial IQs.

Independent studies conducted on everything from rats to college students, Alzheimer victims to people with epilepsy, babies in the womb to fifth graders, from Vienna to California—the jury is in and the verdict unanimous. Listening to classical music enhances brain development, contributes to emotional well-being, even helps the body cope with disease. Researchers widely agree that "it is now no longer appropriate to consider these results as separate phenomena. They all fit into a coherent picture."

Music and the Soul

Why does it all fit? There is a growing consensus in the scientific and psychological communities, represented by the conclusions of Dr. Lawrence Parsons of the University of Texas–San Antonio: "The research shows more clearly than ever that music is represented in mechanisms widely distributed throughout the brain rather than localized in a single region as are other kinds of information, such as visual or movement information."

Long ago, Plato (428–348 B.C.) came to similar conclusions: "Musical training is a more potent instrument than any other, because rhythm and harmony find their way into the inward places of the soul." Perhaps the discovery that, unlike other information, music is "widely distributed throughout the brain" is modern man's way of saying that music finds its "way into the inward places of the soul."

Doctors and hospitals seem to agree. Parents of newborns are sent home from hospitals with free music discs to play for their babies. And it's not kid music. Our latest hospital music disc is all classical music intended to nurture the brain—or is it the soul?—of our new baby. The nonneutral effects of music begin early; midwives urge pregnant mothers to listen to classical music—for their own sakes and the babies'. Baby Einstein videos, significantly, do not have U2 or the Beatles playing in the background. It's music that falls under the broad designation of "classical."

Young men who get a charge from pop music need to sit up and listen. Researchers without concerns for the spiritual or moral effects of pop music on you have overwhelmingly concluded that the effects of music range widely throughout the brain and, thus, profoundly affect the entire individual. And if Plato was correct, these effects go even deeper. Music has a powerful effect on your soul.

So is music neutral? Dr. Max Schoen in his book *Psychology of Music* wrote, "Music is the most powerful stimulus known among the perceptive senses. The medical, psychiatric and other evidences for the non-neutrality of music is so overwhelming that it frankly amazes me that anyone should seriously say otherwise."

Music and the Bible

But does the Bible agree? Choices that a young man makes about his music would certainly be easier if the Bible simply said not to listen to this kind of music, only to this kind. Because it does not, however, many Christians have concluded, "Music can be considered morally neutral" (David Scheer, *PG: A Parental Guide to Rock*, p. 167). Christians may disagree, but no one who reads his Bible can deny that it says an enormous amount about music.

Large portions of the Bible were written specifically to be sung along with instrumental accompaniment. The psalmist clearly commends instrumental music, telling us to "make music to the LORD with the harp," and if the harp isn't quite manly enough for you, he adds "trumpets and the blast of the ram's horn" (Ps. 98:5–6). Next he calls "the sea . . . and everything in it" to join in the music, "the world, and all who live in it" (98:7). Then he invites rivers to join in with clapping and the mountains to "sing together for joy" (98:8). This wonderfully varied panoply of musical sound is to be offered "before the LORD" (98:6, 9).

Music in the Bible, as nearly as I can tell, is always about worship. It has the power to thrill us, to lift us above ourselves, to elevate our verbal expression, to hold before our affections an object of worship. In Psalm 98, everything that is said about worship must be understood in light of the opening phrase "Sing to the LORD," repeated throughout the psalm, concluding with "sing before the LORD" in the final verse. From my reading of Scripture, this priority of music's being created and offered "to the LORD" and "before the LORD" is the consistent message of the Bible.

Put simply, music is worship. And absolutely nothing about worship in the Bible is neutral. Get it fixed in your mind that music is worship, and I'm convinced that most of the discord about music will be harmonized.

Music and Religion

The theologian of the Reformation, John Calvin (1509–64), wrote, "We know by experience that music has a secret and almost incredible power to move hearts," and so Calvin versified psalms and employed Louis Bourgeois to create psalter tunes appropriate for the worship of God. Music's power to affect people's hearts is "secret and almost incredible," which is why we don't all agree—but also why music is so potentially dangerous.

But it's not only Christian theologians of the older and wiser stripe who knew this about music. Keith Richard of the Rolling Stones, in a *Newsweek* article (January 4, 1971), once called Mick Jagger "the Lucifer of rock, the unholy roller," and marveled at his "demonic power to affect people."

Notice the religious character of Keith Richard's words. Since in the Bible music and worship go hand in hand, it's no wonder that music exerts its mysterious power and secret force over us, and that people on either side of the divide speak of music in religious terms.

Derek Taylor, former press officer for the Beatles, was quoted in a *Saturday Evening Post* article (August 1964), "It's as if they'd founded a new religion. They're completely anti-Christ. I mean, I'm anti-Christ as well, but they're so anti-Christ they shock me, which is not an easy thing."

But many are quick to protest: Aren't lots of oldies songs just about having fun? Besides, they're not head-bashers like the stuff kids listen to today. We don't want our kids to think God is a spoilsport. Why not let our young men feel the "good vibrations"? Why not? Because in the Bible, music is always about worship. And musical sounds and genres, apart from lyrics, are carefully crafted to fit whatever the theology of that worship is.

Shortly before his death, John Lennon candidly reflected on the music genre he helped to popularize: "Rock music has got the same message as before. It is anti-religious, anti-nationalistic and anti-morality. But now I understand what you have to do. You have to put the message across with a little more honey on it."

Remember the secret power of music? Add honey to it and you have a force like a tidal wave to change hearts, to woo minds, to alter the entire course of a culture. It's the honey that has deceived many a young man over the years. It has deceived an entire culture, including a generation of well-meaning Christians. And it may be deceiving you.

Paul Johnson in an article for *National Review* attributed the decline of religious morality in the West in the last half-century to "the destructive spirit of the 1960s, that disastrous decade, [which] has never quite been laid to rest. Its victims and addicts are still influential at all levels of society, and the consequences of its ravages continue to unfold."

Included in those "victims and addicts," alas, may be some Christians who fondly think back on those days and jest that the sixties weren't all that bad. Yet Johnson goes on to observe that as a result of the sixties, "Christianity is much weaker."

Christianity is weaker because it was powerfully under attack by a new culture, by a new philosophy of life, by a new religion. Open a secular history textbook and you will read dispassionate analysis citing "four young men who helped create the 1960s cultural revolution." You will read how "popular culture, especially music, both expressed and stimulated the new dissent," or how this or that pop song was the "anthem of youth rebellion," and you will read about "the strong sexual cast" of the music of the "New Left," as cultural revolutionary C. Wright Mills termed it.

Still, many Christians persist in saying, "I see no danger," as they plop in their favorite oldies album and escape back into "the magical mystery tour."

Music and Sex

Secular historians candidly admit that "rock was the music of the rebellious young, the trade mark of youthful cultural revolt," and they seem to agree that the sexual revolution had its most powerful ally in rock 'n' roll. Note that identifying a particular music genre as "the trade mark of youthful cultural revolt" is tacit admission that music is not neutral. But what characteristics make one music genre such a powerful ally of cultural dissent?

Rock music and its derivatives are designed to make you reckless, to give you a throbbing sense of invincibility, an adrenaline-pumping notion of power and freedom, to lower your moral resistance, to urge you to act on what you feel, to throw off restraint, and to live outside of the boundaries. It's also designed to hit you in the face with sex.

But don't take my word for it. Chris Stein, lead guitarist and founder of New Wave band Blondie, stated about rock music what he thought was obvious: "Everybody takes it for granted that rock 'n' roll is synonymous with sex." Frank Zappa agreed and even offered a reason: "Rock music is sex. The big beat matches the body's rhythms."

Andrew Loog Oldham, manager of the Rolling Stones, put it this way: "Rock music is sex, and you have to hit [teenagers] in the face with it." Oldham discovered Mick Jagger at a London nightclub and was so taken with the "commercial prospects of Jagger's sexuality" that he cut a deal to make himself manager of the superstar.

Rock music emerged out of the sexual revolution, and then became the ubiquitous transmitter of its ideals. As such, it must bear a great deal of the responsibility for the decades of moral decline that persists in its wake. Just as music and worship always go together in the Bible, so rock music became the liturgical music of a new religion, one whose idol is still sexual freedom.

You know what it does to you. How it makes you feel, what it encourages you to think about. It's why you like it. If you have spiritual wits about you, you already know which music is "orgiastic," as Dr. Howard Hanson put it. Therefore, any young man who takes seriously Paul's urging to "avoid sexual immorality" (1 Thess. 4:3), to avoid it so much that there is not even a hint of sexual immorality given quarter in your heart, the young man who guards his heart because he knows that it is the wellspring of life (Prov. 4:23) will not allow music designed to awaken sexual desire to have its secret power over his life.

Music Ennobles or Degrades

Keep this clear in your mind. There are two paths in life: God's and the world's. A path that leads to heaven and one that leads to hell. The music you listen to will make one or the other of these paths attractive. "Good music can move our hearts to love God," author Josh Harris wrote. "Ungodly music can entice us to love sin. The musicians we listen to become our companions, and God says the companion of fools will suffer harm" (Prov. 13:20). Honestly ask yourself: what music makes the straight and narrow King's Highway look attractive?

Answer the question; then brace yourself like a man and change your listening habits. If God takes sin so seriously that he tells us to cut off our hand and gouge out our eye if either makes it easier to sin, then a Christian young man will not hesitate to cut off music that makes sin feel good.

Still, some Christians demand quantitative proof. I suppose they think music is like plumbing or solving square roots. You don't have to be a gastroenterologist to know that eating food saturated in fat produces bad effects on your health. So it is with music. It will produce good or bad effects on your soul. Philosopher and statesman Boethius (480–ca. 524) put it bluntly: "Music is a part of us, and either ennobles or degrades our behavior."

Music will inevitably produce its ennobling or degrading effect on your life. So what kind of life do you want to live? Pull up your chair at the smorgasbord of music and feast on it. But know this: your choices in music will predispose you for a life of contentment—or of ruin. If you want to live a reckless life, there's music aplenty to fit that approach to life, just as there are irreversible consequences of such a reckless life. If you want to live life in the fast lane, a life of glitz and glamour, there's music for you. If you want to live a defiant, rebellious life, there's music aplenty for you. If you want to live a life with low expectations, with low demand on your mind, there's no shortage here, either. But make no mistake. For good or for ill, music profoundly shapes your life.

Even apart from lyrics, the music you listen to either aids you in worshiping God or aids you in bowing down to false gods. If you're serious about living your life at full attention before the face of God, then stop listening to music that makes you content with the world, that makes you slouch or swagger, that degrades you and makes you effeminate. Begin today to cultivate a love of the rich canon of music that reflects the splendor and beauty of God and that ennobles you and awakens high and grand aspirations in your soul.

Resolves

- To be honest with myself about the secret power of music on my soul
- To avoid music that makes me content with common things
- To cut off all music that makes me feel reckless or invincible
- To cut off all music that arouses inordinate sexual thoughts and desires
- To cultivate more appreciation for music that has stood the test of the ages

Scripture Memory

"Worship the LORD with gladness; come before him with joyful songs."

Psalm 100:2

For Discussion

1. In discussions about music, why is it not helpful to argue that music is neutral?
2. Listen to a rock or other pop-music song with your dad, and read the words carefully as you listen. Discuss whether you could honestly thank God for the effect it has on you.
3. Listen to more musical genres and ask whether the music, regardless of the lyrics, draws you closer to God and whether you can honestly glorify him by listening to it.
4. In your listening, discuss whether the music ennobles or degrades you, whether it helps you to be a man or makes you effeminate.

"My Song Forever Shall Record"

My song forever shall record
The tender mercies of the Lord;
Your faithfulness will I proclaim,
And every age shall know your name.

Psalm 89, The Psalter, *1912*

For Further Study/Listening

Psalms 108, 138; classical guitarist Christopher Parkening, cellist Yo-Yo Ma, trumpeter Wynton Marsalis; composers Bach, Palestrina, Vivaldi, Purcell, Handel, and beyond

YOUNG MEN: THEIR WORDS AND MANNERS

15

THE FORCE OF SPEECH

James 3:1–12

Tiller Steering

When my daughter reluctantly agreed to go and take her driver's permit test, a requirement in Washington State, she flunked it. I couldn't believe it. It's supposed to be a fall-off-a-log simple test. Indulge me for a moment. My daughter is not stupid. She was president of honor society, was a National Honor Society Scholarship nominee, was a Washington Commended Scholar, graduated *summa cum laude* from high school, and was offered attractive scholarships from colleges. So what happened?

"It was a question about steering," she answered tearfully.

"Steering?"

"Yes. It asked which way I was supposed to turn the steering wheel if I wanted to go that way," she explained, pointing left.

"And you missed that question?"

"I checked 'right,' " she sniffed, "and it was the wrong answer."

"Why did you check 'right'?" I asked, making my voice sound as patient as I could manage.

"Because when I want to turn the sailboat to port," she said, pointing left, "I move the tiller to starboard (she pointed right), just like you taught me. I guess it's not the same with a car."

I studied her face. She was dead serious. "No, honey, it's not," I managed at last. I knew that I had my work cut out for me if she was ever going to learn to drive a car.

James tells us that managing our tongue is something like steering a sailboat. Compared to the rest of a vessel, the rudder is small, a tiny fraction of the weight and bulk of the rest of the boat's parts. Similarly, your tongue is minuscule compared to the rest of your body. But don't be deceived. A ship with a faulty rudder runs before "stupid winds" making "quaint voyages," as poet Stephen Crane put it, completely at the mercy of wind and tide, soon to be utterly destroyed on rocks and shoals.

So a young man who doesn't know which way to turn the tiller, who has a faulty tongue, who "boasts of great things," will create great destruction for himself and for those whom he speaks to and about.

Words, Words, Words!

Men with too much time on their hands tell us that the average man speaks 17,000 words per day. Do the math. That works out to 6,188,000 words per year. Multiply by seventy; in a lifetime, that's a massive number of words for which to give an account. Moreover, the wise man in Proverbs tells us that when words abound, so does sinning (Prov. 10:19).

In a given day, you and I say lots of things with those 17,000 words—some things are kind and helpful; many are sinful. James says that your tongue and mine, though a very small part of our anatomy, like the rudder on a ship, can steer us into safe harbor, into peace and rest, health and service, kindness and love, or it can steer us into destruction and ruin. And it's always real people who are either helped or hurt by all those words. Thus, a wise young man will train himself to speak as though others are listening. They always are.

I overheard an interesting verbal exchange while my sons worked out at the harbor one afternoon. As a curious passerby watched the workout, he said to a woman standing nearby, "Whose idiot kid is that one?" pointing to a young man enjoying some late-workout, goofball antics in his kayak.

The woman replied coldly, "He's mine."

I cringe to think how many times I have been in that man's place, all because I've failed to control my own tongue.

We've all heard the ditty, "Sticks and stones may break my bones, but names [words] will never hurt me." Oh, yeah? It's doggerel nonsense. Wounds from sticks and stones usually heal. Damage done with words can last forever. Perhaps a more accurate axiom goes like this: "The pen is mightier than the sword." But surely this can't be true. With a sword you can persuade a man to save his life by drastically altering what he intended to do. And if he won't do your will, you can whack his head off with the sword. Surely a pen can't do that. Yet the axiom remains. Why? Because you write words with a pen. And with those words you can change not one man's thinking but the thinking of entire nations, and not just for the moment but for generations to come.

Sword or Pen?

John Bunyan faced the sword of King Charles II because he refused to stop committing the "crime" of unlicensed preaching. No amount of kingly sword-wielding would do, not even threatening to exile Bunyan to the American colonies. Fearless, the humble tinker stood firm. So for Bunyan it was off to the damp old Bedford jail on a wide stone bridge that spanned the River Great Ouse—for twelve long years.

The sword won out, right? Wrong. During those twelve years Bunyan had a pen, and with it he wrote nine books; the greatest was

The Pilgrim's Progress, second only to the English Bible in number of copies published over the centuries, and never out of print since 1678. Few would attempt to understate the influence that this book has wielded over the centuries, and still wields in the hearts and minds of any who read it.

The pen is emphatically more mighty than the sword. With a pen Bunyan wrote words—words that imaginatively taught and adorned the gospel of Jesus Christ, words that showed men the pathway to heaven. It would be impossible to overstate the power of words—whether written or spoken.

In Bunyan's spiritual autobiography, *Grace Abounding to the Chief of Sinners*, he recorded an episode in his life that underscores the power of words. While plying his trade as a tinker, a traveling repairman of pots and pans, his seventy-pound portable anvil over his shoulder, Bunyan happened upon some women sitting in the sun, chatting. Moving nearer, he began eavesdropping. He records the profound impression that their speech had on him:

> But upon a day the good providence of God did cast me to Bedford, to work on my calling; and, in one of the streets of that town, I came where there were three or four poor women, sitting at a door in the sun, and talking about the things of God; and being now willing to hear what they said. But I may say, I heard, but I understood not; for they were far above, out of my reach. Methought they spake as if joy did make them speak; they spake with such pleasantness of Scripture language, and with such appearance of grace in all they said, that they were to me as if they had found a new world, as if they were a people that dwelt alone, and were not to be reckoned amongst their neighbors.

They're Listening

Think back on recent conversations with your friends. What were you talking about? What did you laugh at? What was the tone of that conversation? If an unbeliever had been listening in, would he have heard anything that would make him say that you spoke as if joy did make you speak? Would he have heard the Bible in your words? Would he have heard words full of grace and kindness toward others? Would he have had any reason to think that you had found a new world, that by your conversation you were not like other young men?

Bunyan's account should sober you. It should make you cringe. Imagine if your unsaved neighbor could log on and track a week's worth of your speaking. What would he hear? Ungrateful, impatient speaking to your mother; disrespectful comments about your father; unkindness expressed to your siblings; gossip about peers and competitors; crude locker-room jokes; jokes at sleepovers; sexual remarks designed to lower the bar, to break down the barriers; lying to someone to cover your sinning.

If you are honest with yourself, you must admit that your casual conversations fall far short of the biblical standard for your speaking and would rarely if ever lead someone to Christ and salvation. The fact is, it's not a private world; others are listening to you—always.

Fire from Hell

The problem is so ubiquitous and intractable that theologian John Calvin wrote, "Since the tongue cannot be restrained, there must be some secret fire of hell hidden in it." Fire out of control is a destructive force. How much more destructive, then, is fire right out of hell! When your conscience begins to awaken to the scorching harm you're daily doing with your tongue, you should feel the singeing fire of hell in that realization.

Jesus said in the gospels, "I tell you that men will have to give account on the day of judgment for every careless word they have spoken" (Matt. 12:36). You and I speak nearly half a billion words in our lifetimes. How many of them are idle, careless, or—worse—unkind, hateful, untrue, even foul?

When I was a kid, a friend of mine and I used to stay up late at night and create our own radio mystery programs. They weren't very original—the great train robbery was one of them—but we created elaborate sound effects and faked the voices of our characters, all to our own great amusement, if to no one else's. I'll never forget the first time I heard my voice on that tape recorder. I was shocked. It couldn't be my voice, I thought. It sounded so strange. Do I really sound like that?

Maybe you've experienced the same thing. What will it be like on the judgment day to hear my voice? What will it be like to have to hear my gossip, my boasting, my false piety as I elaborate on the sins of others, my harsh, angry words, my unkind speech of every kind, played back for me and all to hear again? What will you think when your coarse jesting, your locker-room language, your jokes full of sexual innuendo are played back on the great day? Know now that you will "give account" for all these words on the day of judgment. This is a horrific thought. But it is true, and I'm certain that it's calculated to be a goad in your side so that you will bend your might and bring your tongue under control.

The Ugly Truth

But it's not simply a matter of clamping your hand over your mouth and not saying proud, stupid things in public anymore. Christ said, "For out of the overflow of the heart the mouth speaks" (Matt. 12:34b). You're saying the things that you're thinking deep in your being. Face the ugly truth: In and of ourselves, we are hopeless sinners, in bondage to our sins, and without the power of will needed to reform ourselves. Thus, you and I must be changed by the power of God from the inside out. In this as in all other matters of the heart, you must seek the Lord earnestly to change your heart and then to help you in controlling your tongue.

But you could be sitting around for a very long time waiting for the internal change to happen. Meanwhile, your tongue continues to set "the whole course of [your] life on fire" (James 3:6).

So where to begin? Even though sin comes from within you, James relentlessly blames your tongue, and throughout Scripture we are repeatedly urged to put off, to mortify, sin; and in the same stroke of the pen, the inspired writers urge us to put on the corresponding righteousness we have been lacking. This all happens by God's grace and power, of course, but no young man has ever learned to master his tongue without making it his first priority to do so.

What kind of restless evil, what kind of deadly poison, what kind of great boast, comes from your lips? Isolate it. Stare it in the face. Is it youthful pride, expressed in boasting? Then put boasting to death, and as you do, ask yourself what corresponding righteous speech ought to take boasting's place. Be specific as you answer your own question. Write your answer down. Even rehearse what you ought to say in front of the mirror. It will help. Replace your boasting with complimentary speech to and about others. On the highest level, replace your boasting with words of praise, adoration, and gratitude to Jesus Christ: boast in the Lord. No words could be more appropriate.

The Christian young man who is serious about self-control and leadership must start here: tame your tongue and you will be able to "keep [your] whole body in check" (James 3:2). Fail here and you will leave a "world of evil" in your wake (3:6).

Resolves

- To make myself accountable to my dad for my speech
- To pray daily for power to control my tongue
- To read God's Word daily and so fill my mind and heart and speech with his words

Scripture Memory

"My dear brothers, take note of this: Everyone should be quick to listen, slow to speak and slow to become angry. . . . If anyone considers himself religious and yet does not keep a tight rein on his tongue, he deceives himself and his religion is worthless."

James 1:19, 26

For Discussion

1. What circumstances do you find yourself in that make it easy for you to sin with your tongue?
2. What specific sins of your tongue do you need to put off?
3. What would the corresponding righteous speech be for each?
4. How will you make yourself more accountable for your speech?

"O God, My Faithful God"

Keep me from saying words
That later need recalling;
Guard me, lest idle speech
May from my lips be falling:
But when, within my place,
I must and ought to speak,
Then to my words give grace,
Lest I offend the weak.

Johann Heermann, 1630

For Further Study

Read Proverbs 10 and 11; look up, read, and discuss other passages on the tongue.

16

THE FORCE OF GRATITUDE

Luke 17:11–19

Yawning Ingratitude

In the first English novel, *Robinson Crusoe*, published in London in 1719, Daniel Defoe takes the reader on a whirlwind of forbidden voyages, pirate attacks, and shipwreck and desolation, finally hurling his protagonist up on a deserted island for twenty-eight years, two months, and nineteen days. Why did this happen? Ingratitude. The entire conflict in the story is set in motion when teenage Crusoe grows discontent with his family—especially with his father.

Defoe's young man was like so many others before the tale and since. Crusoe's was a loving Christian home, not rich, but not poor either. In the golden mean of comfort, he grew up with plenty of material things and was sheltered from the harsher difficulties of life. Like most young men in your comfortable world, Crusoe was never forced to go hungry. He had a nice home, plenty of clothes, a good education, and probably more than enough leisure time for sports and recreation.

Nevertheless, greedy for adventure and fortune, restless and ungrateful Crusoe defied his father's authority and ran off to gain wealth and fame at sea. Defoe tells a universal tale of young men who crave independence, who, with their newly acquired learning and strength, long to rule their world for themselves.

I suspect that you have felt this tug at your own heart. I also suspect that you have been given a great deal more than most young men in the world. And I suspect that you, too, lack gratitude remotely proportionate to what you've been given.

It is the plague of the prosperous Western world. But it gets worse. Though they've grown up with so much, most young men are hungry for more, and many even feel that they deserve more. Renowned Victorian preacher Charles Haddon Spurgeon said this of ungrateful people such as you and me: "You say, 'If I had a little more, I should be very satisfied.' You make a mistake. If you are not content with what you have, you would not be satisfied if it were doubled." Ungrateful people are always discontent, and will remain so as long as they remain ungrateful.

How often do your parents have to remind you to say "thank you"? How often are you ungrateful for the many things they do for you, and the many things they buy for you? A U.S. Department of Agriculture study found that raising one child from infancy to fiscal independence costs parents $237,000—in real dollars. Your parents could be spending the cash on other things—such as a Ferrari—but they're happily spending it to feed and clothe you. Next time you're ungrateful for common everyday blessings, those wonderfully ordinary gifts from a loving heavenly Father, generously bestowed by a loving earthly father and mother, consider what a financial liability, what a fiscal parasite, you are.

Twenty-eight years was a long time for Crusoe to reflect on the sins of his youth. At last Defoe's rebellious young man concluded, "All our discontents spring from the [lack] of thankfulness for what we have."

As it did for Crusoe, ingratitude for everyday gifts festers away at your joy, robs you of contentment, bars you from loving fellowship with your parents and siblings, and dries up your devotional life with God.

Ingratitude and discontentment are like infectious disease bacteria, dividing and multiplying, feeding voraciously on your inner man, until they have overrun your affections and spread throughout your entire being. Do with ingratitude and discontentment what you would do with infectious disease: wash your hands of them; get clear of the source of them.

There is only one sure cure for ingratitude for and discontentment with everyday gifts. And you will need to take massive daily dosages of that cure. The cure is heartfelt, verbal gratitude actively expressed. Petition your heavenly Father for more of that life-giving cure. Start by praying this prayer of holy discontent along with Puritan poet George Herbert: "Thou that hast given so much to me, Give one thing more—a grateful heart."

Big Problems

Ingratitude for ordinary blessings develops an intractable habit of ingratitude, one that is seldom broken even when confronted with extraordinary blessings. In Luke 17:11–19, we are given an account that illustrates the second kind of ingratitude: ingratitude after a special mercy, after an extraordinary deliverance. In the gospel account of the healing of the ten lepers, we see not one but ten men miraculously delivered from the most dreaded disease of the ancient Near East.

Leprosy was not chicken pox. By all accounts, it was a horrific disease. How would you like having a health condition that gradually rotted away not only your skin but whole fingers, your nose, your ears? Entire limbs gradually decayed away under the ravages of this disease. What's more, rotting flesh puts off a disgusting odor. Because of the stench and the contagion of the disease, victims of it were driven out of their village, shunned by their families, forever to live with other lepers as discarded outcasts. So potent a disease was leprosy that it took the Black Death of the fourteenth century to check its progress.

A leper's condition was hopeless. There was no cure. There was absolutely nothing you could do to change yourself. Worse still, leprosy was a disease that perversely forced you to look on while your body decomposed *before* you died. At the last, you ended your miserable days in an excruciatingly lonely death.

Moreover, leprosy had no respect for rank or station. Young or old, rich or poor—anyone could contract the dreaded disease. No king could eradicate his leprosy by royal decree. No general could kill it with sword or spear. No rich man's money could buy a cure. Like death, leprosy was the great leveler.

There was, however, one good thing about having leprosy. You knew that you had big problems. All ten of the men in Luke's account had serious problems, and they knew it. It's easier to cry for help when you know how badly you need it. These men desperately needed help.

Imagine the thrill when they caught sight of Jesus off in the distance. What hope must have sprung instantly into their benighted world. They'd heard about Jesus. Who in Judea hadn't? He could help sick people, maybe even heal people with leprosy. No wonder they called out in loud voices when they saw Jesus. Hoping beyond hope, ten desperate men must have made quite a racket as they called out, "Jesus, Master, have pity on us!" (Luke 17:13).

And he did. Suddenly, without fanfare, Jesus healed them. He told them to go and show themselves to the priest, and as they turned to go, their wretched disease vanished. Jesus had heard their cry. They were clean, free from the disease, free from the stigma of it, from the gnawing isolation of it all.

Nine Out of Ten

If the story ended here, it would be much like many other wonderful accounts of the power of Jesus to heal the sick. But the

Holy Spirit seems to have something else for us in this historical account.

One of the men, a Samaritan, when he saw that he had been healed, turned back to Jesus. One out of ten. Several important things happened next that ought to help you and me understand how to be truly grateful.

First, this Samaritan leper "came back, praising God in a loud voice" (Luke 17:15). How different from the drive-by, no-eye-contact, grunting "thanks" that young men sometimes offer. Like this leper, you must turn, come back, and say words of gratitude that cannot be mistaken. Anything less is ingratitude.

Second, because this man was truly grateful, he showed it in unmistakable ways. He turned, came back, and "threw himself at Jesus' feet and thanked him" (Luke 17:16). Like every other dimension of your Christian faith, gratitude is not merely an internal matter. By its very nature your thanksgiving must be expressed in obvious ways, ways that others will notice. You can be sure that everyone around Jesus knew that this one man was overflowing with thanksgiving. By his voice and by his posture he made sure of this. Grateful people always do.

Notice that Jesus did not have to prompt this man to make some begrudging expression of his thanks. Why not? Because the man was truly thankful. When you leave your mother or father no option but to prod you with, "What do you say?" your silence is proof of your ingratitude.

Third, gratitude is rare. Ten were healed. Nine went their way. Only one returned to say "thank you." Alas, like the nine, most young men are ingrates. But why is this? Perhaps because gratitude requires honest humility.

Humility and Gratitude

"Gratitude is not only the greatest of virtues," wrote Cicero, "but the parent of all the others." Thus, it comes as no surprise that the virtues of humility and gratitude are so closely connected.

But most young men are not humble. Most young men are proud. They imagine that they are strong, that they are invincible, that nothing can stand in their way, that they are self-made.

When this one leper expressed his thanks in word and posture, he did so because he understood that he was none of those things; he understood his great need. He knew just how sick he was, how utterly unable he was to heal himself. This is where his leprosy was to his advantage. Who with this horrible disease would not be thankful if they were healed of it? But then, of course, nine other lepers were healed yet remained ungrateful. So it is with you and me. How quickly we forget who we really are, our sin, our great need, our utter inability to save ourselves from death and hell. Alas, how much we are like those nine.

Pride and Ingratitude

It's not shyness, or even being tongue-tied, that keeps most young men from expressing their thanksgiving. It's pride that keeps young men from expressing their thanks. Pride keeps you from valuing the gift of God, his love pitched on you from all eternity, his choosing you to be his "precious treasure," as John Calvin called you, his sending his Son to redeem you from sin and judgment, his sending the Holy Spirit to regenerate your heart and mind, to make you a new creation in Christ Jesus.

I doubt that you've been delivered from leprosy, though perhaps God has delivered you from some other disease. But every healthy young man is in the grip of a serious disease, one that has the most horrific consequences. Though God has delivered you from sin and death, judgment and hell, all too often young men are not grateful in proportion to the greatness of their deliverance.

We cringe at the nine who scorned to say "thank you" when they had received so much from Jesus. It reflects so poorly on their character. Meanwhile, we men often do the same thing—but on the heels of an even more splendid deliverance. Such ingratitude likewise reflects poorly on our character.

We note the ingratitude of the nine and think less of them for it, but more importantly by far, Jesus took note of it. "Were not all ten cleansed?" he asked. "Where are the other nine?" (Luke 17:17). What might he say about you and me? "Have not I lavished on you, young man, my love and grace, my forgiveness and righteousness? Where, young man, is your thanksgiving?"

So which ought you to be? The answer is obvious. Give up your pride, and be like the one outcast leper. Throw yourself at Jesus' feet and in a loud voice, obvious to all, say how thankful you are for his countless gifts of love to you.

Gratitude That Runs Deep

There is yet another level of gratitude: gratitude when there seem to be no ordinary blessings, gratitude when there is no special mercy shown, gratitude expressed in the midst of affliction and despair. You've heard stories of persecuted Christians who live in grinding poverty, whose lives are in constant danger, yet who smile and seem full of humble thanks to God. Let's be honest. You and I are pretty bewildered by this.

Perhaps one of the greatest examples of this level of gratitude is seen in the life of seventeenth-century German pastor Martin Rinkart. From 1618 to 1648, armies of the Holy Roman Empire, bent on crushing Reformation Christianity, wreaked havoc throughout Germany, descending on whole villages, at times not leaving a man, woman, or child alive in their wake. Historians tell us that more than a third of the population of Germany died in this Thirty Years' War.

By 1636, Pastor Rinkart's village of Eilenburg in Saxony had become little more than a plague-infested wasteland. Rinkart had conducted funerals for 4,480 of his parishioners, including his wife and all his children. One of few men left alive in the village, in peril of his life, Rinkart sought relief for his grief-devastated flock. "Come, my children," he urged the few who remained, "we can find no mercy with men; let us take refuge in God."

179

Unlike the leper who had just been delivered from sickness and death in Luke's account, Rinkart was far from any such deliverance. War would rage on for another twelve years. Caught in the maw of the brutalities of war, he and his flock, I am sure, found themselves more than a little perplexed by the devastation and death on every hand. Nevertheless, Rinkart's faith was such that he looked past all the woe, and while still in the deepest trials, he managed to pen one of the church's greatest thanksgiving hymns. Think of his story as you read aloud these lines from his hymn:

> Now thank we all our God
> With heart and hands and voices,
> Who wondrous things hath done,
> In whom his world rejoices;
> Who from our mothers' arms
> Hath blessed us on our way
> With countless gifts of love,
> And still is ours today.
>
> O may this bounteous God
> Through all our life be near us;
> With ever-joyful hearts
> And blessed peace to cheer us;
> And keep us in his grace,
> And guide us when perplexed,
> And free us from all ills
> In this world and the next.

Now consider, with shame, how often you fail to meaningfully express gratitude for "countless gifts of love," for daily blessings or for special graces, how often you have been like the nine lepers.

Notice further how Rinkart calls you to a gratitude expressed with "heart and hands and voices." I wonder whether he might have even had the grateful leper in mind when he penned those words, his heart so overflowing with thanksgiving that he "prais[ed] God in a loud voice" and "threw himself at Jesus' feet and thanked him" (Luke 17:15–16).

Ingrates will always think that such expressions of gratitude are too extravagant. But true gratitude springs from the heart, overflows in sincere speech, and floods the world with tangible deeds. Because you know that you ought to be grateful for "countless gifts of love," cultivate grateful feelings in your heart, take grateful words on your lips, do grateful deeds with your hands.

Resolves

- To stop, turn, and look someone in the face when I thank him
- To say "thank you" in a complete, developed thought ("Thanks, Mom, for a great dinner. You're the best cook ever.")
- To practice using a more thankful tone of voice
- To show my gratitude by specific acts of kindness
- To write a note or call loved ones to whom I owe thanksgiving
- To pray regularly together as father and son

Scripture Memory

"Give thanks to the LORD, for he is good; his love endures forever."
Psalm 107:1

For Discussion

1. What are the three parts of gratitude? Discuss why it must have all three parts.
2. What are the three levels of gratitude? Which kind of ingratitude are you most often guilty of?
3. Discuss the differences between being grateful when someone has given you a gift (the leper) and being grateful while in the midst of suffering (Rinkart).

"Now Thank We All Our God"

All praise and thanks to God
The Father now be given,
The Son, and him who reigns
With them in highest heaven—
The one eternal God,
Whom earth and heav'n adore;
For thus it was, is now,
And shall be evermore.

Martin Rinkart, 1636

For Further Study

Psalm 100; Philippians 4:6; Colossians 2:7; 3:15; 1 Thessalonians 5:18

17

THE FORCE OF GOOD MANNERS

Leviticus 19:32

Stand Up

After an intensely gripping battle scene in a movie version of one of maritime novelist Patrick O'Brian's tales, the camera swept over the fallen on the bloody decks of the *HMS Surprise*. As the clash of fighting faded away, silence descended over the theater. My friend's nearly deaf father, who had served as a high-casualty tail-gunner on a B-17 in World War II, leaned over to his fourteen-year-old grandson. At the top of his voice, he broke the somber stillness: "Sure glad I joined the Air Force!" Mortified, the young man scrunched down in his seat.

Young men naturally revere themselves, but having respect for and showing it to old folks who do this kind of thing comes tougher. Let's be honest. For young men, having and showing respect for just about everyone on the planet comes hard—mothers, sisters, women in general, siblings—showing respect for others is the most unnatural thing for most young men.

But disrespect for others, especially elderly folks, is not some minor sin to be winked at. Leviticus 19:32 connects showing respect for elders and showing respect for God. What's more, the text gives you lesson one in how to change your internal thinking from self-absorption to respect for others: "Rise in the presence of the aged."

Whom do you speak with the minute the worship service ends at your church? Think about it. How many widows do you shoulder past getting to your friends? How many old men in wheelchairs do you cut off as you get in line for coffee or a doughnut? How many elderly folks have you intentionally avoided eye contact with because you had more important people to visit with? None of this equates to standing in the presence of the aged.

Standing to one's feet is the universal gesture of respect and honor. "All rise!" barks the bailiff in every courtroom in the land as the judge takes his seat at the bench. When the President enters the room, Democrat and Republican congressmen rise as a gesture of respect for the man or at least for his office. When a bride starts down the aisle on the arm of her father, everyone rises to their feet.

Rising to your feet shows respect. Real men who read and obey their Bibles stand up in the presence of elderly people; so it used to be, and so it must still be if you are to "revere your God" (Lev. 19:32). Standing in the presence of the aged shows respect, like kneeling in the presence of God. But the devil wants you to believe the utter nonsense that "bodily posture makes no difference." Satan desperately does not want young men to believe, as C. S. Lewis put it, that "whatever their bodies do affects their souls."

Young men want respect. They want to be thought grown up and independent. Ironically, in their mad dash to gain the approval of others, many young men show disrespect for others. According to Moses, however, showing respect to the elderly is nonnegotiable for young men who are serious about honoring God. You start by standing to your feet.

Respect and Fishing

A high school senior I'll call Joe lacked community service on his application to West Point. His school counselor asked him if he did anything to give back to the community. Joe furrowed his brow, shrugged, and said, "No."

"Haven't you ever done anything to help somebody in your neighborhood?" the counselor probed.

Joe, prompted by the counselor, gradually began telling about a lonely old man who lived down the road. "His wife died when I was pretty young," he explained, and then Joe stopped.

"Well, what did you do for him?" urged the counselor, her pen poised over his application.

"Nothing, really."

The counselor looked exasperated.

"Sometimes I'd call him," offered Joe.

"Calling an old man's good," she said. "But it's not enough to count as community service. What else have you got?"

"Like I said, nothing, really. Only I'd call and ask if he wanted to go fishing."

"And what would he say?"

" 'Pick me up at five,' he'd say."

"Driving elderly people around on errands is community service!" declared the counselor.

"His eyes aren't as good as they used to be," continued Joe. "So he can't drive himself like he—" Joe broke off.

"Like he what?"

"Well, like he used to do when I was a kid."

Joe went on to explain that it was this old man who had first taught him how to bait a hook, and where the best spots in the lake were for catching the big ones.

"So you sort of feel obligated to take the old man fishing," said the counselor, "because he took you fishing. That works."

Joe frowned. "He's my friend," he said simply. "I go fishing with him because he's my friend. We spend whole days together in the summers fishing on the lake because we're friends. That's all."

"Joe, don't you see? That's community service," the counselor said eagerly. "Put it down."

Joe's eyes flashed and color rose on his cheeks. "He's my friend. I do it because he's my neighbor and he's lonely, and he loves fishing. I don't do it to get points on an application."

The United States Army found a good man when it found Joe. He went to West Point, became an intelligence officer, and fought for freedom in Iraq. I suspect that he spent his off-duty time looking around for a lonely old widower and a wide spot in the Euphrates.

For Joe, "rise in the presence of the aged" meant spending time with an old friend out fishing. If you want to show reverence for God, stop looking past the elderly person in the pew in front of you, or who shuffles past on his way home from the bus stop. Will it be inconvenient? Yes. Obedience always is for sinners. Get on with it. Honor the aged. Reverence God.

What You Miss

Though an old man may go home from church as lonely as he came, the one who really loses when you ignore elderly folks is you. Frank Starr is eighty-seven years old, is hard of hearing, and likes to shake hands. Because Frank has Parkinson's disease, his prolonged handshakes really shake. Frank also loses his train of thought and breaks off for long stretches, looking at you with his watery eyes—still holding your hand. Young men get uncomfortable holding the flinching hand of a silent old man.

One day after a sermon on dying, I grasped Frank's hand and settled in for one of our visits. Seemingly out of the blue, haltingly, he began talking about the war.

"I jumped into Holland," he said, his hand grasping mine and tugging me toward him.

"In the war?" I asked. He nodded. "Were the Germans there?"

After looking at me for a moment, he replied, "Yes."

"Were you afraid?" I asked.

"No," he said simply, as if it were an irrelevant question.

"Were the Germans shooting at you?"

Again he paused, looking at me with his large watery eyes. "They shot down the plane ahead of ours."

"Was it a fighter plane?"

"No," he replied. Still he gripped my hand. Another long silence. "It was full of soldiers," he continued at last, "paratroopers, like me."

I wasn't sure what to say. I felt like he was telling me something intensely important. "Did you have an M1 Garand?" It was a silly thing to ask, but it was all that came to mind.

"An M1? No, it was a small one."

After another long pause, he continued. "The Dutch people were dancing all around us." Another pause. "They were so happy, they were dancing. I could hardly get clear of my parachute."

"But the Germans were nearby," I said. "They'd just shot down the other plane. Weren't you afraid they'd shoot you?"

He looked at me as if across a divide over which I could not cross. "No," he said. "I was a soldier."

The next Sunday his wife handed me a large envelope. I opened it and unfolded yellowed newspaper clippings from the 1940s and Frank's service record. He had served in the 82nd Airborne Division and had fought in many major battles of the European theater. On September 19, 1944, he had been wounded in Holland and was decorated for it.

After the worship service, Frank picked up the story and told how he'd not been able to hear so well ever since serving for a time in a tank. He tried to explain just how loud things were when they fired the tank, and how the recoil propelled every man right off his seat. I'd seen his service record and knew that he'd earned a Purple Heart and other medals. I asked Frank about his medals.

"Medals?" he said. "Don't remember that," he concluded simply.

Believe me, you are the one who loses when you ignore old men, when you refuse to obey God's command to show respect to the elderly, when you are so wrapped up in your petty teenage world that you have no time to be transported back in history, when you're so enslaved to artificial thrills that you have little interest in being enlarged by hearing an eyewitness give you a peek at what World War II was really like.

"When I Was a Kid . . ."

Thanks to a philosophy called Romanticism, championed by the French Enlightenment thinker Jean Jacques Rousseau, society has come to believe that youth is supreme and that wisdom resides with the young. So Henry David Thoreau could write, "I have always been regretting that I was not as wise as the day I was born." Modern education is fueled by this absurd philosophy. Young people are supposed to be masters of their own destiny, shapers of their own course of study, arbiters of wisdom and knowledge. The wisdom of the ages found in old books is held in contempt. Add to Rousseau a dash of pop psychology, and students are left alone to compound ignorance as they get more deeply in touch with the child within.

Because our culture uncritically assumes all this, you are further encouraged to do what you naturally do anyway: hold the aged in contempt. But this is not the Bible's view. In Proverbs, gray hair is a crown of glory (Prov. 16:31), and in today's text you are commanded, out of reverence for God, to show honor to elderly folks.

But what about the irascible old man who begins every sentence with, "When I was a kid . . . ," who scowls and sneers and gripes about everything? There are fewer of these than the inflated caricature suggests; nevertheless, they're out there. And God commands you to show respect even to them, yes, to rise in their presence and so "revere your God." It won't be easy. Obedience in a fallen world rarely is. But that cynical old man will have one less thing to be cranky about: you've shown him respect.

Manners Matter

Converging on the door of the bank with a woman, a young man stepped aside and held the door open for her. "You're doing this because I'm a woman!" she said accusingly.

"No, I'm doing it because I'm a gentleman," replied the young man.

Blend Rousseau with Betty Friedan and feminism, and you have a formula for the death of gentlemanly good manners. Egalitarianism run amok demands that everyone be treated the same—especially women. This kind of cultural nonsense lobs a pipe bomb at good manners. Young men used to be taught to make eye contact with adults and greet them with deference and respect, to square their shoulders and say, "Yes, sir." Young men were taught to hold the door for women, and to rise when a woman entered the room. They were taught when to remain silent and when and how to speak. All this has almost entirely disappeared from societal expectation. No wonder we've produced a generation of raw-meat barbarian males.

Feminists insist that traditional good manners were ways by which men subjugated women. Women and children who survived the sinking of the *Titanic* would not have agreed. Good manners are gestures that make tangible your obedience to the Bible's commands to love your neighbor, to lead like a man, to use your strength to protect and provide for women, children, and the elderly. Good manners are the daily outworking of loving Christian obedience. Let's explore several important habits that you must master if you're going to put into practice what the Bible teaches about manhood.

The telephone. Greet the person who answers your call and immediately identify yourself clearly. Next, ask politely whether now is a good time to speak with the person you are calling. All of this is guided by the knowledge that the telephone is often an interruption, that you are intruding on a family, and that you're aware that the person you are calling might be occupied. Never play guessing games on the phone. Respect the time of the person you have just disturbed from

189

what he was otherwise doing. Assume that what he was doing when you called is more important than what you called about.

The table. My grandfather used to jab his fork into stray hands caught reaching across the table! Don't reach. You may have the metabolism of a nuclear reactor, and may feel like you're starving to death come mealtime, but be patient. First, hold the plate for any woman or child seated next to you; then serve yourself. Don't pick through the serving plate for the largest, juiciest chicken breast. Gently help yourself to the one closest to your side of the plate. Don't chew with your mouth open. No elbows on the table. Don't talk with your mouth full. Be guided by making your eating nonintrusive on everyone else's eating.

Sidewalks. In the Middle Ages, a gentleman protected women by placing himself on the pavement where he would be in the way of the rubbish that might be tossed out of upper-story windows. How does this translate to today? A man always walks on the traffic side of the sidewalk. In this way his clothes get splattered with mud when a passing car hits a puddle. Or worse, if a car careers out of control, he is the one struck and killed, not the woman. In other words, a man puts himself in the position of protecting the woman, of inconveniencing himself for her convenience.

Doors. Most women are capable of opening doors on their own, but it is a gentleman's privilege to lighten her burden, even in things that she can do for herself. What's more, rising when a woman enters the room, or pausing and opening a door for her, reminds a man that he is not the center of the universe. All good manners require a real man to put himself in second place, while actively placing someone else in the first place.

Speech. "Children are to be seen and not heard," my parents used to tell me. I remember squirming and flinching, desperate to blurt out my jokes and comments and generally dominate conversation. I'm appalled at children—usually boys—who thoughtlessly barge into adult conversation. This is bad manners, and it stems from boys' thinking they are equal with adults. Young men ought to refer to adults as "Mr.," "Miss," and "Mrs." until in rare cases they are asked to call an adult by his first name. Don't call adults "guy"! Greet adults with complete sentences, make eye contact, and don't mumble. For example: "Good evening, Mr. Smith. My name is Winston Churchill. I'm pleased to meet you." If the adult initiates a handshake, shake his hand, but in most cases a young man ought not to initiate handshaking. After visiting, conclude with, "It was nice to have met you."

Misusing manners. Finally, avoid showing respect merely as a means of showing the world what a big shot you are. As you begin loving your neighbor by practicing the discipline of good manners, it is tempting to "do your 'acts of righteousness' before men, to be seen by them" (Matt. 6:1). Some young men "show respect" by attempting to put on an affected semblance of equality with adults: pushy handshaking and speaking with adults as though it's a given that they're on the same level. This is not good manners but simply pseudo-respect employed as a cover for youthful arrogance, the back door to thinking more highly of oneself than one ought. At the end of the day, it is uglier, more inappropriate, more disrespectful, because it perverts deferential behavior into yet another way of revering self instead of God.

Practice good manners from the heart: love your neighbor; revere your God.

Resolves

- To begin rising in the presence of the aged
- To begin thinking less about others' showing respect to me and more about my showing respect to others
- To humbly develop daily habits of good manners

Scripture Memory

"Rise in the presence of the aged, show respect for the elderly and revere your God. I am the LORD."

Leviticus 19:32

For Discussion

1. What habits of bad manners do you need to change?
2. Discuss other ways that good manners could be applied in other areas of your life and behavior.

"How Firm a Foundation"

E'en down to old age all my people shall prove
My sovereign, eternal, unchangeable love;
And when hoary hairs shall their temples adorn,
Like lambs they shall still in my bosom be borne.

Rippon's Selection of Hymns, *1787*

For Further Study

Leviticus 19:13–18; Proverbs 16:31; 20:29

18

THE FARCE OF COOL

Matthew 20:20–28

Cool Turkeys

Picture in your mind the equivalent of a teenage male turkey trying to be cool to impress the girls. When he thinks he's found that special girl turkey, the one he wants to spend his life with—you know, the cute one in brown and black feathers, batting her eyelashes, that maddeningly alluring grin on her beak—he simply has to impress her. But it can't look like he's doing it on purpose. Even in the turkey world, that's just not cool. What better way to impress her than to look bigger than the chump turkey next to him? So he swells out his tail feathers, preening and strutting, trying to pretend that none of this is put on; it's just who he is. But furtive glances her way give him away.

To those of us who are profoundly relieved to have the more overt forms of this male behavior behind us, teenage male cool looks pretty much like mating season on a turkey farm.

You may not like this, but let's explore the equivalent of this behavior in young men. Consider one moment in the ever-changing fashions that exert pressure on young men who desperately want to be cool. In many circles it's obligatory that cool males wear: slinky basketball shorts, large enough to be worn simultaneously by all the guys in your neighborhood; the correct boxer shorts to be copiously revealed above the sagging waistline; the right pro-football jersey, wide and flowing and extending well below the knee; and their hair longish in the front, swooping over one eye so that, in an effort to see, the chin must jut defiantly upward. You get the idea.

None of this happens randomly. It is the inevitable uniform of cool. But it's not just clothes that make the cool dude. You have to master the slouching, swaggering shuffle, the half-closed eyes, the slack jaw, the studied indifference and boredom shown on the face and in the tone of voice that makes you a cool dude.

Cool Isn't Cool

"Watching teenage boys trying to be cool," one man observed, "is an adult spectator sport." Teenage boys trying to be cool lose the ability to see this. Hold cool at arm's length and it becomes clear that the Herculean effort to be cool is uncool in the extreme. Nevertheless, many young men feel that they must make the effort.

For many, cool posture and attitude is an unstudied announcement that you feel yourself to be profoundly inadequate. Nagging deeply below the subconscious of many would-be cool teenage boys is the fear that if they really had it, they wouldn't need to make the effort.

Think cars for a moment. Young men who drive monster trucks—or who wish they could drive monster trucks—fail to see that they might just as well wear an oversized T-shirt printed with: "I'm excessively insecure in my manliness, and so I'm driving this great big truck to draw everyone's attention to me, and to what a great big man I want them to think I am." To compensate for feeling so small and insignificant, these males make their tail feathers so big that they fairly cry out in the streets that they really are big shots—really!

This is classic immodesty. Immodest people dress and carry themselves in order to stand out, to shock, to allure, to draw as much attention to themselves as possible. Girls usually do this with provocative necklines and skirt lengths (and a panoply of other subtleties). Guys prefer the swaggering bravado derived from prowess in sports or from being seen behind the wheel of the correct muscle car. Either way, importance is measured by the unimportant things: physical features or horsepower under the hood.

None of this fits well with loving your neighbor as yourself, with seeking greatness by humbly serving those in need all about you, with drinking the cup our Lord drank, with using your strength to bear the burden of the weak.

Cool Culture

Teen cool is a setup for a fall. And it starts by making you care too much about peers, about what everyone else is doing, about things that are valued by only a few and for only a brief moment.

Cool thus robs you of enthusiasm for the things that endure, for great events in history, for heroes, for unique places and customs, and for great ideas. Cool enervates creativity and curiosity and leaves you slouching and sullen in a world where God calls you to be riveted with fascination at all that lies before you and around you.

Entertainment and amusement are largely responsible for making sulky indifference seem so cool. Pop culture and all its technological distractions—movies, computer games, television, cell phones—sap your enthusiasm and make you yawn at the enduring things.

Moreover, the conduit of popular culture is also the principal means by which the gurus of cool dictate to you what's cool today—but stay tuned; things will change. They're good at all this, especially when you desperately want what they're selling. They're pretty good at it when you're just blissfully ignorant of the scam—but *you* are not.

195

Like sin, cool has a thousand faces. Thus, there's no easy formula to avoid the enervating effects of cool. Instead, you must develop spiritually informed discernment that equips you to identify and root it out in its varied forms.

In the Jazz Age, for instance, cool was a devil-may-care hedonism that created a world that looked like an amusement park. In F. Scott Fitzgerald's *The Great Gatsby*, after a summer of "riotous excursions," Nick Carraway had reached the limits of his ability to tolerate the Roaring Twenties with that decade's version of cool: "I felt that I wanted the world to be in uniform and at a sort of moral attention forever."

Peerless Cool

Travel the world and you will observe that young people in almost every country wear the uniform of their school. I taught in a school overseas where all sixteen hundred students wore their school's uniform. And when I lead students on history tours of the United Kingdom, they're impressed by the classy uniforms that all British students wear.

When American educators began investigating the value of school uniforms, however, you would have thought, by the outcry, that basic constitutional rights were in jeopardy. In the midst of the flurry, one perceptive cartoonist raised an essential question of the debate. He drew five schoolkids of various shapes and sizes, standing shoulder to shoulder, all wearing baseball cap backwards, baggy, drop-crotch pants, and oversized T-shirts, collectively intoning the mantra in a single cartoon bubble: "If they make us wear uniforms we'll all look the same."

Of course, they already did look the same. Cool already has its uniform, but it's a uniform fashioned by entertainers, by the media, and by teen peers, by others desperately trying to impress others with how cool they think they are. The peer pressure is enormous.

There is, however, a new twist to modern-day cool. "In the old days you had to be like everyone else in order to be like everyone else," writes Douglas Wilson. "But this new generation coming up is media-savvy and street-smart-hip; they have to be like everybody else so that they can be different from everybody else." This is where the media makes things so ridiculous. Teens who want to be cool "have been massaged into thinking they are striking a blow for individual liberty and freedom of choice whenever they ask for money to buy just what all the other nonconformists are buying."

It takes little scrutiny to see through the absurdity of all this, but then being cool makes you ignorant of many things that are abundantly obvious to parents, pastors, future employers, college admissions counselors, even more thoughtful peers.

As one *World* magazine news brief illustrates, succumbing to peer pressure can be self-destructive: "One foolish sheep, leaping from a cliff, started a doomed stampede resulting in about 450 dead animals and a grievous loss to one Turkish town. Nearly 1,500 sheep took the plunge."

Stop dressing for cool. Sit up, and wear the uniform of your true calling. Stop clambering after cool, or get ready for the plunge.

Cool Lingo

The cool look has a cool language, and it demands verbal conformity. Cool is a package deal. Few have captured this as memorably as the ape King Louie in the Disney classic Jungle Book.

Picture the double-jointed romping of the ape king as he sings, "You! I wanna be like you," and recall the double reverse in the dizzying ambiguity of the final lines. We're not sure, in the end, who is supposed to be aping whom. So it is with conformity when fashioned by cool. Picture two young men coming to their senses about being cool: "I was trying to talk and walk like you," says the first. "No way, I was trying to talk and walk like you," says the other guy.

Not only do you want to be like, and walk like what's cool, young men who cast their eye in cool's direction inevitably find themselves aping the lingo of cool. One of the most destructive effects of cool is that it requires a young man to stop talking in clear, understand-

YOUNG MEN: THEIR WORDS AND MANNERS

able language. It's as if he has reverted to the pre-verbal stage of toddlerhood or, worse, the nongrammatical communication of a brute. Grunts and head-bobbing, with an occasional hand gesture, are all that remains.

Nowhere is the effect of cool on language more obvious than when a young man speaks with adults. Teenage cool demands that you turn away and mumble when your mother or father speaks to you. Vagueness is the highest verbal good in the hip world of teenage speech. Crisp, clear, unequivocal speech is the vice to shun.

The Bible, however, says, "A man of perverse heart does not prosper; he whose tongue is deceitful falls into trouble" (Prov. 17:20). You are not at liberty to deceive with your words by grunting or mumbling. The gurus of cool may tell you otherwise, but God's Word tells you that deceitful communication starts as a heart problem—one that plunges you into trouble.

Consequently, when my sons ask to go somewhere with friends and there is a hint of vagueness about who, what, when, where, how, and why, the answer is always a crisp, clear, unequivocal "No."

Cool and Self-Love

Whether you teeter on the brink of cool because you feel profoundly insecure in your manliness or because you are so self-deluded that you actually believe you are the greatest hunk of male meat out there, either way, cool is the by-product of self-love.

In one of William Shakespeare's lesser-loved sonnets, he bemoans self-love and calls it what it is: sin. So all-absorbing is self-love, he even hints that it is on a par with being possessed by the powers of darkness:

> Sin of self-love possesseth all mine eye
> And all my soul, and all my every part;
> And for this sin there is no remedy,
> It is so grounded inward in my heart.

Elsewhere, Shakespeare refers to this animal self-love as the worst of sins. Here he proceeds with punishing honesty, laying down just how vain and ugly the delusion of self-love makes an individual:

> Methinks no face so gracious is as mine,
> No shape so true, no truth of such account;
> And for myself mine own worth do define,
> As I all other[s] in all worths surmount.

If words such as *cool* were in the vocabulary of Shakespeare, I'm sure he would have used *cool* to describe his strutting persona in these pathetic lines. A cool kid thinks that his face is the most attractive, he thinks that his body is the true version of maleness, he thinks that his opinion counts more than everyone else's. In short, a cool dude defines his own self-worth and ranks himself more worthy than everyone else in the universe.

It's not until he owns up to all this ugliness about himself that he reads his self-love rightly, finally concluding, "Self so self-loving were iniquity." One secular Shakespeare scholar suggested that this sin of self-love is "not quite the same as selfishness. In Christian morality it is the opposite of loving one's neighbor, and hence, a sin against Christ's greatest commandment."

The Back Door to Cool

God's call to young men is clear. He calls you to humbly love your neighbor—not to be cool. C. S. Lewis suggests that by the virtue of humility God "wants to turn the man away from self to [God] and to the man's neighbors." But this kind of "self-forgetfulness" is obliterated by the self-absorbed cool that enervates many young men.

Let's face it. We men have a pretty hard time forgetting ourselves. Cool, in all its stages and forms, is the living, breathing expression of how intractable our self-love is. We're consumed with wondering what others are thinking of us, obsessed with worry that others might not be giving us credit for our accomplishments. It's no exaggeration to say that many young men are enslaved, body and soul, to being cool.

What is the solution to all this? You've heard people try self-deprecation, or false modesty. The Tempter wants you to think that putting aside your cool swagger and putting on humility requires you to lie. So the devil suggests that if you're serious about this humility business, you need to tell people that even though you're quite good at algebra, you don't know binomials from binoculars. Or, if you're an accomplished bagpiper, that your playing sounds like a flock of geese getting smashed by a freight train. This "humility" always rings a bit false— and is another back door to cool.

Cool and true humility are mutually exclusive. We know what cool looks like. Lewis helps us to see what true humility looks like. He suggests that a man is truly humble when "he could design the best cathedral in the world, and know it to be the best, and rejoice in the fact, without being any more (or less) or otherwise glad at having done it than he would be if it had been done by another." Your heavenly Father wants a man "to be so free from any bias in his own favor that he can rejoice in his own talents as frankly and gratefully as in his neighbor's talents."

Cool Slavery

Slouching cool bars you from this true humility, and it bars you from true masculinity. Guys who slouch don't step up and serve their neighbor. It doesn't occur to them to care about the needs of those around them, let alone roll up their sleeves and meet those needs with their strength.

Cool makes you look in the wrong direction. It makes you ask the wrong questions about life. Instead of asking how you can use your strength to serve others, cool sets you up to look around with a yawn and ask, "What's cool today?" Thus, cool emasculates young men because it requires them to throw their strength away on the relentless pursuit of cool.

"Diligent hands will rule, but laziness ends in slave labor" (Prov. 12:24). A young man who would heed the call to be a leader must break the chains of cool today. Diligent men are leaders. Being cool is the opposite of being diligent. Slouching is the opposite of standing tall. Shuffling indifference is the opposite of taking initiative, sweating, getting dirty, and getting an important job done, and done well.

Enslaved to cool, a young man loses his curiosity about God's vast and fascinating world. A cool kid is indifferent about gaining knowledge, about developing skills, and about learning to work, and work hard. Henry Wadsworth Longfellow wrapped up a famous poem written to young people with the imperative, "Learn to labor and to wait" —probably because he saw how prone young people are to laziness and impatience.

Predisposed to laziness by the low-demand posture of cool, many young men never learn to labor, and so they slouch into unproductive oblivion. They've done little or no good for their neighbor, and have lived to be missed by no one but themselves.

Coincidence that it is, *cool* rhymes with *fool*. No employer, government, general, or church willingly entrusts a fool with important, exciting, and challenging duties. If you develop the habitual posture and attitude of cool, you will be of little use to either the City of Man or the City of God.

Be cool and get ready for a life of slave labor. Be a man and get ready for a life of thrilling leadership, a life of loving your neighbor as yourself, of drinking the cup our Lord drank, of seeking greatness by humbly serving those in need—a life of using your strength to bear the burden of the weak.

Resolves

- To turn my back on what's cool
- To replace cool posture and attitude with humble service

YOUNG MEN: THEIR WORDS AND MANNERS

Scripture Memory

"Pride goes before destruction, a haughty spirit before a fall."

Proverbs 16:18

For Discussion

1. Why do soldiers wear uniforms, stand at attention, and learn "No excuses!" speaking and behavior?
2. Look up definitions of *cool* and discuss why cool is incompatible with important things.

"Father, I Know That All My Life"

I ask thee for the daily strength,
To none that ask denied,
A mind to blend with outward life,
While keeping at thy side,
Content to fill a little space,
If thou be glorified.

Anna L. Waring, 1850

For Further Study

Proverbs 18:12; Romans 12:1–2; Philippians 2:5–8

YOUNG MEN: THEIR HEROES AND LOYALTIES

19

HONOR THE KING

1 Peter 2:9–17

Kings or Frauds

More than 230 years ago, our founding fathers decided that the biblical injunction to honor the king no longer included King George III of England. In some expression of solidarity with those men, if you're like my sons and me, you and your father enjoy celebrating the Fourth of July.

There's something wonderfully invigorating about the flames, the smoke, the creative ballistics, the innovative use of firecrackers and bottle rockets, not to mention the sparkler bombs. If you're at all like we are, you get a considerably greater kick out of your own backyard adaptations of fireworks than the highly sophisticated fireworks bursting over your city or town square. Large quantities of hot dogs, potato salad, chips, soda, watermelon, and homemade apple pie help round out one of the most enjoyable days of the summer.

The text before us, however, seems to imply that we could get a bit off track here if we're not careful. Peter suggests that we have a higher loyalty, that we are from a different nation, a "holy nation" (1 Peter 2:9), that we are "aliens and strangers in the world" (2:11). What's more, the text strongly suggests that we are to submit "for the Lord's sake" to the earthly king (2:13), and in a crowning blow, you and I—Americans— are even commanded to "honor the king" (2:17). This posed problems for our more thoughtful founding fathers. It poses problems for you and me, too.

Born and reared in egalitarian America as most of us have been, we have fairly limited experience with kings and royalty, though it is not for that reason any less negative. So were the experiences and opinions of Huckleberry Finn and the runaway slave Jim, in Mark Twain's classic American novel, when their raft was boarded by two men claiming to be a king and a duke.

It doesn't take Huck long to make up his mind that "these liars warn't no kings nor dukes, but just low-down humbugs and frauds. Take them all around, they're a mighty ornery lot." Over the next days, poor Huck and Jim learn more about just how ornery these frauds were. In a flourish of comic irony, Twain has Huck wish that they could "hear of a country that's out of kings." But Jim still thinks their king is the real article, though he laments that "dise one do smell so like the nation." Huck decides not to break it to Jim that these were not the real thing because "it wouldn't 'a' done no good: you couldn't tell them from the real kind." At the last Jim says it best: "dese kings o' ourn is regular rapscallions." Thus, Twain humorously explored the official American distaste for kings and nobles and, ironically, the curious fascination we have with them and all things royal.

Kings Loom Large

Reluctantly, I confess to some of that fascination. A number of years ago while teaching at Lavengamalie College in the tiny South Pacific kingdom of Tonga, I twice encountered the king of Tonga. He was hard to miss. In a tropical island nation where importance was calculated with a tape measure around the middle, and where the king was most definitely the most important man, he was inevitably also the largest. As he got older, his English doctor, with shameless insensitivity to local custom, ordered him to lose a considerable amount of his hundreds of pounds of royal girth—or else.

One of my sightings of this great man was on a narrow side street in the capital town of Nuku'alofa. Flanked by the jogging Tongan army, and the ubiquitous mob of pigs, he was the largest human being I had ever seen—and he was dutifully trying to ride a bicycle. I pitied that bicycle. Maybe he suffered with an eating disorder, or maybe it was cultural gluttony; nevertheless, this man was a professing Christian and, by all accounts, a kind and benevolent ruler. Perhaps I didn't catch him at his royal best, but I had no twinges of longing to live under his or any other monarchy, and I remain grateful to be an American—and to celebrate July 4.

Americans have long had problems with kings. In political theory we despise them. But in actual fact, we have a curious fascination with them. I am no exception. Nor, on the other hand, am I a groupie of the British royal family. So perhaps meeting the most celebrated member of that family one dark and dreary morning in Scotland not long ago thrilled me more than it should have.

A Chat with the Prince

It was early April and raining, but this was Scotland, so it was no delicate spring shower. Wind-driven rain pummeled the medieval ramparts of Edinburgh Castle and struck my numbing face like tiny bolts of electricity. Along with a colleague, I was responsible for leading some fifty high school students on a historical study tour of Britain. Our students huddled together on the drenched cobblestones of the wide parade ground in front of the Great Hall. The shivers and hurt looks on their faces suggested that they were seriously reconsidering their enthusiasm for this adventure. The only advantage I could find in the cold and wet was that there wasn't another tourist in sight.

I had led tours of this castle before, and the weather was, frankly, not unusual. But this time something was decidedly different. The turrets and battlements were lined with armed police wearing fluorescent green raingear. Police motorcycles roared into position, creating a perimeter. Scots guards flanked a luxurious green Bentley. Reporters and cameramen hovered on all sides of the scene. Something was definitely brewing.

"The Great Hall is closed," a guard informed us in a clipped Scots brogue. "We regret any inconvenience."

I felt cheated. The Great Hall was one of our principal objectives. There, in 1560, under the disapproving scowl of Mary, Queen of Scots, the Scottish Parliament had approved John Knox's Scots Confession. And it contained one of the most impressive collections of weapons—claymores, pikes, suits of armor—north of the Tower of London. And here we were stuck out in the pouring rain while some bigwig strolled through at his leisure.

Then I saw him. I don't read the tabloids, but I recognized the long nose, wide ears, and—forgive me—gawky features of Charles, Prince of Wales, heir apparent to the British Crown. What's more, instead of ducking into the plush interior of his Bentley, he turned and strode toward our sopping-wet huddle of students, a Scots guard trotting beside him holding aloft a Black Watch tartan umbrella over the royal head.

"Welcome to Great Britain," he said with that wide smile of his. "From where in America have you come?"

His question made me feel a bit conspicuous. As he spoke he shook hands with each of our students, some of the boys circling around to press his flesh again at the other end of the line. For several moments he stood within arm's reach, chatting with our students about their travels, their school, and his snow-skiing with William and Harry in our North Cascade mountains only months before. The dreary day had been transformed into a day that each of us would speak about for years to come, perhaps for our lifetimes.

While cameras chattered on every side, reporters cornered several of us to get details about our school and students. Back at the youth hostel that evening, students gazed in wonder at their photograph with the prince in *The Scotsman* and eagerly read about their school and about what they were supposed to have said that morning in their encounter with Prince Charles. They excitedly watched the evening news on the television, breathlessly hoping to see themselves shaking hands with the next king of Britain.

Why All the Brouhaha?

We're Americans. So why this level of honor given to someone else's king? He's not going to be our king. We believe in republican ideals, remember? What's more, why such euphoria if we are "a royal priesthood, a holy nation" (1 Peter 2:9), and our citizenship is ultimately in heaven?

Democratic Americans are probably impressed by the romanticized view of old-world medieval castles, courtly love, royal pageantry, and all the idealized notions we entertain about what an incredibly wonderful life it would be to have everyone wait on us, to have everyone applaud when we nod and intone a few words, to have all the wealth, luxury, and status, to wield royal power, to speak and see people obey our every whim. What a life!

For whatever the reasons, meeting royalty impresses us—it impressed my students; it impressed me. Here I am writing about it several years later. Considering what rapscallions so many kings have been, however, I wonder whether all this fascination is not curiously misplaced.

Political history refers to the king of Macedon as Alexander the Great, but the Holy Spirit in Daniel's prophetic words calls him a "shaggy goat" (Dan. 8:21). How turned around we have it when we lionize kings and men considered great in the world's eyes. After all, few if any Alexander the Greats of the world will be in heaven. Conversely, think, with shame, about the boredom and indifference that often marks our worship of the King of kings.

Few Kings

In 1661, when ailing Samuel Rutherford was ordered to appear and answer charges of high treason before the royal court of another royal Charles, the double-dealing King Charles II, the saintly pastor sent a reply that seems more appropriate to someone who sees his way clearly when it comes to kings. Knowing that he was dying, he tersely replied that he had a summons from a higher court and Judge, "and I go where few kings and great men come."

Why do we heap so much honor on earthly royalty and great men, but when it comes to honoring and bowing before the splendor of King Jesus, our prayers are so anemic, our praise so pedestrian, our gratitude so superficial, our love so diluted? Why so much thrill for what is partial at best, so full of tyranny and injustice at the worst? I wonder if it is because we simply don't see clearly. And why don't we? Because clear sight in this instance requires a different set of eyes. We need our vision cleared by a firmer grasp of divine truth and by stronger faith.

If we had faith like Rutherford's, we could then see "the King there in his beauty, without a veil between." We would feel that there was no price too high, no sacrifice too great, if only we could spend all our days with him. Not just occasionally bump into him at one of his castles, but walk with him in the cool of the evening, speak to him without ceasing, and know that he would never weary of our requests, that he would listen and answer every word. For the young man with this kind of faith, nothing would compare with listening to this King's sweet voice, sitting down and eating and drinking with him, working, playing, communing with him in every dimension of life. If we had more faith, we would clamor to be in his presence, to hear his voice, to see his smile, to feel the warmth of his hand in ours. We would do what some of my students did: run to the end of the line to see the prince up close again, to clasp his hand in ours once again.

One of the Few Kings

On another July 4, this one in the year 1552, John Calvin, the theologian of the Reformation, wrote a letter to fifteen-year-old King Edward VI of England. Calvin had dedicated a book he had just written on Psalm 87 to the young Protestant king. "You will find [Psalm 87] contains a very profitable lesson for your Majesty," wrote Calvin.

The profitable lesson that Calvin had in mind for Edward applies to young men living under a monarchy or a republic, or living in the days of the Reformation, or living in the modern world.

"You know, Sire," wrote Calvin, "how much danger kings and princes are in, lest the height to which they are raised should dazzle their eyes, and amuse them here below, while making them forgetful of the heavenly kingdom."

The evil of which Calvin was warning Edward regularly intoxicates more than just kings. A thoughtful young man knows this.

"Now, in the present Psalm," continued Calvin, "mention is made of the nobleness and dignity of the Church, which ought so to enrapture both great and small, that no earthly honors and possessions should hold them back, or hinder them from aiming to be enrolled among the people of God."

Calvin proceeded to tell Edward what a great thing it was to be a king. "Nevertheless, I have no doubt that you reckon it beyond comparison to be a Christian. It is, therefore, an invaluable privilege that God has vouchsafed you, Sire, to be a Christian king."

Calvin concluded by calling Edward "to employ all [his] energies to [Christ's] honor and service." We too, in ultimate loyalty to the King of kings, ought to "submit [ourselves] with all humility and reverence beneath the spiritual scepter of his gospel."

A Castle or Low-income Housing?

When Calvin wrote his July 4 letter, it was merely another day on the calendar. But what should a Christian young man think now

211

about celebrating our Fourth of July and all that it represents? You have privileges and temporal advantages, and arguably even spiritual ones, that result directly from our American republican ideals, from our free-market economy, from our constitutional freedoms. Go ahead. Have another hot dog. Enjoy the fireworks. Be grateful for American freedom and for those who bought it with their lives.

But know this. Your ultimate citizenship is a heavenly one, so high and splendid that no earthly kingdom or republic even begins to measure up to this nation. Yes, you are to honor earthly authorities in proportion to their roles, but ultimately you are to fear God and give the loftiest honor to the King of kings.

Your obligations to honor your nation and earthly leaders will come into proportionate clarity when the eyes of your faith are wide open to the surpassing wonder of being a citizen of heaven, part of a royal priesthood, a child of the King. He promises you that what is his is yours, that you are heir of all that is, and that he has prepared a place that will make Edinburgh Castle, or any other earthly royal residence, look like Hooverville housing next to what he has for you in Emmanuel's land.

Long live the King!

Resolves

- To regularly remind myself, when I see someone who is great in the world's eyes, how small that person is next to my God
- To cultivate a stronger faith in the unseen world of heaven and eternity
- To read my Bible with an increasing sense of surpassing wonder at what it contains
- To pray regularly together as father and son

Scripture Memory

"But you are a chosen people, a royal priesthood, a holy nation, a people belonging to God, that you may declare the praises of him who called you out of darkness into his wonderful light."

1 Peter 2:9

For Discussion

1. What people or things do you give too much honor to?
2. How might your role as an American come into conflict with your role as a Christian?
3. Discuss a particular activity or person that is very important to you, and compare your enthusiasm for it (or that person) with your enthusiasm for Christ.

"Glorious Things of Thee Are Spoken"

Savior, if of Zion's city
I, through grace, a member am,
Let the world deride or pity,
I will glory in thy name:
Fading is the worldling's pleasure,
All his boasted pomp and show;
Solid joys and lasting treasure
None but Zion's children know.

John Newton, 1779

For Further Study

Read Psalm 72; use a concordance and look up other biblical passages about kings.

20

HONOR, FAITH, AND COURAGE

Exodus 3:7–11

Since many men face monumental challenges at some time in their lives, Christian men will train early to face conflicts with courage and faith. This chapter is written by a young man who has faced dangers in real-world combat that few of the rest of us can imagine. David Uthlaut, First Captain and Brigade Commander at West Point, served as 101st Airborne Division Rifle Executive Officer in the initial ground assault in Iraq in April 2002. Later deployed as a Ranger Platoon leader, David fought Taliban terrorists in remote mountains in Afghanistan. While in command on the ground, David was wounded in the same battle that took the life of one of his men, a celebrated pro-football star turned soldier. Later, David received a Purple Heart, two Bronze Stars, and an Army Commendation Medal for valor in combat. Read how one courageous man learned to use his strength to serve his country in war—but ultimately to serve Christ.

A Grim Challenge

Spying a small Afghan village in the distance, my platoon of approximately forty men piled out of our modified pickup trucks at a fork in the canyon. I began surveying the surrounding ridgelines, peering through both the early-morning fog and the haze of my crystallized breath. Red-eyed and road-weary from over eight hours of bouncing over rocky crags and treacherous cliffside trails throughout the night, my platoon of Rangers trudged on past me.

As my men began taking inventory of all equipment they would need for the upcoming trek, I recognized the look in their eyes. They were thinking the same thoughts I was: despite our current state of discomfort, the 8,000 feet at which we currently stood looked remarkably pleasant compared to the white-capped peaks extending over 2,000 feet above us. Smoke curled from mud-and-timber huts in a nearby village. I noticed other plumes of smoke and orange glows spotting the wooded slopes of the mountain we were preparing to climb. These could just be local villagers scraping out a living in these barren mountains. Or they could be enemy insurgents waiting in ambush. This could turn out to be a really bad day.

A significant proportion of the Rangers under my leadership had signed up to serve our country specifically because of the attacks on America on September 11, 2001. They believed as I do that the same terrorists who had funded and trained the attackers on that fateful day would strike again and that they would stop at nothing short of their own death to accomplish their twisted mission.

As far as my men and I were concerned, we would much prefer to root them out and kill them on their turf than to have them come after our families and loved ones in our home country. This logic had brought us to where we currently stood—miserable and in a precarious situation, yet still doing our part to "keep the wolf from the door" in America. Again, I scanned my platoon. These Rangers are the steely-eyed heroes that legends are made of; they are men of crystal focus, gallant heart, and iron will.

215

I checked my map a final time, folded it, and slid it into the top of my rucksack. Gnawing on a brittle piece of Powerbar, I gathered my squad leaders to make final preparations for our ascent. My orders had been to search out and destroy remnants of the Taliban taking refuge in these remote hills, and we were going to do it—or give it our all in the attempt. Next, we would hunker down and set a trap to catch any other stray terrorists moving through the area.

Every man knew that the terrain, the bitter elements, and the constant danger would push us to the limits of our endurance and skills. We would be challenged physically and mentally. Inwardly I prayed that I would be up to this challenge as a leader, and that, with God's help, we would accomplish our objective and I would not fail my men.

"We're moving out in ten minutes," I told my squad leaders.

"Who Am I?"

At times God asks us to take on tasks that we believe are manifestly beyond our capabilities. Moses certainly realized the enormity of the task that God had placed before him. He was supposed to waltz right into Egypt, a country from which he had fled years earlier for killing an Egyptian, and ask for an appointment with the ruler of the land—the mighty Pharaoh. Furthermore, he was to tell this powerful king to set free the people of Israel, the slave workforce that kept the kingdom rich, or else God would bring terrible plagues upon Egypt. Imagine the courage that this task would require.

Moses' response was a human response, one that any of us would have adopted, given the circumstances. He essentially told God, "You've got the wrong guy; pick someone else." To be sure, Moses was fearful for his own life because of his exile status, but he also felt that he was not the right choice to take on this task because of his own personal shortcomings. He did not believe he had the eloquence of speech to effectively carry God's message to Pharaoh.

Moses, however, forgot two very important things about God. He forgot that God doesn't make mistakes, and that God himself would speak the message to Pharaoh. God would be using Moses only as a human vessel to carry the message. Nevertheless, God had pity upon Moses by allowing him to take his brother Aaron along with him to help him speak, but God did not change the mission he had for Moses or take it away from him.

When Doubt Sets In

Once we have accepted the tasks set before us, the battle does not cease to be fought. It has, in fact, only just begun. The Bible tells us that God will give us the strength to succeed (Josh. 1:5), but he never tells us that it will be an easy road. In fact, he tells us that we should expect to face trials and setbacks (James 1:2–4).

As my platoon began to ascend the jagged Afghan peaks, burning lungs strained by the altitude and weighed down by eighty to a hundred pounds of equipment each, many of us began to question the wisdom of the mission we had been given. If we came under attack, how would we fight effectively? I must admit that I had my own doubts.

By God's grace, we faced no enemy resistance that day. Either they had seen us coming and decided to fight another day, or they had departed long before our arrival. Either way, we were relieved to have avoided a fight in those miserable conditions. Our search of the villages scattered along the slopes also proved relatively uneventful, turning up nothing more than a few hunting weapons and disjointed information about the enemy from the villagers. Having no further intelligence to redirect us, we passed on through to the highest portion of the surrounding terrain, where we would have ideal overwatch of the avenues of approach into and out of the canyon.

Our unit reached the heights in its entirety, having successfully completed the climb and the first portion of our mission, and not one of my soldiers had uttered a complaint the entire time. Just as we thought things might get a little easier, the temperature dropped; our sweat began to freeze, and snow began to fall—for the next three days— and God placed a new set of challenges before me on top of that ridge.

Moses had his share of doubts, which set in shortly after embarking on his mission from God. The Bible does not tell us just how Moses and Aaron were able to enter Egypt and earn themselves the right to speak before Pharaoh, but that must have been an extreme challenge by itself. Once they did make their demands to the king, Pharaoh basically laughed in their faces and told them to get back to work with their slave brethren. On top of that, Pharaoh mandated that the slaves no longer be provided with straw to make bricks, a cruel morale-crushing order that enraged the Israelites. So here you have Moses and Aaron, returning from an unsuccessful visit to Pharaoh, having seemingly done nothing but worsen the situation for the very people they were attempting to help. And now not even the Israelites wanted their help.

I can hear Moses now, looking wistfully up toward the heavens and saying, "See, God, I told you that you had the wrong guy. And now look what has happened because of this . . . ." Actually, it went a little more like this: "O Lord, why have You brought harm to this people? Why did You ever send me? Ever since I came to Pharaoh to speak in Your name, he has done harm to this people, and You have not delivered Your people at all" (Ex. 5:22–23 NASB).

Moses is certainly considered one of the giants of faith, as evidenced by his lengthy mention in Hebrews 11, but at this moment he exhibits natural human doubt about the divine plan. God's plan may have seemed flawed up to this point, but God always had a clear view of the future and of the bigger picture, neither of which Moses was privy to. This is the point at which Moses had to let go of his doubts and put his complete faith in God—just as you and I must do.

The Sustained Fight

After nearly a week in the mountains, with minimal shelter and scanty food rations, my platoon finally returned to our base camp to refit and get some rest. Less than twenty-four hours later, however, we boarded helicopters for a similar mission in another part of the country. There we were greeted by weather and terrain that looked all too familiar, but this time we were more confident of our ability to handle whatever was thrown at us.

This time we made better use of the terrain, paid the villagers for hot food and shelter, and made arrangements to help the village with civil-affairs projects. Our relationship with the villagers was much stronger as a result, and they were more forthcoming with intelligence about the enemy we were facing. This cycle continued throughout the deployment, each successive challenge making us stronger and increasing our level of self-confidence.

On a personal level, God was mentally preparing me to sustain storms of even greater proportion. Our battalion lost a soldier to an Improvised Explosive Device (IED) blast midway through that deployment, a soldier who had previously been in my company and was close to many of the soldiers I worked with.

On successive deployments and in other parts of the global war on terror, I lost many more soldiers I worked with and friends I'd gone to school with. Some of these losses have been more difficult to handle than I could have imagined. The majority of the enemy fire I have personally come in contact with also came after this deployment, and having undergone much emotional and mental strain beforehand helped me keep my wits about me under fire. The levels of adrenaline and pure fear associated with being shot at or having mortar rounds land close by are difficult to express in words. Being able to overcome human frailty in these situations is a true blessing from God and a testament to his grace.

I am a work in progress, and so are you. God often has to put us through the grinder in order to chip away some of our sinful tendencies. Some of the most life-changing experiences for me have been the most humbling experiences as well. When God takes away my pride and causes me to realize my own shortcomings, that is when I am most willing to turn to him and rely on him for guidance. That state of dependence is exactly where God wants us, where he can use us most effectively.

Moses and the Israelites eventually made it out of Egypt. God even did them the favor of wiping out all the Egyptians who pursued them, planning to slaughter them in the desert. But if they thought it was going to be smooth sailing from there, they were greatly mistaken.

Moses dedicates a significant portion of Exodus, Leviticus, Numbers, and Deuteronomy to chronicling the ups and downs of the Israelite people in the desert. In the end, these people proved to be so "stiff-necked" that God decided that they would never see the Promised Land that they had been seeking since their departure from Egypt. Only two men, Caleb and Joshua, passed the tests of faith in order to warrant their entrance into the Promised Land.

Let us not sell Moses short—it was he who had borne the brunt of the desert trials year after year, sustaining the constant grumbling of the people of Israel and interceding with God time and time again so that he would not wipe out the entire race. Without Moses' faith and perseverance, not one Israelite would have ever made it even out of the desert. When Moses stepped up and accepted the extremely difficult mission from God, he paved the way for Israel to become a nation of their own, and eventually for Jesus to come to earth.

Weapons and Ammo

The first step in being mightily used of God is to identify the strengths that God has given you. God has bestowed on each one of us a unique set of talents so that we might better serve and glorify him. The body of Christ is made up of many members (1 Cor. 12:12), and each of these members has a different role to play within the church. What is yours?

But remember, gifts can be used for good or for evil. A man in charge of leading other men could lead them to heaven or to hell. You must set about to use your gifts for godly purposes, to lead others to heaven.

Next, you must learn to obey orders and accept the specific mission that God has for your life. As with my mission in Afghanistan and with Moses' mission in Egypt, God's mission for your life may be very different from what you imagine. But once God makes clear to you how he has determined to use you, there's but one thing to do: pick up your rifle and move out.

How does God make clear to you what he wants you to do? One important way is through prayer. Are you talking to God on a regular basis to see what mission and purpose he has for you?

When the day comes for you to fulfill your mission, you'll need to know how to use your weapons. So you must be gaining skill with them now and making sure you've got plenty of ammunition for the fight ahead. Fit to fulfill your mission, you will be Satan's greatest human enemy, and he will attack you at every curve in the road. Satan hopes to cut you down with trials; God intends to strengthen you with these trials for the tougher times ahead. Train with your weapons so that you're prepared to withstand the tough times that God has promised you.

My combat missions have certainly not been for the faint of heart. But in a life worth living there are seemingly impossible missions that are worth the risk of undertaking for the benefit of others. Doing what we can to bring terrorists to justice and helping to establish peace, order, and freedom in countries that have never known these things is one of those worthwhile missions. Strengthening and preserving those freedoms at home is another. If this is true in a just war, how much more so in the spiritual missions that God calls young men to engage in.

When God calls you to do difficult and dangerous tasks, never forget that God doesn't make mistakes and that God himself will speak and act through you. Just as God was using Moses as a human vessel to carry his message to Pharaoh, so he wants you to trust in his strength to fight his battles and to fulfill the mission he has for your life.

Will you train yourself for the battle ahead? Will you prepare for the challenge? Or will you be faint of heart?

Resolves

- To identify the strengths that God has given me
- To become expert with my spiritual weapons now
- To seek and prepare for God's kingdom mission for my life

Scripture Memory

"You who have made me see many troubles and calamities will revive me again; from the depths of the earth you will bring me up again."

Psalm 71:20 ESV

For Discussion

1. What is courage?
2. Which areas of your life are most susceptible to attack?
3. How can you adequately train yourself for the conflicts that loom ahead?

"Fight the Good Fight"

Fight the good fight with all thy might;
Christ is thy strength, and Christ thy right;
Lay hold on life, and it shall be
Thy joy and crown eternally.

John Monsell, 1863

For Further Study

Exodus 14; Deuteronomy 32

21

HONORING REAL GREATNESS

Philippians 3:17–21

"Pay Attention!"

Steve Kelley, sportswriter for the *Seattle Times*, recently recollected the advice his father used to give him when they sat together watching the Philadelphia Phillies at Connie Mack Stadium. "Pay attention," his dad would say when Willie Mays came to bat. "You're watching greatness. You don't want to forget this."

I remember sitting on "Tightwad Hill" with my uncle, watching the farm club Tacoma Twins, cheering wildly as I peered through the binoculars. The next day after school, I'd grab my bat and try my best to imitate the swing of those heavy-hitter wannabes. For the record, no matter how hard I tried, I wasn't wired for baseball greatness. "You can't put in what the Lord's left out," quipped the trainer in the classic film

Chariots of Fire. When I would come to bat at neighborhood games, as if on cue the outfield moved in, or just squatted down and waited until I finished flailing the air. Through all this, however, I have figured out something important: I pay attention to men I think are great, and I desperately try to be like them. And so do you.

Kelley's dad was right about one thing: you don't want to forget greatness. We must sit up and "pay attention" to real greatness. But what makes someone worthy of this attention? What makes someone truly great, a worthy hero, someone you should never forget, someone you should hold in the highest regard, someone you should imitate?

All Men Honor Heroes

"Any nation that does not honor its heroes," said Abraham Lincoln, "will not long endure." In an age when debunking heroes has become as American as apple pie and hot dogs, an age of flag-burning ingratitude, an age of pompous disdain for the past, an age that chants "Hey, hey, ho, ho, Western culture's got to go," we should cringe at Lincoln's prophetic words. Maybe we've come too close. Maybe we're there already. Maybe we are a people that mocks at real heroes and, in their place, is now bowing down before the real villains.

Nineteenth-century Scottish historian Thomas Carlyle wrote, "Hero-worship cannot cease till man himself ceases." In the fifth century, Augustine referred to men as *homo adorans*, man made to adore, to worship, to venerate heroes. Thus, kings and generals are followed by their adoring armies even into the jaws of death. "Once more unto the breach, dear friends," cried Shakespeare's Henry V as he rallied his men before the battered walls of Harfleur, "or close the wall up with our English dead!" In the first century B.C., Julius Caesar was so adored by his legions that they were prepared to cross the Rubicon and march in defiance against Rome and Pompey. Or the young Alexander the Great motivating thousands to fight and die so that he might spread Greek culture and language—and rule the world in the bargain.

224

The literature of Western civilization is the fascinating saga of great achievement, an enduring celebration of heroes. Great poetry praises the deeds of heroes, real or imagined, from the three hundred Spartans at Thermopylae, to the bloody triumphs of Beowulf, to the dragon-slaying Red Cross Knight of Edmund Spenser's epic allegory, to the six hundred courageous men of Alfred, Lord Tennyson's Light Brigade, even to the humble heroics of J. R. R. Tolkien's mythical Frodo the hobbit—it all fires the blood and fascinates the imagination.

One thing is overwhelmingly clear: You and I were made to adore heroes. We pay attention with all our being to great men.

Beware of False Heroes

This ingrained tendency to adore heroes, however, poses particular challenges for young men growing up in a culture inundated by glitzy, muscle-bound icons of popular culture and the sports arena. Pop culture particularly plays on your love of heroes. It could not survive without it. The icons of entertainment demand your worship. They live and die for it. So it has always been.

Many historians argue that the history of the world is the history of men following heroes. It would be just as accurate to say that the history of the world is the history of young men blindly following the wrong heroes, following unworthy examples, whose vices are tragically compounded in their fawning worshipers.

So who are your heroes? In today's reading, Paul urges the Philippian Christians to "join with others in following my example" (Phil. 3:17), that is to say, follow the right men, set up heroes for yourself, and be like them. Speak as they speak; do as they do. The Bible often speaks this way. Twenty-eight times we are told to imitate others, often to follow Christ the Captain of our salvation, but fully seventeen of those times we are commanded to follow other men, such as Paul, as they heroically follow Christ.

Paul, here, is in earnest. This is no casual advice, take it or leave it. No. He reminds us, "I have often told you before and now say again

225

even with tears" (Phil. 3:18). Why with tears? Why so earnest? Because "many live as enemies of the cross of Christ" (3:18). Because an earthly hero has his mind "on earthly things" (3:19). And the young man who chooses to follow worldly heroes, to applaud at their entertainment, to listen to their music, to cheer at their achievement, to spend his money on their products, to paper the walls of his bedroom with their posters should not be surprised if he follows those heroes right into the jaws of hell. From this, you and I are duty bound to draw the line in the sand. This is no trivial matter. Don't follow the enemies of the cross of Christ. "Their destiny," Paul declares without equivocation, "is destruction" (3:19). As will be yours if you follow them.

Moreover, the more impressed you are by the status and achievement of unbelievers, by their sophisticated good looks, by their clothes and shoes, by their posture and swagger, by their prowess in sports, by their associations, by their way of speaking, and by their money and fancy cars, lavish houses, planes, and yachts, the less you will be able to separate out their vices. Soon they won't seem like vices at all. At the last their vices will be yours. Know that their end will be yours as well. Fully expect to become like those you adore.

"We are all creatures of imitation," wrote nineteenth-century Anglican bishop J. C. Ryle. "Precept may teach us, but it is example that draws us." And since those examples can draw us from both directions, you must beware of the tendency to go easy on the parts of your sports or music heroes' lives that you know are sinful.

Do you honestly think that you will be unaffected by the foul language, the unfaithful living, the hostility to truth, or the swaggering arrogance of your worldly heroes? I doubt it. And the more impressed you are with their achievement, the more likely you are to embrace other elements of their lifestyle.

Don't expect to see it coming like a tidal wave. It all happens gradually. Rarely does a young man, like yourself, who is growing up in a Christian home, plunge headlong into sin with his back against all that he has been taught. Generally, it happens little by little, one single what's-the-big-deal step at a time. "The road to hell," observed C. S. Lewis, "is a gradual one."

The best way to avoid the gradual road to hell is to cultivate honor for and imitation of truly worthy heroes. Here's one of mine.

Fight to the Death

I've thought a good deal lately about one of my heroes. P-47 World War II fighter pilot John Hemminger lived with his wife and three children on American Lake, a five-minute bicycle ride from my childhood home. I was the neighbor kid who always hung around in the summer, fishing, swimming, and doing woodworking projects in the basement. Along with the stray dogs that attached themselves to kindhearted Mr. Hemminger, I, too, adopted the Hemminger family as my own.

My mother's rule was that I couldn't go swimming unless the thermometer read seventy degrees. I soon figured out how to nudge it up with the hair dryer, and then I'd hop on my bike and off to the Hemmingers. I always tried to time things so that I could sit down for the usual lunch fare of grilled cheese sandwiches, soup, Gravenstein applesauce, dilly beans, and smoked salmon. Nobody did homemade applesauce like Edna Hemminger, and nobody did salmon like John Hemminger.

John Hemminger was a man of deeds and not words, and so I rarely heard him speak about the war, and never about his role in it. I was forced to piece things together from pictures and from stories told by others about his role in that great conflict.

"The greatest catastrophe in history," Stephen Ambrose called World War II, and "the most costly war of all time." In April 1945, 300,000 Americans attacked the Japanese island of Okinawa, while the U.S. Navy was pounded by 350 kamikaze planes. We lost thirty-six ships. In human life, the casualties were beyond staggering: 49,200 men in one battle. The Japanese lost 112,129 human lives at Okinawa. Still they fought on.

Germany surrendered in May, but by summer, it appeared that Japan would fight on until not one Japanese soldier remained alive. A full-scale Allied invasion of Japan seemed the only option, but it was an invasion that would have cost a million American soldiers their lives. President Truman opted to drop two atomic bombs on Japan in hopes of breaking the enemy's will to fight to extermination. It was as if the entire nation had become kamikaze flyers.

Fighter-Pilot Greatness

In 1941, after the Japanese attack on Pearl Harbor, America joined the war, and can-do men such as John Hemminger were desperately needed to fight. He said goodbye to his childhood sweetheart, Edna Mae Firch, and joined up.

The picture of him that I will always have in my mind is of a quiet young man in a leather bomber jacket, a shy, boyish grin stretching across his handsome features, posing with his beloved P-47, affectionately dubbed *Edna Mae*. Though he was called on to do highly dangerous and daring feats, there was no hint of the cocky, swaggering dog fighter in his looks or carriage.

John Hemminger loved machines. I can only begin to imagine his fascination at first sight of his P-47's Pratt and Whitney eighteen-cylinder, 2,800-horsepower engine, or the heart-pounding thrill when he first accelerated into the heavens at his plane's maximum speed of 433 mph.

He was a gentle, peace-loving man, so I particularly wonder what his first thoughts were when he laid eyes on the eight 12.7-mm Browning machine guns bristling from the wings of his P-47, a machine engineered for killing. One thing I'm sure of: there was no better cared-for fighter plane than his, and probably none more skillfully used for its designed purpose.

John Hemminger was credited with the last P-47 kill of the war. By some accounts, he and the Japanese pilot were slugging it out somewhere over the blue waters of the Pacific on September 2, 1945, while

American top brass accepted the Japanese unconditional surrender onboard the USS *Missouri*. The facts are unclear because John Hemminger rarely spoke about the war, and boasting was something he never did.

What is clear is that John Hemminger, along with a generation of other Americans, was a humble servant hero who did his duty, and then, unlike many with whom he fought, he returned home. Bidding farewell to his P-47 *Edna Mae*, he married his beloved Edna Mae, raised his family, and lived a long, seemingly insignificant life. John Hemminger and his dear wife were not bombastic about their faith in Christ, but few people have more consistently lived out the Lord's injunction to love their neighbor as themselves. Consequently, their home was a quiet, contented one, filled with stability and service.

In the world's eyes, after the war John Hemminger lived an ordinary life. Some might have called it boring. But not to the dozens of missionaries he supported and took fishing when they were home, and whose decrepit cars he repaired, rebuilt, or replaced, often at his own expense. And all done hush-hush, so that no one would give him credit for his latest acts of generosity.

True Greatness

Jesus told his disciples that if they wanted to be great, they must become servants. He didn't tell them to become great baseball players, or inventors, or CEOs, or powerful politicians, or celebrity pastors, or best-selling authors—or even fighter pilots. "Whoever wants to become great," Jesus said, "must be your servant" (Matt. 20:26). If you want to be great, you, too, must be a servant. John and Edna Hemminger were great Christians because they were great servants.

My hero John Hemminger died of Parkinson's disease on December 27, 2006. His wife, Edna Mae, suffered for decades with multiple sclerosis before her homegoing. But I never heard either of them complain. They bore their trials with patience—even with smiles. Nor did I ever hear either of them speak critical words about others. I think they were simply too busy, in Christ's name, loving and serving their neighbors. Pay attention, young man. This is true greatness.

You probably don't need to travel to faraway places to get to know and honor servant heroes. I suspect that in your church, neighborhood, and extended family there are several John and Edna Mae Hemmingers. Such folks help unmask the masquerade of what passes for greatness among modern celebrities. Pop icons and all their vainglorious glitter look pretty irrelevant next to great people such as these—but only if you train your eye and your affections to know and honor genuine greatness.

Glitz or Glory

Let's face it. It's far easier to talk about being impressed with servant greatness than it is to actually be so. I wonder whether the normalization of sin is the reason. "Worldliness is what makes sin look normal," wrote David Wells, "and righteousness look odd." Hence, venerating worldly heroes sets us up to begin feeling that humble, holy living is out of touch, not much fun, certainly not cool.

Here again, you must pay attention. When you honor heroes who live worldly lives, you should expect to gradually become more impressed with their worldliness. Meanwhile, your worldly hero's lifestyle will increasingly seem to be the normal way of things. And since no one wants to be odd, everyone wants to think of himself as a normal guy, so gradually you will wink at their vices, embrace their values, and imitate their ways. Finally, Paul's point in Philippians 3:17–21 is that if you do this, when the dust settles, you will share in their destruction.

Puritan Jeremy Taylor described the incremental decline that a young man should expect to pass through if he forges friendships with worldly heroes and their sin: "First it startles him, then it becomes pleasing, then easy, then delightful, then frequent, then habitual, then confirmed, then the man is impenitent, then obstinate, then resolves never to repent, and finally he is damned."

On the judgment day, all that worldly glitz, all that superficially impressive lifestyle will be unmasked. And if you have been duped by a false hero, by one whose mind is on earthly things, it will be far too late to halt the cycle of decline. You must do it now.

Join with others in following the example of great Christians—such as John and Edna Mae Hemminger. The Bible is full of them, and so is church history. Pay attention to them.

Throw in your lot with the truly greats. Know your citizenship. Paul says that it is "in heaven" (Phil. 3:20). Know that most of the world's heroes are frauds. Their power, their prestige, their wealth is all borrowed and will someday be swept away with them. "Their destiny is destruction" (3:19). No real man would throw in his lot with losers like that.

You, young man of God, were predestined for a glorious body, transformed by the infinite power of the Lord Jesus Christ. Make him your ultimate hero, honor those who honor him, and resolve that he will have no worldly rival.

Resolves

- To cut off all known influences that become rivals to Christ
- To adore and worship God alone
- To examine the worldly influences I have allowed myself that could become sinful

Scripture Memory

"He who walks with wise men will be wise, but the companion of fools will be destroyed."

Proverbs 13:20 NKJV

For Discussion

1. Who are the quiet, humble, outwardly unimpressive great people in your life whom you need to get to know?

2. What steps will you take to imitate servant heroes?
3. Discuss with your father areas in your life where false heroes may have crept in (sports, music, film, hobbies, politics).

"The Son of God Goes Forth to War"

A noble army, men and boys,
The matron and the maid,
Around the Savior's throne rejoice,
In robes of light arrayed:
They climbed the steep ascent of heav'n
Through peril, toil, and pain:
O God, to us may grace be giv'n
To follow in their train.

Reginald Heber, 1827

For Further Study

Psalm 119:63; Matthew 16:25–26; 1 Corinthians 15:33

YOUNG MEN: THEIR WITNESS

22

THE POWER OF THE HOLY SPIRIT

Acts 15:25–40

Pussyfoot Witness

I recently received a whispered e-mail from a graduate during the first week of his freshman year at a secular university. Jim's e-mail began something like this: "My new roommate is sitting at his desk across the room from me, right now, and you'll never believe what he's doing. Reading a Bible he checked out of the library!"

Frankly, Jim was not a graduate I was expecting to hear from. But here was his e-mail. I was thrilled; God was hemming Jim in. His whispered e-mail continued. "What should I do? I mean, I know whatever I do, I've got to be extremely careful—say just the right thing. I need to plan this all out and approach him in just the right way."

I e-mailed back and suggested that he not worry too much about all that. "Ask him if he understands what he's reading," I suggested, "then tell him what God has done for you." I explained that I thought it was the devil's lie prompting him to stammer and halt around for just the right words, that it was the fear of man that suggested such things, not the fear of God. I reminded him that it's the power of God that saves sinners like his roommate, not "wise and persuasive words" (1 Cor. 2:4), nor our clever techniques, nor our sophisticated arguments. Nor our silence!

Then I changed tacks. I asked Jim whether he was reading *his* Bible and urged him to make the most of this opportunity to "make [his] calling and election sure" (2 Peter 1:10). A few days later, he stopped by my classroom after football practice and we talked. I gave him a copy of *Mere Christianity*. "But make sure you're reading your Bible first," I told him.

Jim did speak to his roommate and brought him to church, even bought him his own Bible. God had plopped an honest, serious-minded seeker after truth into a dorm room with a church kid who was more or less indifferent about his Christian profession. How odd of God to put a real seeker into a room with a worldly wannabe. Or was it? In God's sovereign design, he may have been killing two birds with the proverbial single stone. Such is the mystery and power of God to bring in his sheep, one from a far country—and a local stray.

What to Say?

You may be like Jim. He was terrified at the prospect of speaking about God, Jesus, and the Bible with a guy who was a double major in physics and chemistry, the sort of honor student whom classmates laugh at for being a left-brained, geeky type—until exam time. None of that mattered when the Spirit of God was on the move in his soul. When the Holy Spirit begins wooing a young man to Christ, that young man will leave his books and hunt down a Bible in the university library, open it, and begin devouring it.

You've been tempted to be silent many times and for many reasons. But one reason that ought never to weigh in is that you don't know what to say, that you'll probably say the wrong thing and mess things all up.

The story of a chain-gang member known as "Biker Bob" illustrates the point. When Biker Bob was eight years old, his grandmother took him to Sunday school. Little Bobby was incorrigible. He did everything he could to disrupt the Bible lesson. He broke crayons, threw crackers, and probably made the teacher cry. She may have even prayed that he'd stop coming.

As a teen, Biker Bob started using drugs, dropped out of school, lived a life of crime, and eventually joined the Hell's Angels, spending hot summer evenings doing drugs with other hard-living bikers.

Late one night after hours of partying, things got out of hand. A friend overdosed on heroin and started screaming for help. His own mind numb with narcotics, Biker Bob began racking what remained of it, when suddenly he thought of the Bible stories from Sunday school. Haltingly at first, he began telling of David and Goliath, then of Moses and the crossing of the Red Sea, of Jesus born in Bethlehem, of his miracles, his parables, his arrest and beating, his death on the cross, his resurrection and promised return.

Early in the morning, seemingly unaffected by the stories, the doomed biker's ravings ended, and he died. But Biker Bob began to live. While listening to his own imperfect retelling of Bible stories that he had not heard for twenty years, God was at work.

If the Spirit of God can convict and save a drug-befuddled sinner by his own profoundly flawed recollections of Bible stories told while bringing comfort to a dying friend, never blame your reluctance to witness on not knowing what to say.

And what of the Sunday school teacher? Her telling of those Bible stories was probably not perfect, either. But God delights to use flawed people such as that teacher—and you and me. She had no idea that God would use her faithful teaching to convert the worst little monster in her class—so is the mystery of God's saving providence.

The Parson's Converted!

Don't misunderstand me. The more you know of Christian theology, history, and apologetics, the better. You should strive to be a rigorously informed Christian, equipped to proclaim Christ to all comers. But in your witness, it is essential that you be a Christian young man who knows his Bible and who depends entirely on the power and sovereignty of God.

In 1842, William Haslam was a young Englishman who cared little about the Bible. He was looking for a socially respectable way to have a comfortable income and do next to nothing to earn it. Ordained into the Anglican clergy, he found his ideal profession in the parish of Baldhu, Cornwall. John Newton a generation before had estimated that there were ten thousand parishes in the Church of England and that nine thousand had unbelieving ministers. Haslam was in the majority. Soon after his installation, however, just when he was hoping to settle into his life of ease, the Spirit of God began to trouble him.

His distress increased, until one Sunday morning he mounted the pulpit, opened to the sermon text for the day, and read, "What think ye of Christ?" (Matt. 22:42 KJV). While commenting on the text and comparing it with other like texts, a light seemed to break on his troubled soul. What had seemed vague and unimportant before now shone with clarity on his mind: the reality of sin and judgment, of Christ and redemption, of the new birth, of righteousness and sanctification, of eternal life and heaven.

In the midst of the sermon, one of Haslam's parishioners suddenly leapt to his feet. "The parson's converted! The parson's converted!" The rest of his congregation joined in with hallelujahs. The story of Richard Haslam, the parson converted by his own sermon, powerfully illustrates the sovereignty of God in saving a sinner, even when that sinner happens to be the preacher.

On-the-Knees Conviction

But there's more to the story. Haslam picks up the thread in his own account: "On the Monday after my conversion, our weekday service was filled to excess. I was telling of how God pulled me out of a desolate pit, when someone began crying aloud for God's mercy. This was followed by another, then another, until preaching was impossible. I cannot tell how many found peace that night, but there was great rejoicing." Haslam started midweek gatherings in a local cottage, and the Spirit continued to work, some hearers falling to the floor with conviction.

Haslam's account continued: "I gave out a hymn and went among the 'slain of the Lord.' After about an hour, someone suggested that we should go to the school-room, as it was getting dark. When I reached the place, I found it impossible to get in, for all was full and a crowd hung about the door. I finally climbed in through the window and stood on a table."

Then Haslam moved among the crowded gathering, pointing them to salvation in Christ alone and praying. As some found peace with God and offered praises to him, Haslam was forced to ask them to leave to make room for others who surrounded the school, desperate for salvation. The meeting stretched late into the night.

Famous in church history, the Cornish Revival of the 1850s spread rapidly throughout the region, Haslam and others preaching in the open air throughout Cornwall. Large crowds, rich and poor, high and low, fell under the convicting and saving power of God's Spirit.

One dramatic example occurred at Mount Hawke in 1852. Haslam's text was from John 3:16: "For God so loved the world, that he gave his only begotten Son, that whosoever believeth in him should not perish, but have everlasting life" (KJV). Haslam preached a simple sermon and later recorded what followed: "A mighty power of the Spirit of the Lord came upon the meeting and several hundred fell on their knees simultaneously."

All this began in a backwater part of England, in a parish with an ill-trained, unconverted minister, with modest gifts at best. Haslam's story is confirming evidence of Paul's words in 1 Corinthians 2:4–5: "My message and my preaching were not with wise and persuasive words, but with a demonstration of the Spirit's power, so that your faith might not rest on men's wisdom, but on God's power." In your witness, you're not called to be clever; you're called to believe and be faithful.

Fear God, Not Kings

Nor are you called to be silent out of fear of man. And because the apostle Paul did not depend on his own wisdom, he was free of the fear of man in his evangelism. J. I. Packer's description of Paul's "intransigent refusal to modify his message in order to suit circumstances" is a timeless model for all who are reluctant to bear witness for fear of man.

But what if you're called to preach before a man whose favorite response was "Off with his head"? That's precisely what happened to Hugh Latimer in January of 1530. He was called to be chaplain to Henry VIII. Warned by a courtier to "speak as he speaks," saintly Latimer entered the service of one of the most notorious monarchs, responsible for beheading two of his six wives. Over fifty thousand people had reasons to mourn the loss of someone who died at the command of this tyrant, including notables such as Sir Thomas More and William Tyndale.

Being chaplain to Henry was as likely to result in Latimer's losing his head as it was to be offered tea in England. Understandably, Latimer trod softly during his first months in court, justifying his reticence to speak on the basis "that prudence is necessary." Months passed, and Latimer felt increasingly uncomfortable about not speaking with the king about the condition of his soul.

Then one day in November, while reading in the writings of the early church fathers, Latimer came across this passage by Augustine: "He who for fear of any power hides the truth, provokes the wrath of God to come upon him, for he fears men more than God." Smitten, Latimer read on, this from St. Chrysostom: "he is not only a traitor to the truth who openly for truth teaches a lie, but he also who does not pronounce and show the truth that he knoweth."

The good chaplain later wrote of these rebukes, "They made me sore afraid"; they "troubled and vexed me grievously in my conscience." He resolved to declare the truth as taught in Holy Scripture, and he knew that it was likely to cost him his life. "I had rather suffer extreme punishment," he wrote, "than be a traitor unto the truth." Boldly, Latimer set his pen to paper.

"Your Grace, I must show forth such things as I have learned in Scripture, or else deny Jesus Christ. The which denying ought more to be dreaded than the loss of all temporal goods, . . . honor, and all manner of torments and cruelties, yea, and death itself, be it ever so shameful and painful." I think I would have avoided giving Henry ideas. But holy Latimer was in earnest.

One of the first things he raised with the king spoke directly to the heart of the Reformation, *sola Scriptura*: "Your Grace promised by your last proclamation that we should have the Scripture in English. Let not the wickedness of worldly men divert you from your godly purpose and promise." This was not the way to speak to Henry VIII, not if you valued your life.

Yet Latimer was just warming up. Critical of many of Henry's clerical advisers, Latimer said that they "hinder the Gospel of Christ," that through these false teachers it was really Henry who "would send a thousand men to hell ere [he] send one to heaven." Undaunted by Henry's divine right, Latimer pressed on: "I pray to God that your Grace may do what God commandeth, and not what seemeth good in your own eyes."

Men who frowned at the wrong moment lost their heads in Henry's court. But Latimer was undaunted. Confronting Henry's mistaken understanding of his temporal authority over the church, Latimer spoke of the two spheres of authority and charged Henry, self-declared supreme head of the Anglican Church, to "make not a mingle-mangle of them." A century later, eighteen thousand Christians would lose their lives for denying that the king of England was the head of the church. For now, Latimer lived on, preaching regularly before the king. After one bold sermon, a friend told Latimer, "We were convinced you would sleep tonight in the Tower." Latimer replied, "The king's heart is in the hands of the Lord."

Impossible as it seems, Latimer survived Henry, but in October of 1555, by order of Henry's Catholic daughter, Bloody Mary, Latimer and his friend and fellow preacher Nicholas Ridley were bound to the stake before Balliol College where Wycliffe had once taught. As the flames were fueled, Latimer said to his friend, "Be of good comfort, Master Ridley, and play the man. We shall this day light such a candle, by God's grace, in England, as I trust shall never be put out."

So must you "play the man" before a hostile world, a world more interested in laughing at you, for the moment, than burning you at the stake. "Let the world deride or pity," John Newton put it in the hymn "Glorious Things of Thee Are Spoken."

Power of the Gospel

A friend of mine became a Christian because a man cared so much about the lost that he vowed to confront everyone he met with Jesus. "Do you know Jesus?" this man asked my friend Ray. God used that unadorned, unafraid, and, yes, unsophisticated witness to save Ray.

You may be reluctant to witness because talking about Jesus doesn't sound very cool. You're waiting until you have sophisticated, intellectual answers to give. Christians tend to sound simpleminded, so you're waiting until you find words that will give intellectual credibility to Christianity.

You may already feel the pull to be known as a thinking Christian, one with sophisticated answers that will trump the world's disdain for the gospel—and for you. I recall the words of a twenty-something girl nearing the end of her three-month L'Abri experience in Switzerland. Pirouetting around the table as we cleaned up after a meal at one of the chalets, she bemoaned her return to family and church. "How can I fit in there," she asked, "now that I am a thinking Christian?"

Wherever you go, you will fit in best if you are a humble, grateful Christian, one who cares that those around you are lost and desperately need to be saved. Let me suggest three things to shape your witness:

First, depend on the power of the Word of God in your witness, and shape the conversation so that you are reading or quoting God's Word. Never be ashamed of the world's disdain for what John Calvin terms the "seemingly rude simplicity" of the Bible. It is sharper than any two-edged sword. It alone can change a sinner's heart.

Second, know the power of prayer. Depend on the supernatural power of God to change sinners' hearts. Pray that God "will open the eyes of their understanding, soften their hearts, renew their natures, and move their wills to receive the Savior" (J. I. Packer).

Finally, bear witness to what Christ has done for you. "The LORD is gracious and righteous; . . . when I was in great need, he saved me" (Ps. 116:5–6). The Bible is full of this kind of witness. Be guided by a humble, grateful sense of what God has done for you, and cultivate a deeper desire that God would do the same for the distressingly lost all around you.

Resolves

- To point the lost to Christ by my life
- To be ready always to bear verbal testimony to faith in Christ
- To care more about witnessing to the lost than about being ridiculed by them
- To pray regularly together as father and son

Scripture Memory

"For it is by grace you have been saved, through faith—and this not from yourselves, it is the gift of God—not by works, so that no one can boast."

Ephesians 2:8–9

For Discussion

1. Discuss why you often think of what to say only after the opportunity is gone.
2. Plan out key passages of Scripture that you want to memorize so that you will have the words to say (see "For Further Study" below).
3. Role-play a conversation with an unbeliever.

"And Can It Be That I Should Gain"

Long my imprisoned spirit lay
Fast bound in sin and nature's night;
Thine eye diffused a quick'ning ray;
I woke, the dungeon flamed with light;
My chains fell off, my heart was free;
I rose, went forth, and followed Thee.

Charles Wesley, 1738

For Further Study

John 6:35–40; 14:6; Romans 3:23; 6:23; 10:9; *Evangelism and the Sovereignty of God*, by J. I. Packer

23

THE POWER OF THE HOLY BOOK

Isaiah 55:1–13

If you're into computers, weapons systems, or airplanes, you'll want to hear Jim Price's story. While majoring in physics in college, Jim was awarded the Helberg Memorial Award for excellence in engineering. He graduated magna cum laude *with a B.S. in aeronautics and astronautics from the University of Washington and was First Honor Graduate at Air Force Officer Training School. After being commissioned in the USAF, he earned an M.S. in aerospace engineering at the University of Southern California. For his technical contributions to the Kinetic Energy Weapon System, an anti-ballistic missile system, part of the so-called Star Wars program, he was awarded an Air Force Commendation Medal in 1990. He worked on doctoral studies at Cal Tech; then he left to develop missile trajectory software, and to co-found C/S Solutions, Inc., where he develops software for the U.S. Department of Defense. But Jim's story isn't really about Star Wars;*

it's about the transforming power of the Word of God breaking irresistibly on the mind and heart of a man who thought he had it all.

Physics Works!

If you are a young man who has been raised in a devout Christian home, you may never have had to "seek the LORD while he may be found" (Isa. 55:6), because God has done the same for you as he did for David (Ps. 22:9), and made you trust in the Lord as a nursing infant. This is a great privilege—a very great privilege—and something for which I hope you thank God every single day. But no one gets all of God's blessings, and if you've been blessed to know God from infancy, let me tell you of the blessing he's given me—how he turned my life upside down by the power of his Word.

Growing up, my brothers and I received good moral instruction, but no religious instruction of any kind. When I was very young, we attended church regularly for a brief period—mainly, I think, because my father knew it was expected that an up-and-coming young executive would be in church on Sunday. I don't think we ever attended church after I was about ten years old.

In high school, I read Herman Hesse and the Bhagavad-Gita, wrote poetry, cut classes, took drugs, and listened to the Moody Blues. Inexplicably, I failed to become one with the universe. My closest approach probably came in a junior-year physics class—we did a simple experiment that involved rolling a steel ball down a little track shaped like a ski jump. We took measurements and placed a cup where we calculated the ball would land. Now, the ball didn't actually land in the cup, but it gave it a good thrashing—close enough to make me think, "Aha! physics works." I decided to become a physicist. I still remember my older brother's dismay when he came into our bedroom and found a book entitled *Fun with Slide Rules.* He felt we had a certain level of cool to maintain, and I was letting down my side. I could see his point; nevertheless, I cut my hair, skipped my senior year, and went off to study physics.

In due course, I attended college, left college, got married, joined the Air Force, finished college at Air Force expense, worked on several missile defense programs, left the Air Force, started a doctorate, ran out of money, went back to work as an engineer, co-founded a software company, put in many years of very long hours—and one day realized that the company was a success, and that I needed a change of pace.

The Great Book

Now, you may think it odd, or you may think it the most obvious thing in the world, but when I want to relax, I read. And so I did: philosophy, history, literature, whatever caught my fancy. I didn't follow a formal "Great Books" list, but that was basically what I had in mind. In everything I read, I ran across quotations from, and references to, the Bible. Even Christianity's detractors praised it: H. L. Mencken, a famous literary critic and notorious opponent of Christianity, said the King James Version "is probably the most beautiful piece of writing in all the literature of the world." I decided I'd better read it.

I chose the Bible itself with some care. It had to be the King James Version, of course, but I didn't want anything religious. I was reading literature; I wanted a nonreligious Bible. Happily, Oxford University Press publishes just that, in its "World's Classics" series. It's called *The Bible*. Not *The Holy Bible*, mind you, just *The Bible*. It doesn't even look like a Bible. It looks like any other eighteen-hundred-page paperback, with a picture of Abraham on the cover. Perfect. I ordered it from Amazon, standard shipping. When it arrived, two to nine days later, I sat down, turned to Genesis 1:1, and started reading.

From the very beginning, I was fascinated. I thought I knew the Bible, or at least the stories—Adam and Eve, Cain and Abel, Noah's Ark, the Tower of Babel, and so on—but I quickly realized I hadn't known them at all. At best, I knew children's versions (which I had mocked for being childish). I was unprepared for the richness of the real thing. I knew that Adam and Eve had eaten the forbidden fruit, but I didn't appreciate the naked rebellion in the act. I knew that God had exiled them from Eden, but I didn't know that he clothed them first. I knew that Cain had murdered Abel, but I didn't know that the "mark of Cain" was for his protection, not his punishment. I knew "An eye for an eye," but not that it replaced "A life for an eye." Over and over again, where I expected only wrath—this was the Old Testament, right?—I saw justice and mercy.

I knew that Joseph had a coat of many colors, but I didn't know that his own brothers had sold him into slavery. And I didn't know that by so doing they had unwittingly saved themselves, and all Egypt, from a terrible famine many years later. When Joseph told his brothers, "Ye thought evil against me; but God meant it unto good" (Gen. 50:20 KJV), I was awed. For the first time, I felt a real sense of the sovereignty of God, who could move history so that even the wicked actions of human beings accomplished his purposes.

This was nothing like the God I expected. Clearly, the Israelites hadn't understood him, either. Did ever a people get into more trouble with their own God? Given the choice, they obviously preferred their neighbor's god, Baal, which they understood. Every ancient culture had a Baal—except, apparently, the one that produced the Bible. How strange.

Facts Are Facts

The commentary in the back of my "World's Classics" edition turned out to be useless. I quote: "The story of the Tower of Babel is a nice example of how an oppressed people can make fun of their imperial overlords." Well . . . okay. Apparently the author of Genesis was a Marxist. The deeper I got into the Old Testament, the more inane, then disrespectful, then outright offensive the commentary seemed. I put the big paperback aside and started reading a proper, black-leather, gold-trim, India-paper, "Holy" Bible. My wife was, I thought, a bit alarmed at this. In truth, so was I. On whose behalf, exactly, was I taking offense?

I wasn't having too much trouble with the King James English, but I decided to get a modern translation to help me over the rough spots. Not wanting to wait two to nine days, I headed down to Borders, found the Bible section . . . and came to a screeching halt. I had no idea that there were so many translations. How to choose? How else? I went home, got on the Internet, and started reading up on Bible translation. You never know where a Google search will take you, and I ended up getting launched on an extended study of the Bible itself. I learned two things that greatly affected my thinking.

First, I learned that there's really no doubt that the Bible has been accurately transmitted. With respect to the Old Testament, its accuracy is verified by the Dead Sea Scrolls, which are practically identical to independent copies made a thousand years later. With respect to the New Testament, there are incomparably more and earlier copies of those writings than we have for, say, Homer or Plato or Aristotle, all of which were sitting on my bookshelf with nary a doubt raised by anyone as to their essential accuracy.

Second, I learned that the Bible was at least on a par with other ancient documents, considered strictly as history. For example, the Hittites were unknown outside the Bible until archaeologists confirmed their existence in the 1890s. Likewise, the pool of Bethesda. Indeed, by the standard methods that historians use, there's at least as much reason to believe that Jesus was resurrected as there is to believe that Caesar crossed the Rubicon. That profoundly changed things. For better or worse, I think like an engineer. Facts are facts.

Atheism or the Real World

I started reading the New Testament along with the Old. I found the person of Jesus Christ to be immensely challenging. In one story, a temple officer sent to arrest Jesus comes back empty-handed, saying, "No one ever spoke like this man!" (John 7:46 ESV). I agreed. I was certain that no one could have made him up. In one place, Jesus says, "Come to me, all who labor and are heavy laden, and I will give you rest. Take my yoke upon you, and learn from me, for I am gentle and lowly in heart, and you will find rest for your souls" (Matt. 11:28–29 ESV).

In another place, he says, "On that day" (he's speaking of the last day) "many will say to me, 'Lord, Lord' . . . . And then will I declare to them, 'I never knew you; depart from me, you workers of lawlessness' " (Matt. 7:22–23 ESV). I had never read anything so hopeful as the invitation, nor so chilling as the dismissal.

I should note that I wasn't troubled by the miracles. Physicists almost unanimously agree that the universe we observe hasn't always existed. Why it suddenly began to exist is, by definition, a metaphysical question, and a perfectly good answer is given by Genesis 1:1: "In the beginning, God created the heavens and the earth" (ESV). Even skeptics acknowledge that this is the explanation to beat, especially since the universe appears to have been "fine-tuned" for life. Since the alternatives all boil down to, "In the beginning, nothing created the heavens and the earth," I had never been able to take atheism very seriously. And if God existed, the miracles certainly weren't a problem.

In any case, the miracles were clearly part and parcel of the gospel accounts. Strip them out, or "naturalize" them, and what's left makes no sense. There's nothing to attract and keep the disciples, nothing for the crowds to get excited about, nothing for the Pharisees to get alarmed about, no crucifixion, no resurrection, no fearless apostles, no Bible, no Christianity. But like the universe, Christianity obviously existed.

Conscience Takes a Beating

I kept reading. I made it through Matthew and Mark more or less without incident, but my conscience was taking a beating: Jesus says that "everyone who is angry with his brother will be liable to judgment" (Matt. 5:22 ESV), and "everyone who looks at a woman with lustful intent has already committed adultery with her in his heart" (5:28 ESV), and "love your enemies and pray for those who persecute you" (5:44 ESV). I had considered myself a pretty good person, but Jesus set the bar so much higher than I had ever imagined.

Luke finally did me in. Jesus says, "The good person out of the good treasure of his heart produces good, and the evil person out of his evil treasure produces evil, for out of the abundance of the heart his mouth speaks" (Luke 6:45 ESV). The verse hit me like a hammer. I thought of all the times I had been rude and snide and sarcastic—to perfect strangers, to people I loved, and worst of all, to people who worked for me, who couldn't even answer in kind. What did that say about my heart? In the very next verse, Jesus asks, "Why do you call me 'Lord, Lord,' and not do what I tell you?" (6:46 ESV). I had no defense. He had just told me why. I spoke "out of the abundance of [my] heart," that was the problem. I could bite my tongue and edit my e-mails, but that didn't make me good; it just made me polite. I wasn't just someone who sinned; I was a sinner. I sinned as naturally as I breathed. It was my nature to sin—it came straight from my heart. And finally, I understood what Jesus meant when he said that "unless one is born again he cannot see the kingdom of God" (John 3:3 ESV).

This Was Personal

That was the end of my "academic detachment." Suddenly, this was personal; I could no longer even pretend that I was "just reading the Bible." If Christianity were true, I had to become a Christian. If Christianity were not true, I had to know. One of the Web sites I had stumbled upon in my Bible researches included a general introduction to Christianity. I dug up that site again and devoured it. The site frequently quoted the works of C. S. Lewis, an Oxford scholar who had famously reasoned his way from atheism to faith. I read his book *Mere Christianity* and found it extremely helpful. I was struck by how rational Christianity really is—the great doctrines of Christianity are simply a logical working out of what the Bible tells us about Christ. The conclusions are extraordinary only because the data are. After all, if Christ's resurrection is a fact—and all subsequent history screams that it is—then something absolutely stupendous took place that first Easter morning. It's a fact of inconceivable importance, it affects everything, and no system of thought that ignores it or downplays it can possibly be correct.

A Rebel Laying Down Arms

There are mysteries, certainly: one of the great Christian doctrines says that Christ is both human and divine. Well, according to modern physics, light is both a wave and a particle. I couldn't picture that, either, but that didn't make it any less true. Did I expect to fully understand God, when I couldn't fully understand his creation?

And that, really, was that. I found that I believed—in the perfectly ordinary way I believed anything—that the Bible was the Word of God and that the Christian doctrines drawn from it were true. Moreover, there was no going back; I couldn't un-believe those things even if I wanted to. My only choice was whether to act on them or not. My problem wasn't doubt; it was inertia. I had a very comfortable life; becoming a Christian would change things, God only knew how. At the very least, I saw stormy weather ahead in my marriage. But Jesus says, "If anyone would come after me, let him deny himself and take up his cross daily and follow me. For whoever would save his life will lose it, but whoever loses his life for my sake will save it" (Luke 9:23–24 ESV).

In the end it wasn't difficult. As Lewis wrote, "I chose, yet it did not really seem possible to do the opposite." I went to my knees, asked Christ to forgive my sins, and told him I was his, to do with as he pleased. I didn't want anything from God; I had no expectations at all. I just surrendered, a rebel laying down arms. Externally, nothing had changed—internally, nothing was the same. I had new desires, new motives, new goals, new joys, new sorrows; I saw everything in a new light. "Therefore, if anyone is in Christ, he is a new creation. The old has passed away; behold, the new has come" (2 Cor. 5:17 ESV).

On the following Easter Sunday, perhaps three weeks later, I attended church for the first time as a believer. I got up early and started getting ready. My wife, I think, had seen this coming. She asked, in the flattest tone of voice I had ever heard her use, "Are you going to church?" I said, "Yes," and got dressed. Though she was not a believer, she had been raised a Lutheran, and when I came downstairs she said, "If anyone says to you, 'He is risen,' you should say 'He is risen indeed.' " My most fervent prayer for the next six months was that she, too, would be saved. And thanks be to God, she was. He is risen, indeed.

Resolves

- To thank God often for his revelation to us in his Word
- To read several chapters of the Bible daily
- To encourage non-Christian friends to read the Bible
- To learn more about the Bible, to be able to defend it as God's Word

Scripture Memory

"So shall my word be that goes out from my mouth; it shall not return to me empty, but it shall accomplish that which I purpose, and shall succeed in the thing for which I sent it."

Isaiah 55:11 ESV

For Discussion

1. By what power was Jim Price converted to Christ? By what means?
2. Does it matter whether the Bible is historically or scientifically accurate?
3. What is the difference between a mystery and a contradiction?
4. Have you ever thought of Christianity as "rational"? Why or why not?
5. What is the relationship between faith and reason?

"The Heavens Declare Your Glory, Lord"

The heav'ns declare your glory, Lord;
In ev'ry star your wisdom shines;

But when our eyes behold your Word,
We read your name in fairer lines.

Isaac Watts, 1719

For Further Study

The New Testament Documents: Are They Reliable?, by F. F. Bruce;
The Old Testament Documents: Are They Reliable and Relevant?, by
Walter C. Kaiser Jr.

YOUNG MEN: THEIR PRAYING AND READING

24

HOW TO PRAY

Psalm 42:1–2

Cold War Terror

It was 1949, and the U.S. Department of Defense was in a whirlwind of strategic planning. Intelligence sources had confirmed the news: the Soviets had just exploded a test version of the atomic bomb. This, combined with their introduction of the Soviet *Tu-4 Bull* long-range bomber, made a Communist first-strike capability on American soil frighteningly real. The Cold War was on, and we were losing. In the weapons and space race, the USSR was years ahead of the USA.

President Harry Truman immediately began planning for a worldwide nuclear conflict. The National Security Council went public in 1950: Put simply, unless the United States caught up, the Soviets would have enough nuclear bombs within four years to do cataclysmic damage to America. The NSC urged Truman to spend an unprecedented 20 percent of the U.S. gross national product on a massive defense build-up—or prepare for a Soviet Communist takeover of America. This was war, and Truman's budget of $50 billion was quickly approved. Troop strength was doubled; new strategic military bases were established; new planes, ships, and tanks were built. But what was really needed was a computerized first-alert early-warning defense system—or America was doomed.

With this kind of threat, conventional military muscle would be of little help. Since late in World War II, engineers had been dabbling in computerized warfare at Massachusetts Institute of Technology, the nerve center of American science and technology. Truman rejuvenated MIT's Project Whirlwind, and the most brilliant engineering minds in America, building on what they had learned about analog computer warfare, began in earnest to develop a digital machine that would become the brain of all U.S. military control functions.

The project came under the command of the U.S. Air Force and was known as Project SAGE, a computer system designed to provide "global oversight and instantaneous military response, a real-time command control system throughout the armed forces," a worldwide warfare video game—only this was no game.

One military analyst called SAGE "the single most important computer project of the postwar decade." Most agree that SAGE was the mother of all computerized satellite warfare. Without it, Americans who survived would be speaking Russian today. The threat was imminent—many believed apocalyptic. Christians were on their knees in prayer.

No God and No Prayer

Meanwhile, in 1949, a gangly sixteen-year-old sweated through his sophomore year of high school. When he was younger, words had flipped around on the page, and when he was learning to write, whole sentences had often come out backwards. In despair, one teacher had flunked him back a grade on the first day of the new school year. By sheer determination, things were better in high school, but reading and writing still required intense concentration. Math class, however, was different.

He loved solving problems. Hidden beneath his learning disability was a brilliant mathematical mind and an indomitable will. Finally, in 1956 he graduated from Seattle Pacific University, married the love of his life, and landed his first real job as a systems engineer for Western Electric, a company with a contract to solve big problems for the Department of Defense. Granted top-secret clearance, he joined the elite defense engineers at MIT. Tensions with Communist Russia intensified.

Then the Soviets launched *Sputnik I*. Many Americans feared that the USSR could also launch ballistic missiles carrying weapons capable of triggering a nuclear holocaust on American soil. One month later, on November 3, 1957, the Soviets did it again. *Sputnik II* was bigger, and this time they came one step closer to manned space travel by launching into Earth's orbit a dog named Laika. Feeling badly outgunned, most Americans were deeply worried, and many prayed.

Work on Project SAGE took on greater urgency. The federal government transferred their bright engineer and his young family to McChord Air Force Base in Washington State, where he crunched numbers, daily adding critical capability to U.S. early-warning defense capability. Solutions came to him at odd times. Working equations in his sleep, he sometimes scrambled out of bed and spent the remainder of the night feverishly scrawling figures and diagrams at the kitchen table, then went eagerly off to work in the morning with his nighttime epiphanies.

Meanwhile, the Soviets had been secretly erecting ballistic missile sites in Cuba, a mere ninety miles from American shores. We wouldn't know until October of 1962 just how desperately the vital work on Project SAGE was needed. Never before in the history of the world had two superpowers stared each other down with such devastating potential for mutual destruction.

Then, when Cold War tensions were at the breaking point, on April 12, 1961, the Soviets launched cosmonaut Uri Gagarin into orbit. On his return, reporters interviewed him. The now-famous atheist cosmonaut said that he'd traveled through space but seen no God.

In a press conference, reporters challenged evangelist Billy Graham, asking him how he explained Gagarin's claim that he'd explored space and seen no God. With disarming good humor, Graham said that the cosmonaut's claim was odd because "I just spoke with God this morning."

In February of 1962, scrambling to catch up with the Soviets, the U.S. launched astronaut John Glenn into orbit. Meanwhile, determined to trust in American ingenuity, on June 25, 1962, the U.S. Supreme Court banned prayer in American public schools. Three months later, Americans faced seven nerve-racking days of staredown with Soviet Premier Khrushchev in the Cuban Missile Crisis. The Soviet finger was poised over the red button, but it was now illegal for teachers to lead their students in prayer.

Hoist on Our Own Petard

Banning public prayer on the basis of an interpretation of the Establishment Clause of the U.S. Constitution is historical and logical absurdity. Return with me to June 27, 1787, when, as in the Cold War, "the fate of America was suspended by a hair." Delegates to the Constitutional Convention were polarized on the great debate over composition and selection of representatives to the bicameral legislature. Opinion was divided, and disagreement was, like the weather in Philadelphia, hot. Men disagreed so sharply that there was even talk of hanging one another. The wrangling prompted the venerable Ben Franklin to speak:

> In this situation of this Assembly, groping as it were in the dark . . . how has it happened, Sir, that we have not hitherto once thought of humbly applying to the Father of lights to illumine our understanding? In the beginning of the Contest with Great Britain, when we were sensible of danger we had daily prayer in this room for the divine protection. Our prayers, Sir, were heard, and they were graciously answered. All of us who were engaged in the

struggle must have observed frequent instances of a Superintending Providence in our favor. To that kind Providence we owe this happy opportunity of consulting in peace on the means of establishing our future national felicity. And have we now forgotten that powerful friend? Or do we imagine that we no longer need his assistance? I have lived, Sir, a long time, and the longer I live, the more convincing proofs I see of this truth—that God governs in the affairs of men. And if a sparrow cannot fall to the ground without his notice, is it probable than an empire can rise without his aid?

This from Franklin, who, though he had a brilliant political and scientific mind, was no bastion of theological orthodoxy. Though Franklin and the constitutional framers did halt and pray for divine wisdom and protection, 175 years later a branch of government created by those framers defied the intention of those framers, clubbing into silence the very means by which those framers found the wisdom to establish our constitutional republic—including its Supreme Court.

Perhaps history has never seen so defiant an act of willingly hoisting ourselves on our own petard. Though "sensible of danger" in the Cold War, America's highest court made a decision that denied even deistic Franklin's conclusions, "that God governs in the affairs of men." Thus, in a stroke of national self-reliance, the high court established faith in man, not in God. The justices made it official that "we no longer need [God's] assistance." The rubble of our national prayerlessness lies all about us.

Government: Teach Us to Pray

A Mallard Fillmore cartoon captured the absurdity of efforts to expunge prayer from public schools with the "Back-to-school tip #35: Don't fall asleep in class . . . The teacher might think you're praying." But it's no laughing matter, and it's no longer just government schools that define and dictate what praying is and where it can and cannot happen.

Now the U.S. military is defining and regulating the "free exercise" of praying by Christian chaplains by actually telling Americans

YOUNG MEN: THEIR PRAYING AND READING

how to word their prayers! Chaplain Lt. Gordon James Klingenschmitt faced court-martial by order of Navy Secretary Donald C. Winter for illegally praying "in Jesus' name" before the White House. In response, the American Center for Law and Justice gathered hundreds of thousands of signatures, seeking an executive order upholding the right of chaplains to pray in accordance with their individual "faith tradition," including the right of Christians to pray in Christ's name.

Should Americans even be having this discussion? Eighty percent of our military consider themselves, in some form or other, Christians. Dozens of concerned congressmen put their support behind a statement that reads: "Hundreds of thousands of Christian soldiers in the military, who look to their chaplains for comfort and support, are being disenfranchised by the 'censorship' of their chaplains' prayers."

Other branches of the military practice the same censorship, requiring chaplains to offer nonsectarian prayer during military ceremonies. Thus, the U.S. government has become the approving authority of prayer in the military. All of which not only violates the basic civil liberties of individual chaplains, but runs roughshod over the original intentions of America's constitutional framers.

Jesus' disciples asked him, "Lord, teach us to pray" (Luke 11:1). Cornered by liberal ideologues, the U.S. government now silences Jesus and usurps his divine role by presuming to teach us how to pray.

Oxhorn Knees

It's easy for us to shake our heads in wonder at how a nation founded on freedom of conscience could stoop to dictating to its citizens what words they can and cannot use in prayer. We click our tongues in disgust at the folly of the military and the high court.

Meanwhile, the devil is on the prowl. Do we have a right to be aghast at government censorship of prayer—while we regularly neglect private prayer? The devil has no problem with your decrying government regulations that violate the Constitution, so long as he keeps you off your knees.

Prayer is hard work, and it's mysterious work. Pushing one of my sons in the swing at the playground when he was three, I watched as he gleefully gazed up into the billowy clouds. Then his grin faded, and he fell silent. "God and Jesus," he mused, his voice trailing off. Then he threw his head back and yelled at the heavens, "Who are these people?"

The spiritual world is filled with mysteries. Prayer is one of those mysteries. The fiery Reformer John Knox defined prayer as "earnest and familiar talking with God." And the Protestant Reformation in Scotland was fueled not only by his thundering preaching, but by his praying.

Genuine prayer isn't happening unless the one praying is earnest, unless he believes that prayer is real and that it is profoundly important. "Prayer cannot draw down answers from God's throne," said C. H. Spurgeon, "except it be the earnest prayer of the man who believes."

Young men are earnest about many things: cars, sports, pizza—all things that pale into insignificance next to approaching God in prayer: adoring him, confessing our sins to him, thanking him, and bringing our supplications to him. You and I will pray more earnestly when we are profoundly "sensible of danger."

I remember as a young boy peering wide-eyed through the skeleton key hole at my grandfather on his knees in the living room. He always prayed out loud, his voice rising and falling in earnest pleading with God. Rarely did he lead us in prayer before a meal without a tremor of earnest emotion in his tone. Elmer Elwood Bond taught me what earnest praying ought to be. After his death at ninety-one years old, my father found piles of handwritten prayer lists with quivering ticks next to each name. Eternity alone will show what rich blessings he cried down on my head with his earnest praying.

Prayer for John Knox was not only earnest but familiar. Not to be confused with overfamiliarity, "familiar talking with God" is that incalculable privilege based on our adoption as sons of God. In prayer, the Christian has the ear not only of the Almighty, but also of a loving heavenly Father. One old Puritan put it this way: "In prayer I can intercede as a son to his father."

It's not overfamiliar prayer, for you and me, because we have a right to it as sons. God is God, infinitely above you and me; there is no sense of casual "me and Jesus" equality in this kind of familiarity. Prayer is familiar because it is family talk, a son speaking to his father with respect and love, bringing shared concerns, agreeing on priorities. It is "familiar talking with God" our Father because Jesus, the Son of God, has stooped down in grace and made us sons of God, sons who cry "*Abba*, Father" (Rom. 8:15–16).

John Knox's grandson, John Welsh, was an intrepid Covenanter field preacher, a man on King Charles II's royal hit list—today his mug shot would be at every post office. Welsh learned earnest and familiar prayer and was so often on his knees for the beleaguered church that after his death, when his body was being prepared for burial, his loved ones found calluses on his knees as hard as oxhorn.

Earnest prayer should affect your posture, but the devil doesn't want you to believe this. C. S. Lewis's archtempter Screwtape wants to persuade you that "the bodily position makes no difference to [your] prayers." Don't believe him. Whatever your body does affects your soul.

Be Sane; Be Wise

"The Christian is at his sanest and wisest when he prays," wrote J. I. Packer. If that is true, then most Christian men are insane fools. Praying seems so odd in a modern world, a world where we have mastered and controlled causes and effects, where we have invented machines, technologies, and medicines with which to control our own destinies. But the Christian young man who is serious about growing up and walking by faith must learn to pray—not only during national security threats like the Cold War. The Christian young man who wants daily victory over his sins, who wants power to defeat the enemies of his soul, must learn to pray without ceasing.

If you want to walk by faith and see the unseen world more clearly, learn to pray as one wise old Puritan prayed: "In prayer I launch far out into the eternal world, and on that broad ocean my soul triumphs over all evils on the shores of mortality. Time with its gay amusements and cruel disappointments, never appears so inconsiderate as then." The more absorbed you are in entertainment and popular amusements, the more incongruous praying will seem and the more unreal and irrelevant heaven and eternity will seem to you. A sane, wise young man will take note.

But praying does another thing for a young man, something that you desperately need. Again, the old Puritan on his knees helps us: "In prayer I see myself as nothing . . . . In prayer all things here below vanish, and nothing seems important but holiness of heart and the salvation of others . . . . In prayer I am lifted above the frowns and flatteries of life, and taste heavenly joys."

Learn to see things as they are. Learn to see yourself as nothing. How? Learn to pray. Daily, disciplined, earnest, familiar, humble, on-the-knees talking with God.

Wisest and Sanest

The dyslexic Project SAGE engineer who flunked fourth grade was my father. While many in the Department of Defense and the Supreme Court were looking to man to solve our national security crisis, he—one of the wisest and sanest of men—was daily on his knees in prayer. "The horse is prepared for the day of battle," wrote the wisest of men, "but victory belongs to the LORD" (Prov. 21:31 NASB). My father overcame his disability and employed his engineering skills in one of the most important national defense projects in U.S. history, but he knew that victory in the Cold War and in life "belongs to the LORD," so he prayed.

I treasure many wonderful memories of my late father, but chief among them will be seeing the soles of his wingtips as he knelt in prayer at the old rocker at the top of the stairway each morning. Perhaps because he had a thorn in the flesh he knew his great weakness, and thus his great need of the arm of the Almighty on his side, and so he prayed. He will always be for me one of the wisest and sanest of men. Lord, teach us to pray as my father prayed.

Resolve

• To pray like this: "Purge me from selfishness, the fear of man, the love of approbation, the shame of being thought old-fashioned, the desire to be cultivated or modern. Take away my roving eye, curious ear, greedy appetite, lustful heart . . . . Then take me to the cross and leave me there. May I never dally with the world and its allurements, but walk by thy side, listen to thy voice, be clothed with thy graces, and adorned with thy righteousness."

From *The Valley of Vision*

Scripture Memory

"Do not be anxious about anything, but in everything, by prayer and petition, with thanksgiving, present your requests to God."

Philippians 4:6

For Discussion

1. What are ways in which you can be more self-disciplined in prayer?
2. For structure to your praying, try using "ACTS": Adoration, Confession, Thanksgiving, Supplication.

"Come, My Soul, Thy Suit Prepare"

Thou art coming to a King,
Large petitions with thee bring;
For his grace and pow'r are such,
None can ever ask too much.

John Newton, 1779

For Further Study

Psalm 62:8; John 16:23; Westminster Shorter Catechism Questions
98–107; *Lord, Teach Us to Pray*, by Alexander Whyte

25

HOW TO READ THE BIBLE

Psalm 119:17–24

Silver Lining

The 1962 Supreme Court ban on school prayer had a positive side: it became a great catalyst to the modern Christian education movement. Now that it was illegal to pray in public schools, tens of thousands of Christian schools began springing up across America. My father left his work on Project SAGE two years after the fateful national prayer ban, and spent the next thirty-seven years as superintendent of Tacoma Baptist Schools.

My first-grade reader was a large-print King James New Testament. As our founding fathers intended, once again, students could pray in school, and they could read, memorize, and study the Bible, the "Law of Christ," as the venerable John Wycliffe fondly called it.

In fourteenth-century England, it was a crime to read the Bible in English—in schools, and even in churches. Undaunted, Wycliffe determined to translate the Law of Christ into Middle English, and then from among his students at Balliol College, Oxford, he would train itinerant preachers and send them to the four corners of the realm with the Bible in the language of the people. Like the bullying Supreme Court, Bishop of London Courtney was not about to tolerate the outrage of vulgarizing the sacred Scriptures. He would do whatever it took to halt Wycliffe.

Royal intervention and an earthquake notwithstanding, Courtney eventually saw to Wycliffe's ejection from his post at Oxford, but not until Wycliffe had implemented his plan. "The Morning Star of the Reformation" was so effective in getting the Bible to the people, and his poor preachers, the Lollards, ranged so widely throughout England and Scotland with the Law of Christ, that one unhappy Catholic priest bemoaned that half of England had succumbed to the "Lollard heresy."

Sola Scriptura

A century and a half later, "The Bible Alone" became the battle cry of the Protestant Reformation. The Bible had its authority not from popes or church councils. "God alone," wrote John Calvin, "is a fit witness of himself in his Word." For the preachers of the Reformation the Bible was everything—the Bible alone, uncluttered by false doctrine, by superstition, or by contradictory interpretations of popes and councils through the centuries.

Hence, chapter 1 of the Westminster Confession of Faith, one of the great Reformed confessions, affirms that the Holy Scriptures were "immediately inspired by God, and by his singular care and providence kept pure in all ages." And since the Bible is "the rule of faith and life," and of "incomparable excellencies, and . . . infallible truth and divine authority," it is to be "translated into the vulgar language of every nation," so that all may know God and his will revealed to man in the Bible.

Thanks be to God, you and I have the Bible in our language. But a young man doesn't have to read very far in his English Bible to realize that it contains some things difficult to understand. So how does a young man set about reading and understanding the Bible?

How to Read

Not surprisingly, the Bible itself tells us how to read its pages aright. Revelation 1:3 says that the man is blessed who reads the words, who hears the words, and who takes the words to heart. Consider this alongside the psalmist's longing prayer, "Open my eyes that I may see wonderful things in your law" (Ps. 119:18), and we're nearer to answering the question of how we're to read Scripture.

Characteristically leaving no stone unturned, the Puritans and Covenanters drafting the Westminster Shorter Catechism asked and answered this important question (no. 90): "How is the Word to be read and heard, that it may become effectual to salvation?" The answer reads: "We must attend thereunto with diligence, preparation, and prayer; receive it with faith and love, lay it up in our hearts, and practice it in our lives."

It may be said of you as Paul said of Timothy that "from infancy you have known the holy Scriptures" (2 Tim. 3:15a). Like me, you may not remember a time when you have not heard the Bible. This is a good thing, though you may not always think so.

"Familiarity breeds contempt," goes the old adage, and familiar as you are with the Bible, some of you may find it a trifle dull, its stories clichés, its style archaic, its rules outmoded. Beware of thinking this way. As essential as food is to your physical life, so the Bible is to your soul.

Feast on it like the psalmist who found incomparable delight in the pages of God's law. The Bible must be sweeter to your taste than honey from the honeycomb (Ps. 19:10b). If it is not, there's only one solution: Open your Bible and "attend thereunto with diligence, preparation, and prayer; receive it with faith and love, lay it up in [your heart], and practice it in [your life]."

270

Read for Freedom

"I run in the path of your commands," wrote the psalmist, "for you have set my heart free" (Ps. 119:32). If you've swallowed pop culture's spin on how uncool it is to live according to the rules, this verse will sound pretty odd. "Doesn't freedom mean that I get to do whatever I want? So how can commands 'set my heart free'?" you ask. "Rules go with slavery, not freedom." Chalk up another lie to the devil.

Though the Law of Christ is divinely inspired, inerrant, infallible, God-breathed, altogether unique, and infinitely above any other book, you must read it according to literary conventions if you want to get its message straight. "Though it is unique, in a structural sense," wrote Charles Colson, "the Bible must be read like any other book: metaphor is metaphor, poetry is poetry, parables are parables. Scripture must be read in context and according to its literary genre."

Reading classic literature in its varied genres is an important preparation for reading your Bible with skill and understanding. It will help you avoid being an Amelia Bedelia interpreter of the Bible. Poor Amelia in the children's books didn't understand figurative language and so made a disaster of dressing the turkey, or pruning the hedge.

Or there's the man who reads his Bible by letting it fall open and blindly placing his finger on a verse. On his first try it fell open to "Judas . . . went away and hanged himself" (Matt. 27:5). Not liking that, he tried again. "Go and do likewise" (Luke 10:37) was the next random piece of instruction. There is a great deal of goofiness that passes for biblical interpretation. Goofy readings might reinforce new ideas, but they won't help guide you into all truth so that you can run in the paths of freedom.

Explicit over Implicit

"We can clear up much of the ruckus over the Bible's seeming contradictions," wrote Charles Colson, "by reading it with careful attention to the literary genres and with respect for the author's intentions." Contrary to postmodern hermeneutics, the author's intentions are critically important in understanding any text. Those intentions are usually not vague and mysterious. When they are, the young man who wants to "correctly [handle] the word of truth" (2 Tim. 2:15) will interpret the less clear passages in light of the explicit ones.

For example, when the poetic wisdom literature reads, "Do not be overrighteous" (Eccl. 7:16), the well-prepared reader will interpret that in light of the explicit instruction throughout the Bible, "Be holy as I am holy." It is not responsible reading of your Bible to take the implicit poetic words of Ecclesiastes over the rest of the Bible's explicit call to holiness.

In a *Time* magazine article, the reporter gleefully exposed the different interpretations that Christians have about the Bible's teaching on wealth. Prosperity preachers concluded that "God wants you rich," while conventional preachers concluded that not only is there no biblical imperative to be rich, the Bible repeatedly warns Christians not to seek earthly riches.

True, the Bible says, "The blessing of the Lord brings wealth" (Prov. 10:22), but heed the genre. This text is poetry, a genre that frequently employs figurative and imaginative language. Thus, the careful reader takes the explicit over the implicit and so compares this text with Paul's explicit instruction concerning wealth: "People who want to get rich fall into temptation and a trap . . . . The love of money is a root of all kinds of evil" (1 Tim. 6:9–10).

No one who takes the explicit over the implicit and observes the Bible's literary genres could ever conclude that "God wants you rich." If, however, they're looking for the Bible to rubber-stamp their pet ideas, they'll find what they're looking for. But if you want to be a workman who is unashamed, who "correctly handles the word of truth" (2 Tim. 2:15), then learn to compare Scripture with itself and let the explicit teaching weigh in more heavily than the figurative passages or the less clear ones.

Hair or Prayer?

"The infallible rule of interpretation of Scripture," wrote the Westminster divines, "is the Scripture itself" (Westminster Confession of Faith 1.9). But what about those controversial passages that people disagree on? "When there is a question about the true and full sense of any Scripture," continued the collective wisdom of the Westminster Assembly, "it must be searched and known by other places that speak more clearly."

Let's put this interpretive wisdom into practice with perhaps the hottest topic in the postconservative evangelical church: the role of women. Paul wrote a scathing letter to the Corinthian church, wherein he deals with sinful practices corrupting church worship. In 1 Corinthians 11, one of the more enigmatic passages in the New Testament, Paul wrote in verse 5 that "every woman who prays or prophesies with her head uncovered dishonors her head," all in the context of its being a disgrace for men to have long hair, but that long hair is a woman's glory and her covering.

Unwilling to search and know what this passage means in light of the ones "that speak more clearly," many interpreters insist that, contrary to centuries of biblical understanding, it's now okay for women to pray and prophesy publicly in Christian worship. But what happens when we compare Paul in chapter 11 with other explicit teaching on women's roles?

Two pages later, Paul wrote with unequivocal clarity on the subject: "As in all the congregations of the saints, women should remain silent in the churches" (1 Cor. 14:33b–34), all in the context of prophesying and doing things "in a fitting and orderly way" in Christian worship (14:26–40).

How does a young man understand Paul's reasoning here? In chapter 11, when Paul speaks of women's praying and prophesying with their heads uncovered, he may merely be employing the rhetorical device of reasoning by analogy. One thing that every reader must agree on, however, is that Paul's discussion of long hair and head coverings is unclear to modern readers. So how to proceed? Go back to the standards: "When there is a question about the true and full sense of any Scripture, it must be searched and known by other places that speak more clearly."

Baptism for the Dead?

Undeterred, modern interpreters choose Paul's enigmatic discussion of women's praying with head coverings as the final word on women's prophesying and publicly leading prayer in church. But what do those same interpreters do when they get to chapter 14, which speaks clearly and without equivocation? They hastily silence Paul's explicit instruction with chapter 11: "Paul couldn't mean 'remain silent in the churches,' " they insist, "because he didn't condemn women's praying and prophesying in chapter 11." End of discussion. The explicit is silenced by the vague and unclear.

When a careful reader, however, follows the guidelines of the Westminster standards and searches out Paul's meaning by comparing these passages with Paul's own instruction in 1 Timothy 2:12, his intention is clear: "I do not permit a woman to teach or to have authority over a man; she must be silent."

You have a choice. You can read your Bible to make Paul agree with postconservative ideas about women's roles in church. Or you can stick with the interpretive standards of the ages and let Paul and the Bible tell us what we need to hear. Put another way, you can accurately handle the Word of truth, or you can silence the explicit instruction in chapter 14 with the implicit discussion in chapter 11. Only one way will lead you to truth. And remember, knowing truth is what sets your heart free.

Still, some ask: "If praying and prophesying in church was wrong for women, why did Paul use it as an analogy without condemning the practice then and there?" But the careful reader will again compare Scripture with Scripture and see whether Paul and other biblical writers reason by analogy without condemnation of false practices in the immediate use of the analogy.

They do. Paul himself does! Turn the page. In 1 Corinthians 15:29, giving instruction on the bodily resurrection of Christ, Paul again reasons by analogy: "Now if there is no resurrection, what will those do who are baptized for the dead? If the dead are not raised at all, why are people baptized for them?"

No orthodox Christian believes in baptism for the dead, and neither did Paul. But just as he did not condemn women for public praying and prophesying in chapter 11, neither does he condemn baptism for the dead here. Search and know. Paul's teaching nowhere supports baptism for the dead—any more than it supports women's publicly praying and prophesying in church. Neither did Moses support making graven images when he records the story of Rachel's stealing of Laban's household idols, but doesn't condemn his idolatry.

Rightly handling the Word of truth means that you are alert to rhetorical methods that Paul and other inspired writers employ to reveal to the reader the person and will of God. God won't show you wonderful things in his law if you read it irresponsibly. Avoid error and mishandling of God's divine Word by taking the explicit over the implicit, by reasoning along with the writer in his context, and by avoiding superficial conclusions when biblical writers employ rhetorical devices in the course of their arguments.

A French Wager

A teenage young man may still feel at a disadvantage because he hasn't lived long enough to go to seminary, to earn a Ph.D. in theology, or to become a scholar. So how are you going to understand the complexities of your English Bible?

Many of my heroes are theologians and preachers, but the Bible was not written for theologians. Its authors wrote to reveal God to the sheep—to you and me. Therefore, you should approach reading your Bible with confidence. Though there are difficult things to understand, God has revealed himself to you in its pages. He's not trying to be obscure. But how does a young man rightly handle passages that some find difficult to reconcile with modern science, or history, or archaeology?

Try using a modification of Pascal's wager when interpreting difficult passages, especially ones whose interpretations might impinge on the power and glory of God. Blaise Pascal, French mathematician, Christian, and contemporary of John Bunyan, wrote his personal thoughts about God and faith in his most famous work, *Pensées*. In his thoughts he offered his famous wager: "If God does not exist, one will lose nothing by believing in him, while if he does exist, one will lose everything by not believing."

Let's try Pascal's wager on Moses. The books of Moses read like authentic history and so are to be believed as a historically accurate account of real events that happened in space, time, and history. I am aware, however, that there are Christian brethren of mine who reject the time element. They don't believe that God created the world in six literal days. Like you, I am no trained theologian, nor am I a cosmologist, so what am I to conclude?

That's where the Pascal wager comes in as a helpful interpretive guide. If error it is, I'm going to choose the interpretation that I'll have the least to answer for if I'm wrong. Therefore, I want to err on the side of the power and glory of God, not on the side of what the naturalists insist could or could not have happened.

For example, when I read in Exodus that God turned all the water in Egypt to blood, the wager approach to interpretation guides me to conclude that, in fact, God, through Moses, turned the water in Egypt to blood, not to water tainted by red clay that made it look like blood. If my interpretation is incorrect, then at least I have erred on the side of giving God his due, and taking the Bible at face value. What harm have I done to the honor of God's power and glory if I read *blood* where the text says *blood*? None whatsoever.

On the other hand, if I explain each of the plagues in natural terms, and I am wrong, I have done great disservice to the name, honor, power, and glory of God. Thus, applying the Pascal wager to difficult passages keeps careful readers of their Bible from dishonoring God.

276

Resolves

- To regularly and systematically read the Bible
- To reject interpretations that lessen God's supernatural power
- To pray regularly together as father and son

Scripture Memory

"All Scripture is God-breathed and is useful for teaching, rebuking, correcting and training in righteousness, so that the man of God may be thoroughly equipped for every good work."

2 Timothy 3:16–17

For Discussion

1. How can you be better prepared when you read your Bible?
2. What will you say to a critic who tells you that the Bible is just like any other book?
3. How will you respond to those who say that biblical writers were ignorant because they refer to things in an unsophisticated way, such as the sun rising or the four corners of the earth?

"The Law of God Is Good and Wise"

The law of God is good and wise
And sets his will before our eyes,
Shows us the way of righteousness,
And dooms to death when we transgress.

Matthias Loy, 1863

For Further Study

Psalm 119; *How Readest Thou?* by J. C. Ryle

26

HOW TO INTERPRET THE BIBLE

Ephesians 1:1–14

Mingle-Mangle

It has been said of the Reformers in England, "Cambridge grew them; Oxford slew them." Hugh Latimer, bishop of Worchester, Cambridge scholar and preacher, royal chaplain to Henry VIII and Edward VI, was one of those who died at the hands of haters of the Word of God and the gospel. Latimer was a preacher of *sola Scriptura*, "the Bible alone," but concerned that some in England misread their Bibles, he urged preachers and laymen alike not to "make a mingle-mangle" of the sacred text.

The Reformation was essentially a return to the sole authority of the Bible and an embrace of what it teaches about how a man is saved and becomes a part of the church. Rome had her teachings on these things, but Latimer and the Reformers found in the actual words of the Bible that salvation was by grace alone. Sinners contribute nothing but their sins.

A young man who is serious about being a Christian will diligently search and know what the Bible teaches about salvation and the grace of God. He must be absolutely clear about the extent of his sins, about the roles of Father, Son, and Holy Spirit in salvation, and about sanctification and the life of holiness to which God has called him. In short, a real man must not make a mingle-mangle of the Bible's doctrine of salvation.

Ability

In Luther's great debate over free will with humanist scholar Desiderius Erasmus, Luther thanked his opponent for going down to the root of the debate: the nature of man. In *The Bondage of the Will*, Luther argues that the fundamental difference between the Roman Catholic view of sin and the Bible's view is that man is in bondage to his sinful nature; this bondage includes his will. His depravity is so total that it makes him not only unwilling but unable to come to God.

Most postconservative American Christians agree that man is depraved, but not so totally that he is unable to come to God, to respond to the universal call of the gospel as an act of his free will. Wittingly or unwittingly, they agree with Jacobus Arminius, sixteenth-century divinity professor at the University of Leyden.

Well-meaning Christians who insist that man is free and able to choose salvation base their view on passages such as Revelation 22:17: "Whoever is thirsty, let him come; and whoever wishes, let him take the free gift of the water of life." Or on Paul's call to the Philippian jailer: "Believe in the Lord Jesus, and you will be saved" (Acts 16:31). The argument proceeds as follows: If the Bible invites whoever wishes to come, and if Paul tells the jailer to believe and be saved, then men must be *able* to come and believe as acts of their free will.

279

Notice carefully, however, that these conclusions are deduced by implication but not from an explicit statement in the text. In neither text, for example, does the author explicitly tell us that men have the ability to come, to thirst, or to believe. It is implicit, Arminians insist, but clearly it is not explicitly taught in these texts. If you genuinely want to know what the Bible is saying, take the explicit over the implicit; otherwise, you will make a mingle-mangle of its teaching on total depravity.

Inability

Compare Scripture with itself on man's depravity, and you will find many explicit texts that clear up any confusion. There is nothing left to inference, for example, when Jesus tells his hearers why they refuse to understand him: "Because you are unable to hear . . . . The reason you do not hear is that you do not belong to God" (John 8:43–47). Clearly, Jesus was teaching that these men's unbelief was based not on a lack of will but on a lack of ability. Turn back a page, and Jesus' consistent message is clearer still: "No one can come to me unless the Father has enabled him" (6:65).

Paul repeatedly makes the same point about the bondage of man's will and his inability to believe as an act of his will: he says that sinners "cannot understand" (1 Cor. 2:14), that "no one . . . seeks" (Rom. 3:10–11), that they "cannot see" (2 Cor. 4:4), that "the sinful mind . . . does not submit to God's law, nor can it do so," and that man "cannot please God" (Rom. 8:7–8).

The words *can* and *cannot* indicate ability or inability; they have nothing to do with wanting or wishing. So when Jesus explicitly declares, "No one can come to me unless the Father who sent me draws him" (John 6:44), he is plainly telling his hearers that no one can come as an act of will; he is unable to do so. Men come when God draws them.

If you genuinely want to know what the Bible teaches about total depravity, find it in the explicit passages. Don't build a theology of free will and ability on implicit texts, especially when the deduced conclusions require you to defy explicit biblical statements.

Cavil at Calvin

We sinners, not surprisingly, chafe when the Bible exposes the depth of our total depravity. Still more, we particularly get our back up when it says that God unconditionally predestined some men to salvation and some to damnation. This goes too far.

When Paul lists predestination, "according to the plan of him who works out everything in conformity with the purpose of his will" (Eph. 1:11), as chief among the blessings we have in Christ in the heavenly realms, we modern American Christians are sure that the text just can't mean what it says.

Thus, we raise two standard objections to predestination: "It makes God unfair," and "How could God blame me for my sins?" After all, if predestination is true, then everything happens "according to the plan of him who works out everything in conformity with the purpose of his will," just as Paul wrote. Paul's statement sounds too undemocratic, and frankly, it offends us.

It offends us because, deep down, we agree with poet William Ernest Henley, who declared, "I am the master of my fate; I am the captain of my soul." More than two thousand years before Henley, Greek dramatist Sophocles observed, "Man desires to be more than man, to rule his world for himself." It's in our fallen nature to entertain exaggerated notions about having godlike power over our own lives. Predestination requires a "steepling plunge," and we desperately squirm and writhe when confronted with it.

John Calvin wrote, "The predestination by which God adopts some to the hope of life, and adjudges others to eternal death, no man who would be thought pious ventures simply to deny, but it is greatly caviled at." To *cavil* is to make frivolous objections to something, objections without foundation.

The most common cavil goes like this: "If predestination is true, then why witness or send missionaries to heathen lands?" Notice, again, how this objection sets aside the clear words of Scripture in favor of a line of human reason.

So long as men cavil, the debate rages on, but it's not because the Bible is unclear about predestination. Read Paul in Ephesians, and wherever the Bible speaks about God's sovereignty and grace you will find explicit teaching consistent with what has come to be called Calvinism. The debate rages precisely because the Bible is so clear, and because what it says is so contrary to what we naturally think about ourselves.

Calvin is correct: biblically informed Arminians cannot deny predestination by name; the word and its parallels appear throughout the Bible. They do, however, redefine the clear meaning of the word and shift the basis of election to God's foreknowledge. They insist that God merely foresaw that some would choose him, so on the basis of men's choice, he chose them. Believe this and you're forced to redefine the clear meanings of words, and you're left scratching your head wondering why, if predestination isn't true, the Bible bothers giving specific answers to man's cavils at it.

Love and Hate

Perhaps there is no more unadorned statement of predestination than Paul's quoting Malachi 1:2–3 in Romans 9:13, "Jacob I loved, but Esau I hated." The careful reader is forced to reject the theory that by *predestination* Paul meant that God passively foresaw that men would choose him and then he chose them. He is forced to reject this theory because of Paul's own words in the Bible. Paul knew that his teaching on predestination would raise this question: "What then shall we say? Is God unjust?" (Rom. 9:14). Paul anticipates the standard human objection: Predestination makes God unjust; things just wouldn't be fair if election were true.

If Arminianism were true, however, Paul would immediately say something like this: "Hold everything! You've misunderstood my entire meaning. When I speak of predestination, I don't really mean predestination. I mean that God just sees that you will have faith and 'chooses' you based on your having already chosen him." But Paul says nothing of the kind. In fact, he raises the bar: "It does not, therefore, depend on man's desire or effort, but on God's mercy. . . . Therefore God has mercy on whom he wants to have mercy, and he hardens whom he wants to harden" (9:16–18).

Read your Bible with integrity, and there's no mingle-mangle here. It's abundantly plain. Nevertheless, men continue to cavil at predestination, and Paul anticipates their next objection: "One of you will say to me: 'Then why does God still blame us? For who resists his will?' " (9:19). Paul is saying in effect, "I know what you're thinking: You think that if what I'm teaching about predestination is true, then God can't blame you or hold you responsible for your sins. You're thinking that if he sovereignly hardens one and chooses another, then it's not fair for him to judge you for your sins."

Again, if Arminianism were correct, Paul would immediately protest, "Hold the phone! That's not what I mean at all!" But he doesn't say this. He is working through a carefully crafted inspired argument based on his certain knowledge that predestination is vein-bulgingly objectionable to proud human beings like you and me.

Here is the ultimate test of whether you've got the Bible's understanding about predestination: Paul's teaching provokes men to object and say that it makes God unjust. Therefore, any theology of salvation that does not prompt that objection is not Paul's teaching and is therefore a mingle-mangle of the Bible's own teaching about predestination.

Why do men have so much trouble here? It goes back to total depravity. We don't like predestination because we don't think we need it. We're not such terrible sinners that we can't make our own choices about our life. Besides, we're Americans, and we believe in self-government, you know, in ruling our world for ourselves. No, this predestination stuff might work in ancient Israel, or in Geneva, or in Scotland, but it's not for us modern Americans.

It's not just Henley or Arminius. Nobody likes predestination. No fallen sinner likes facing the harsh reality of how utterly lost he is and how impossible it is for any of us to be saved by anything we can will, or believe, or do. Jonah got it right: "Salvation comes from the LORD" (Jonah 2:9c)—but we, like Jonah, resent the fact.

Other Troubles with Election

Though it is less likely today, some may have another kind of difficulty with predestination. The devil may raise doubts in a sinner's mind by suggesting to you that there's no use in seeking the Lord, no use in calling out to the Lord to have mercy, because you're probably not elect anyway. So what's the use of attempting to come to God if he has, from all eternity, barred you from his salvation and forgiveness?

The tempter tried this one on John Bunyan, and for a time it worked. But only for a time. Bunyan longed to bask in the sunny side of the mountain that seemed to bar his way from peace with God. Others in Bedford seemed to have found the warm, refreshing pastures of grace and salvation, while he sank in the miry bog of his unworthiness. And when hints of light shone through the narrow passageway to the warm side of the mountain, he was "assaulted with fresh doubts." These doubts came in the form of a question: "Was I elect?" The Scripture seemed clear about these things, but it trampled on all his desire when he read, "It is not of him that willeth, nor of him that runneth, but of God that sheweth mercy" (Rom. 9:16 KJV).

Satan fanned the flames of his doubt with relish. "How can you tell if you are elected?" the tempter whispered in Bunyan's ear. "And what if you are not?" Bunyan had no answer but his groans of despair. "Why then," Satan persisted, "you might as well stop now and strive no further."

Holy Mr. Gifford, pastor of St. John's parish church in Bedford, had taught the poor tinker the whole counsel of God. Bunyan knew his biblical theology. "That the elect only obtained eternal life, I without scruple did heartily agree; but that I myself was one of them, there lay my question."

Then Bunyan heard, as it were, the Lord speak: "Begin at the beginning of Genesis, and read to the end of Revelation, and see if you can find that there was ever any that trusted in the Lord and was confounded." With those words his confusion and perplexity began to vanish.

Take heart in divine sovereignty and predestination. If you are to be saved, it will be God's doing, first to last. But no man who has ever seen his sins and felt his need, who has longed to have peace with God, has ever been turned away. After all, the knowledge of your sins and the desire to be rid of them is also a gift from God. Bunyan took encouragement from this knowledge, and so ought you.

Delightful Doctrine

We might be tempted to think that Jonathan Edwards—the last New England Puritan—was a copper-bottomed Calvinist from birth. But not so. He confesses early doubts and objections to God's sovereignty and predestination in his *Personal Narrative*:

> My mind had been full of objections against the doctrine of God's sovereignty, in choosing whom he would to eternal life, and rejecting whom he pleased; leaving them eternally to perish and be everlastingly tormented in hell. It used to appear like a horrible doctrine to me.

Eventually, Edwards became "convinced, and fully satisfied, as to this sovereignty of God, and his justice in thus eternally disposing of men, according to his sovereign pleasure." He credits the "extraordinary influence of God's Spirit" for the change. "My mind rested in it; and it put an end to all those cavils and objections."

The next stage of Edwards's understanding he described as "a wonderful alteration in my mind, with respect to the doctrine of God's absolute sovereignty and justice, with respect to salvation and damnation; [sovereignty] is what my mind seems to rest assured of." His early conviction deepened into "quite another kind of sense of God's sovereignty. I have often since had not only a conviction, but a delightful conviction. The doctrine has appeared exceeding pleasant, bright, and sweet. Absolute sovereignty is what I love to ascribe to God. But my first conviction was not so."

A man who claims to love God and his Word is not at liberty to begrudgingly concede to any biblical doctrine. The young man who wants to be set free by truth will strive for the maturity that lays aside flawed notions about God and his ways and seeks to find all of God's self-disclosure "pleasant, bright, and sweet," though truth may not look like this at first blush.

If you find yourself still kicking and squalling at the sovereignty of God, do as young Edwards did: seek and know the Lord as he is revealed in the Bible. "The first instance that I remember of that sort of inward, sweet delight in God and divine things that I have lived much in since, was on reading those words, 1 Timothy 1:17 'Now unto the King eternal, immortal, invisible, the only wise God, be honor and glory forever and ever, Amen.' "

Finally, if what you conclude about predestination gives glory to God alone, then you have embraced what the Bible teaches on this grand subject. *Soli Deo Gloria!*

Resolves

- To search, know, and embrace everything the Bible teaches about salvation
- To draw conclusions always on the side of what gives God the greater glory

Scripture Memory

"Praise be to the God and Father of our Lord Jesus Christ, who has blessed us in the heavenly realms with every spiritual blessing in Christ. For he chose us in him before the creation of the world to be holy and blameless in his sight."

Ephesians 1:3–4

For Discussion

1. Role-play the standard objections to predestination and the Bible's answers.
2. What effect does the Bible's teaching on predestination have on evangelism? On worship? On service?

"I Sought the Lord, and Afterward I Knew"

I sought the Lord, and afterward I knew
He moved my soul to seek him, seeking me;
It was not I that found, O Savior true;
No, I was found of thee.

Anon., 1878

For Further Study

Isaiah 46:8–13; *The Doctrines of Grace*, by Philip Graham Ryken

27

HOW TO UNDERSTAND THE BIBLE

Ephesians 3:14–21

World Means "World"?

"Absolute sovereignty," wrote Jonathan Edwards, "is what I love to ascribe to God. But my first conviction was not so."

Let's be honest. Our first conviction is more accurately to hate absolute sovereignty. And if we hate and cavil at absolute sovereignty in predestination, we really get our back up and gnash our teeth at Jesus' dying only for the elect.

But a young man who cares more about what the Bible means than how it at first makes him feel will search and know what it teaches about particular redemption. Called "The Calvin of England," John Owen offered three options for the Bible's teaching on the atonement: Christ died for all the sins of all men, or for some of the sins of all men, or for all the sins of some men. There are no other rational options. So which is it?

Many insist that it is the first: Christ died for all the sins of all men. For them, when the Bible uses the words *all* and *world*, it means every man, woman, and child who has existed or who will ever exist. The *locus classicus* of this position is 1 John 2:2, which says that Jesus "is the propitiation for our sins, and not for ours only but also for the sins of the whole world" (ESV).

Honest Arminians recognize the problems with this conclusion. For example, an Arminian does not think that *propitiation* in 1 John 2:2 means Jesus' actually satisfying the wrath of God for every man, woman, and child. Scrupulous as they are about *world* meaning "world," here they insist that *propitiation* doesn't mean "propitiation"; it means "potential propitiation." Obviously, if Jesus' atonement satisfied the wrath of God for all without exception, there's no more wrath; he sends no one to hell. Since *propitiation* is a legal term meaning "complete satisfaction," the reader who wants to know precisely what the Bible means closely examines the various ways in which the Bible uses the word *world*.

A. W. Pink points out that in the New Testament, *world* (or *kosmos*) "has at least seven clearly defined different meanings." So when Jesus prays in John 17:9, "I pray for them. I am not praying for the world, but for those you have given me," clearly by "world" he means unbelievers, and by "them" and "those you have given me," he means believers, his sheep, the elect. Here, even Arminians must agree that *world* does not mean "all men throughout all time."

Similarly, when Moses records that "all mankind" perished in the flood (Gen. 7:21), no Arminian insists that *all* means "all" and *mankind* means "mankind." Clearly, not every man, woman, and child who ever lived or would live died in the flood. "All mankind" didn't include any of us, nor did it include the eight humans who survived the flood—including Noah.

But what about "For God so loved the world" in John 3:16? Did Jesus mean that his Father sent him to actually ransom, redeem, pardon, atone for, and propitiate—to actually pay the sin debt of—every man, woman, and child in the universe? Return to the context. Jesus was speaking to a Jewish scholar who believed the Messiah was coming just for Jews. Here Jesus was declaring to Jewish Nicodemus that the Messiah has come to save not just ethnic Jews, but the elect from all nations—the world.

Given the varying use of *world* in Scripture, careful readers will interpret passages that, on the surface, sound universal in light of passages that speak more specifically. Comparing John 3:16 and related passages with Revelation 5:9 helps bring clarity: "You are worthy . . . because you were slain, and with your blood you purchased men for God from every tribe and language and people and nation." Notice how particular and specific the language is. Jesus actually "purchased men for God," and he did so without ethnic or racial distinction, pitching his love on men from the whole world.

Sheep Means "Sheep"

John Owen's second option, that Christ died for all the sins of all men, except the sin of unbelief, is favored by other non-Calvinists. This interpretation relieves God of being charged with unfairness, and the only condition of salvation that man contributes is belief. Believe and you have set yourself apart from the rest. But there are serious problems with this view. For starters, the Bible in many places says plainly that the wrath of God is coming for a laundry list of sins, not just for unbelief.

Calvinists believe that Christ actually atoned for all the sins of some men—the elect—that he actually did as he claimed in John 10:11, "I am the good shepherd. The good shepherd lays down his life for the sheep." The language Jesus uses doesn't even hint that he meant he was only potentially or conditionally laying down his life. The words indicate an actual, definite act, accomplished for and applied to specific individuals—the sheep. Sparkling clarity follows when Jesus tells unbelievers a few verses later that "you do not believe because you are not my sheep" (10:26). The sheep believe because they were ordained to eternal life (Acts 13:48), and because Jesus actually—not just potentially—laid down his life for their sins.

Two Critical Questions

In a variety of ways, the Bible answers the critical question, "What must I do to be saved?" It clearly states: "Believe, seek, come, call." But it answers a second critical question about salvation: "Why did I believe?" It answers with equal clarity—we just don't like the answer.

Jealous to protect God's fairness, many nonsensically answer the second question with a variant of the answer to the first. "Why did I believe? Because I just believed." And then they plug their ears. Real men don't read their Bibles this way. The Bible relentlessly answers the question why a sinner believes, so we must hear it: Sinners believe because God chose them, Christ redeemed them, and the Spirit called them.

There's no lack of clarity here. We proud sinners simply don't like the debasement required by the answer. We don't like hearing that we're dead in trespasses and sins, that God predestined some to life and others to damnation, that the elect are redeemed by Christ, their debt paid in full, their guilt and punishment borne on the cross by their Good Shepherd. Nor do we much like hearing that what makes us differ from a lost sinner is the Holy Spirit's effectually calling us out of darkness into the splendid light of the new birth. Believing all that is high-demand. It costs us our pride.

Dead Made Alive

"Born, as all of us are, an Arminian," wrote C. H. Spurgeon, "when I was coming to Christ, I thought I was doing it all myself, and though I sought the Lord earnestly, I had no idea the Lord was seeking me. I do not think the young convert is at first aware of this."

Arminianism, like the flat-earth theory, draws ultimate conclusions based on immediately observable evidence only. Thus, someone who believes in a flat earth does so because what he sees from his observable vantage point looks flat. As Spurgeon suggests, many mistakenly conclude that when a sinner hears the gospel and chooses to believe, his choice is the cause of forgiveness and salvation.

But what makes one man hear, repent, and believe in Christ, while another hears the same sermon but snorts in derision and persists in unbelief? After one such sermon, Luke records that "all who were appointed for eternal life believed" (Acts 13:48). All heard the same sermon, but not everyone believed. This text and many others explain why: God mercifully predestined some to eternal life. That alone is why they believed.

Jesus used the metaphor of the wind blowing where it wishes to explain the mystery of the Holy Spirit's work in salvation, and he used the metaphor of new birth. Just as no one has anything to do with his first birth, so the sinner is born again by the mysterious working of the Spirit, not by anything the dead sinner can will or do. Correspondingly, Paul tells us that we are "dead in . . . transgressions and sins" (Eph. 2:1), but that it is God who makes us alive in Christ by his Spirit (2:4–5).

"Dead men tell no tales," so say pirates, nor can dead men will or do anything pertaining to their salvation. We must be born again, made alive, given the gift of faith by "the Spirit penetrat[ing] into our hearts," as Calvin termed it. Anything short of this gives man credit for the divine work of regeneration in our hearts.

We Call or He Calls?

Though C. S. Lewis was an extraordinary Christian apologist, there were some holes, shall we say, in his theology. One of these reoccurs in the form of philosophical arguments favoring freedom of the will over divine sovereignty. Put simply, Lewis was probably more of an Arminian than he was a Calvinist.

Nevertheless, writers are sometimes at their best when writing poetry or imaginative fiction, so in the Narnia books Lewis wonderfully illustrates the sovereignty of grace and the effectual calling of God's Spirit. In *The Silver Chair* when Aslan tells Jill that he called her out of her world, Jill disagrees. "Nobody called me and Scrubb, you know. It was we who asked to come here. Scrubb said we were to call . . . . And we did, and then we found the door open." Jill, like most, mistakenly thought her calling was what opened the door. Lewis's Lion wisely replied, "You would not have called to me unless I had been calling to you."

Similarly, in *The Magician's Nephew*, Lewis has Aslan utter "a long single note; not very loud, but full of power. Polly's heart jumped in her body when she heard it. She felt sure that it was a call, and that anyone who heard that call would want to obey it and (what's more) would be able to obey it, however many worlds and ages lay between."

As it did for Jill, the power of this call ought to fill us with the deepest wonder at the grace of our God, who alone elects, redeems, calls, and keeps all his sheep so that not one of them is lost.

Flat-Earth Theology

Arians in the early church had trouble figuring out how God could be three and one at the same time, so they rejected the biblical doctrine of the Trinity and, thus, the deity of Jesus Christ. When we frail mortals have trouble grasping high and grand doctrines concerning God, our inclination is to reduce things down to the puny level of human understanding. Error always follows.

From our flat-earth vantage point, predestination makes God not behave as nicely toward all sinners as we think fairness requires of him. Call these systems what you will, adherents insist that it wouldn't be fair of God to do anything more for those who will believe than he has done for those who won't. Thus, they insist that Calvinism can't be right because it violates God's fairness by making him act with favoritism toward some. Consequently, modern evangelism has created several extrabiblical jingles that have become inviolable.

Love and Voting

The first well-intentioned jingle goes like this: "God loves the sinner, but hates the sin." I wonder. After all, it's not the sin that gets thrown in hell. It's the sinner. Nobody wants to be "loved" like that. If God loves in the same way and to the same degree both the man who is saved and the man who will be damned, then *love* and *hate* have no meaning, and we've made a mingle-mangle again.

The Bible, however, uses these terms in precise ways. "Jacob I loved, but Esau I hated" (Rom. 9:13, quoting Mal. 1:2–3). So in Psalm 5:5, God declares that he "hate[s] all who do wrong." Though *all* means "all" to Arminians, *hate* here just can't mean "hate." They insist that God, Christ, and the Holy Spirit are obligated to love all sinners exactly alike and leave the rest up to the sinner. Though heaps of biblical evidence suggests otherwise, the measure of God's love, for them, is its extent, not its effect; it must extend to everyone who ever lives or it's not real love because love is fair.

But is this an accurate understanding of love? No wife would measure the worth of her husband's love by how widely it extends to all women; does her confidence in his love for her come from her knowledge that he loves all women without exception? Of course not! On the contrary, she measures his love by how exclusive, individual, and particular it is, by how he lavishes it on her alone. So Christ's love for his bride is particular, individual, and definite, and is savingly lavished on that bride, the church. Nevertheless, Arminians insist that Christ's love isn't real unless it is the same for all—even the already damned.

The other jingle often used in modern evangelism goes like this: "God cast a vote, Satan cast a vote, and the sinner casts the final vote." Anyone with his Bible open ought to see through this statement like a ladder. Aside from the obvious problem of placing God and Satan on equal terms in their hand-wringing passivity, nowhere does the Bible give man such ultimate self-determination. In all the evangelism recorded in the New Testament, I recall no such nonsense. Though zealous, well-meaning Christians say things like this, we do well to stick with the evangelism of Jesus and the apostles.

Cavils at Calvinism

A frequent cavil at Calvinism insists that its adherents do not care about evangelism and missions. But what of Paul, the quintessential world missionary, who taught these doctrines systematically throughout his epistles? Oft-maligned Calvin himself had a ministry marked by deep concern for the lost, wherein he established an academy precisely for training preachers and missionaries. Harvard, Yale, and Princeton were all established by Calvinists as theological training grounds for Christian preachers and missionaries. What's more, nineteenth-century missions were largely pioneered by a long list of Calvinists.

Another favorite cavil goes like this: If predestination is true, then why pray for the lost? Perhaps no one has more succinctly turned this cavil back on the detractors who raise it than J. I. Packer when he asks how you pray for the lost:

> Do you limit yourself to asking that God will bring them to a point where they can save themselves? I think that what you do is to pray in categorical terms that God will, quite simply and decisively, save them. You would not dream of making it a point in your prayer that you are not asking God actually to bring them to faith. You entreat him to do that very thing. Thus, you acknowledge and confess the sovereignty of God's grace. And so do all Christian people everywhere.

Something about the kneeling posture helps us proud sinners get things right. Perhaps there'd be less mingle-mangle about predestination and sovereign grace if we spent more time on those knees, humbly appealing to God on behalf of dead sinners whom he alone can save.

Does It Matter?

Then comes the final cavil at Calvinism: Calvinism is merely theological wrangling that has no relevance to a Christian's life and calling. But if we truly believe that all Scripture is God-breathed and thus profitable for doctrinal belief and for training in righteousness, then the Bible's teaching on the sovereignty of God must be important for us to understand.

So how ought believing in the doctrines of grace—in the sovereignty of God, total depravity, predestination, definite and particular atonement, and the effectual calling of the Spirit—to affect a young man's faith, devotion, and worship of Christ?

John Bunyan perhaps said it best when he at last saw his sin as a "most barbarous and a filthy crime," and realized that in his depravity he "had horribly abused the holy Son of God." Seeing the depth of your sin and the corresponding depth of electing love and of Christ's substitutionary atonement applied to your miserable life by God's Spirit ought to prompt in you a burning love for the Lord Jesus. Bunyan put it this way: "Had I a thousand gallons of blood within my veins, I could freely have spilled it all at the command and feet of this my Lord and Savior."

Stand fast on these high truths, and feel the force of them. Hold fast to truth, and walk humbly with your God, working out your salvation with fear and trembling, and making your calling and election sure by gratefully pursuing holiness, without which no young man will see the Lord.

Resolves

- To be generous and humble in disagreement with other Christians
- To cultivate a deep sense of wonder and appreciation at the sovereignty of God and all the implications thereof

Scripture Memory

"In him we were also chosen, having been predestined according to the plan of him who works out everything in conformity with the purpose of his will."

Ephesians 1:11

For Discussion

1. What are the two critical questions about salvation identified in this chapter? How does John 1:12–13 answer both questions?
2. Look up other passages that use the words *world* and *all*, and discuss their meaning.
3. How do you resolve the paradox of man's responsibility and God's sovereignty in salvation?

"How Sweet and Awful Is the Place"

Why was I made to hear your voice,
And enter while there's room,
When thousands make a wretched choice,
And rather starve than come?

Isaac Watts, 1707

For Further Study

Matthew 11:25–30; John 6:63–65; 15:16; 17:6–19
What Is a True Calvinist? by Philip Graham Ryken

SELECT BIBLIOGRAPHY FOR FURTHER READING

Confessions, St. Augustine
Saints' Everlasting Rest, Richard Baxter
The Letters of Robert Murray M'Cheyne, Andrew Bonar
Grace Abounding to the Chief of Sinners, John Bunyan
The Pilgrim's Progress, John Bunyan
Commentary on Paul's Epistle to the Romans, John Calvin
Institutes of the Christian Religion, John Calvin
Letters of John Calvin, John Calvin
Personal Narrative, Jonathan Edwards
To a Rising Generation, Jonathan Edwards
Scots Worthies, John Howie
Letters to Malcolm, C. S. Lewis
Mere Christianity, C. S. Lewis
Surprised by Joy, C. S. Lewis
The Chronicles of Narnia, C. S. Lewis
The Screwtape Letters, C. S. Lewis
The Plight of Man and the Power of God, D. Martyn Lloyd-Jones
The Bondage of the Will, Martin Luther
Mortification of Sin, John Owen
Evangelism and the Sovereignty of God, J. I. Packer

Knowing God, J. I. Packer

Pensées, Blaise Pascal

Amusing Ourselves to Death, Neil Postman

Letters, Samuel Rutherford

Trial and Triumph of Faith, Samuel Rutherford

City on a Hill, Philip Graham Ryken

Give Praise to God, Philip Graham Ryken

My Father's World, Philip Graham Ryken

Practical Religion, J. C. Ryle

Thoughts for Young Men, J. C. Ryle

The Complete Works, William Shakespeare

Morning and Evening, Charles Haddon Spurgeon

Logic, Isaac Watts

Lord, Teach Us to Pray, Alexander Whyte

A YOUNG MAN'S HYMNAL

Men are less interested in attending church regularly and even less inclined to commit themselves to ministry responsibilities and leadership in the church in part because there is a significant shift in how Christians worship. Relational songs and emotive choruses have replaced the strong, manly hymns that were sung by men and boys and their families in worship for millenniums. Instead of stout hymns about battles, and triumphant psalms about conquering enemies, and doctrinal poetry calling men to base their lives and deeds on solid biblical foundations, the contemporary church sings superficial songs that make real men feel like they have to act like women in order to be Christians. Young men who grow up under pressure to sing breathy, feminine songs in worship will never be spiritually, intellectually, and emotionally capable of godly leadership in their homes, in Christ's church, or in the world. The following collection of hymns will help men "be done with lesser things" and lift their voices in Christ-honoring, manly worship. (Visit www.cyberhymnal.org for tunes to these hymns.)

- Ah, Holy Jesus (J. Heermann)
- All Praise to God Who Reigns Above (J. Schütz)

- A Mighty Fortress Is Our God (M. Luther)
- Christian, Dost Thou See Them (St. Andrew of Crete)
- Crown Him with Many Crowns (M. Bridges)
- Day of Judgment (J. Newton)
- God Moves in a Mysterious Way (W. Cowper)
- Guide Me, O Thou Great Jehovah (W. Williams)
- How Firm a Foundation (Rippon collection, 1787)
- Immortal, Invisible, God Only Wise (W. Smith)
- Judge Me, God of My Salvation (The Psalter, 1912)
- Lead On, O King Eternal (E. Shurtleff)
- Mighty God, While Angels Bless Thee (R. Robinson)
- Now Blessed Be the Lord Our God (Psalm 72)
- Now Thank We All Our God (M. Rinkart)
- O God Beyond All Praising (M. Perry)
- Once in Royal David's City (C. F. Alexander)
- O Quickly Come, Dread Judge of All (L. Turttiett)
- Pilgrim Hymn (J. Bunyan)
- Rise, My Soul, to Watch and Pray (J. Freystein)
- Rise Up, Young Men of God (W. P. Merrill, alt. D. Bond, 2007)
- Stricken, Smitten, and Afflicted (T. Kelly)
- That Man Is Blessed Who Fearing God (Psalm 1, Psalter)
- The Church's One Foundation (S. Stone)
- The Law of God Is Good and Right (M. Loy)
- The Lord, Great Sovereign (D. Bond, 2001)
- The Son of God Goes Forth to War (R. Heber)
- Though I Can Speak in Tongues of Fire (D. Bond, 2006)

Ah, holy Jesus, how hast thou offended,
That man to judge thee hath in hate pretended?
By foes derided, by thine own rejected,
O most afflicted.

Who was the guilty who brought this upon thee?
Alas, my treason, Jesus, hath undone thee.
'Twas I, Lord Jesus, I it was denied thee:
I crucified thee.

Lo, the Good Shepherd for the sheep is offered;
The slave hath sinned, and the Son hath suffered:
For man's atonement, while he nothing heedeth,
God intercedeth.

For me, kind Jesus, was thine incarnation,
Thy mortal sorrow, and thy life's oblation:
Thy death of anguish and thy bitter passion,
For my salvation.

Therefore, kind Jesus, since I cannot pay thee,
I do adore thee, and will ever pray thee,
Think on thy pity and thy love unswerving,
Not my deserving.

Words: Johann Heermann, 1630
Tune: Iste Confessor, Rouen Church Melody

All praise to God, who reigns above,
The God of all creation,
The God of wonders, pow'r, and love,
The God of our salvation!
With healing balm my soul he fills,
The God who every sorrow stills.
To God all praise and glory!

What God's almighty pow'r hath made
His gracious mercy keepeth;

By morning dawn or evening shade
His watchful eye ne'er sleepeth;
Within the kingdom of his might,
Lo, all is just and all is right.
To God all praise and glory!

I cried to him in time of need:
Lord God, O hear my calling!
For death he gave me life indeed
And kept my feet from falling.
For this my thanks shall endless be;
O thank him, thank our God with me.
To God all praise and glory!

The Lord forsaketh not his flock,
His chosen generation;
He is their refuge and their rock,
Their peace and their salvation.
As with a mother's tender hand
He leads his own, his chosen band.
To God all praise and glory!

Ye who confess Christ's holy name,
To God give praise and glory!
Ye who the Father's pow'r proclaim,
To God give praise and glory!
All idols underfoot be trod,
The Lord is God! The Lord is God!
To God all praise and glory!

Then come before his presence now
And banish fear and sadness;
To your Redeemer pay your vow
And sing with joy and gladness:
Though great distress my soul befell,

The Lord, my God, did all things well.
To God all praise and glory!

Words: Johann J. Schütz, 1675
Tune: Mit Freuden Zart, Bohemian Brethren's *Gesangbuch*, 1566

A mighty fortress is our God,
A bulwark never failing;
Our helper he amid the flood
Of mortal ills prevailing.
For still our ancient foe
Doth seek to work us woe;
His craft and pow'r are great;
And armed with cruel hate,
On earth is not his equal.

Did we in our own strength confide,
Our striving would be losing;
Were not the right man on our side,
The man of God's own choosing.
Dost ask who that may be?
Christ Jesus, it is he,
Lord Sabaoth his name,
From age to age the same,
And he must win the battle.

And though this world, with devils filled,
Should threaten to undo us,
We will not fear, for God hath willed
His truth to triumph through us.
The prince of darkness grim,
We tremble not for him;
His rage we can endure,

For lo! His doom is sure;
One little word shall fell him.

That Word above all earthly pow'rs,
No thanks to them, abideth;
The Spirit and the gifts are ours
Through him who with us sideth.
Let goods and kindred go,
This mortal life also;
The body they may kill:
God's truth abideth still;
His kingdom is forever.

Words: Martin Luther, 1529
Tune: Ein' Feste Burg, Martin Luther, 1529

Christian, dost thou see them on the holy ground,
How the powers of darkness rage thy steps around?
Christian, up and smite them, counting gain but loss,
In the strength that cometh by the holy cross.

Christian, dost thou feel them, how they work within,
Striving, tempting, luring, goading into sin?
Christian, never tremble; never be downcast;
Gird thee for the battle, watch and pray and fast.

Christian, dost thou hear them, how they speak thee fair?
"Always fast and vigil? Always watch and prayer?"
Christian, answer boldly: "While I breathe I pray!"
Peace shall follow battle, night shall end in day.

"Hear the words of Jesus, O my servant true;
Thou art very weary, I was weary, too;

But that toil shall make thee some day all Mine own,
At the end of sorrow shall be near my throne."

Words: Andrew of Crete, 660–732
Tune: St. Andrew of Crete, John B. Dykes, 1868

Crown him with many crowns,
The Lamb upon his throne;
Hark! How the heav'nly anthem drowns
All music but its own,
Awake, my soul, and sing
Of him who died for thee,
And hail him as thy matchless King
Through all eternity.

Crown him the Lord of love;
Behold his hands and side,
Rich wounds, yet visible above,
In beauty glorified:
No angel in the sky
Can fully bear that sight,
But downward bends his burning eye
At mysteries so bright.

Crown him the Lord of peace;
Whose pow'r a scepter sways
From pole to pole, that wars may cease,
Absorbed in prayer and praise:
His reign shall know no end;
And round his pierced feet
Fair flow'rs of paradise extend
Their fragrance ever sweet.

Crown him the Lord of years,
The Potentate of time;
Creator of the rolling spheres,
Ineffably sublime:
All hail, Redeemer, hail!
For thou hast died for me:
Thy praise shall never, never fail
Throughout eternity.

Words: Matthew Bridges, 1851
Tune: DIADEMATA, George J. Elvey, 1868

Day of Judgment! Day of wonders!
Hark! The trumpet's awful sound,
Louder than a thousand thunders,
Shakes the vast creation round.
How the summons
Will the sinner's heart confound!

See the Judge, our nature wearing,
Clothed in majesty divine;
You who long for his appearing
Then shall say, "This God is mine!"
Gracious Savior,
Own me in that day as thine.

At his call the dead awaken,
Rise to life from earth and sea;
All the pow'rs of nature,
Shaken by his looks, prepare to flee.
Careless sinner,
What will then become of thee?

But to those who have confessed,
Loved and served the Lord below,

He will say, "Come near, ye blessed,
See the kingdom I bestow;
You forever
Shall my love and glory know."

Words: John Newton, 1774
Tune: St. Austin, *Bristol Tune Book*, 1876

God moves in a mysterious way
His wonders to perform;
He plants His footsteps in the sea
And rides upon the storm.

Deep in unfathomable mines
Of never failing skill
He treasures up His bright designs
And works His sovereign will.

Ye fearful saints, fresh courage take;
The clouds ye so much dread
Are big with mercy and shall break
In blessings on your head.

Judge not the Lord by feeble sense,
But trust Him for His grace;
Behind a frowning providence
He hides a smiling face.

His purposes will ripen fast,
Unfolding every hour;
The bud may have a bitter taste,
But sweet will be the flower.

Blind unbelief is sure to err
And scan His work in vain;
God is His own interpreter,
And He will make it plain.

Words: William Cowper, 1774
Tune: DUNDEE, Scottish Psalter, 1615

Guide me, O thou great Jehovah,
Pilgrim through this barren land;
I am weak, but thou art mighty;
Hold me with thy pow'rful hand;
Bread of heaven, bread of heaven,
Feed me till I want no more,
Feed me till I want no more.

Open now the crystal fountain,
Whence the healing stream doth flow;
Let the fire and cloudy pillar
Lead me all my journey through;
Strong Deliverer, strong Deliverer,
Be thou still my Strength and Shield,
Be thou still my Strength and Shield.

When I tread the verge of Jordan,
Bid my anxious fears subside;
Death of death and hell's Destruction,
Land me safe on Canaan's side;
Songs of praises, songs of praises
I will ever give to thee,
I will ever give to thee.

Words: William Williams, 1745
Tune: CWM RHONDDA, John Hughes, 1907

How firm a foundation, ye saints of the Lord,
Is laid for your faith in His excellent Word!
What more can He say than to you He hath said,
You, who unto Jesus for refuge have fled?

Fear not, I am with thee, O be not dismayed,
For I am thy God and will still give thee aid;
I'll strengthen and help thee, and cause thee to stand
Upheld by My righteous, omnipotent hand.

When through the deep waters I call thee to go,
The rivers of woe shall not thee overflow;
For I will be with thee, thy troubles to bless,
And sanctify to thee thy deepest distress.

When through fiery trials thy pathways shall lie,
My grace, all sufficient, shall be thy supply;
The flame shall not hurt thee; I only design
Thy dross to consume, and thy gold to refine.

Even down to old age all My people shall prove
My sovereign, eternal, unchangeable love;
And when hoary hairs shall their temples adorn,
Like lambs they shall still in My bosom be borne.

The soul that on Jesus has leaned for repose,
I will not, I will not desert to its foes;
That soul, though all hell should endeavor to shake,
I'll never, no never, no never forsake.

Words: John Rippon, 1787
Tune: FOUNDATION, Traditional American melody, J. Funk's *A
Compilation of Genuine Church Music*, 1832

Immortal, invisible, God only wise,
In light inaccessible hid from our eyes,
Most blessed, most glorious, the Ancient of Days,
Almighty, victorious, Thy great Name we praise.

Unresting, unhasting, and silent as light,
Nor wanting, not wasting, Thou rulest in might;
Thy justice like mountains high soaring above
Thy clouds which are fountains of goodness and love.

Great Father of glory, pure Father of Light,
Thine angels adore thee, all veiling their sight;
All praise we would render; O help us to see
'Tis only the splendor of light hideth thee!

Words: Walter Chalmers Smith, 1867
Tune: JOANNA, Traditional Welsh hymn melody

Judge me, God of my salvation,
Plead my cause, for thee I trust:
Hear my earnest supplication,
Save me from my foes unjust.
O my soul, why art thou grieving?
What disquiets and dismays?
Hope in God; his help receiving,
I shall yet my Savior praise.

For my strength, my God, thou art:
Why am I cast off by thee
In sorrow of my heart,
While the foe oppresses me?

Light and truth, my way attending,
Send thou forth to be my guide,
Till, thy holy mount ascending,
I within thy house abide.

At thy sacred altar bending,
God, my God, my boundless joy,
Harp and voice, in worship blending,
For thy praise will I employ.
O my soul, why art thou grieving?
What disquiets and dismays?
Hope in God; his help receiving,
I shall yet my Savior praise.

Words: *The Psalter*, 1912
Tune: BLAENHAFREN, Traditional Irish Melody

Lead on, O King eternal,
The day of march has come;
Henceforth in fields of conquest
Thy tents shall be our home:
Through days of preparation
Thy grace has made us strong,
And now, O King eternal,
We lift our battle song.

Lead on, O King eternal,
Till sin's fierce war shall cease,
And holiness shall whisper
The sweet amen of peace;
For not with swords loud clashing,
Nor roll of stirring drums,
But deeds of love and mercy,
The heav'nly kingdom comes.

Lead on, O King eternal:
We follow, not with fears;
For gladness breaks like morning
Where're thy face appears;
Thy cross is lifted o'er us;
We journey in its light:
The crown awaits the conquest;
Lead on, O God of might.

Words: Ernest W. Shurtleff, 1888
Tune: LANCASHIRE, Henry Smart, 1836

Mighty God, while angels bless you,
May a mortal sing your name?
Lord of men as well as angles,
You are every creature's theme.
Alleluia! Alleluia! Alleluia!

Lord of every land and nation,
Ancient of eternal days,
Sounded through the wide creation
Be your just and lawful praise.
Alleluia! Alleluia! Alleluia!

For the grandeur of your nature,
Grand beyond a seraph's thought,
For created works of power,
Works with skill and kindness wrought.
Alleluia! Alleluia! Alleluia!

But your rich, your free redemption,
Dark through brightness all along,
Thought is poor, and poor expression,

Who dare sing that wondrous song?
Alleluia! Alleluia! Alleluia!

Brightness of the Father's glory,
Shall your praise unuttered lie?
Fly, my tongue, such guilty silence,
Sing the Lord who came to die.
Alleluia! Alleluia! Alleluia!

From the highest throne in glory,
To the cross of deepest woe,
All to ransom guilty captives,
Flow my praise, forever flow.
Alleluia! Alleluia! Alleluia!

Words: Robert Robinson, 1774
Tune: ALLELUIA (LOWE), Albert Lowe, 1868

Now blessed be the Lord our God,
The God of Israel,
For he alone doth wondrous works
In glory that excel.

And blessed be his glorious name
To all eternity;
The whole earth let his glory fill.
Amen, so let it be.

His wide dominion shall extend
From sea to utmost sea,
And unto earth's remotest bounds
His peaceful rule shall be.

Yea, all the kings shall bow to him,
His rule all nations hail;
He will regard the poor man's cry
When other helpers fail.

Words: Psalm 72, Scottish Psalter, 1650
Tune: McKEE, Harry T. Burleigh, 1939

Now thank we all our God
With heart and hands and voices,
Who wondrous things hath done,
In whom this world rejoices;
Who from our mothers' arms,
Hath blessed us on our way
With countless gifts of love,
And still is ours today.

O may this bounteous God
Through all our life be near us,
With ever joyful hearts
And blessed peace to cheer us;
And keep us in his grace,
And guide us when perplexed,
And free us from all ills
In this world and the next.

All praise and thanks to God
The Father now be given,
The Son, and him who reigns
With them in highest heaven—
The one eternal God,
Whom earth and heav'n adore;

For thus it was, is now,
And shall be evermore.

Words: M. Rinkart, 1636
Tune: Nun Danket, Johann Cruger, 1647

O God beyond all praising, we worship you today
And sing the love amazing that songs cannot repay;
For we can only wonder at every gift you send,
At blessings without number and mercies without end:
We lift our hearts before you and wait upon your word,
We honor and adore you, our great and mighty Lord.

Then hear, O gracious Savior, accept the love we bring,
That we who know your favor may serve you as our King;
And whether our tomorrows be filled with good or ill,
We'll triumph through our sorrows and rise to bless you still:
To marvel at your beauty and glory in your ways,
And make a joyful duty our sacrifice of praise.

Words: Michael Perry, 1982
Tune: Thaxted, Gustav Holst, *The Planets*, 1918

Once in royal David's city
Stood a lowly cattle shed,
Where a mother laid her baby
In a manger for his bed:
Mary was that mother mild,
Jesus Christ her little child.

He came down to earth from heaven
Who is God and Lord of all,
And his shelter was a stable,
And his cradle was a stall:
With the poor, and mean, and lowly,
Lived on earth our Savior holy.

And through all his wondrous childhood
He would honor and obey,
Love and watch the lowly maiden
In whose gentle arms he lay:
Christian children all must be
Mild, obedient, good as he.

And our eyes at last shall see him,
Through his own redeeming love;
For that child so dear and gentle
Is our Lord in heav'n above,
And he leads his children on
To the place where he is gone.

Not in that poor lowly stable,
With the oxen standing by,
We shall see him, but in heaven,
Set at God's right hand on high;
When like stars his children crowned
All in white shall wait around.

Words: Cecil Frances Alexander, 1848
Tune: IRBY, Henry J. Gauntlett, 1849

O quickly come, dread Judge of all;
For, awful though thine advent be,

All shadows from the truth will fall,
And falsehood die, in sight of thee:
O quickly come, for doubt and fear
Like clouds dissolve when thou art near.

O quickly come, great King of all;
Reign all around us and within;
Let sin no more our souls enthrall,
Let pain and sorrow die with sin:
O quickly come, for thou alone
Canst make thy scattered people one.

O quickly come, true Life of all,
For death is mighty all around;
On ev'ry home his shadows fall,
On ev'ry heart his mark is found:
O quickly come, for grief and pain
Can never cloud thy glorious reign.

O quickly come, sure Light of all,
For gloomy night broods o'er our way;
And weakly souls begin to fall
With weary watching for the day:
O quickly come, for round thy throne
No eye is blind, no night is known.

Words: Lawrence Tuttiett, 1854
Tune: MELITA, John B. Dykes, 1861

Who would true valour see,
Let him come hither;
One here will constant be,

Come wind, come weather.
There's no discouragement,
Shall make him once relent,
His first avowed intent
To be a pilgrim.

Whoso beset him round
With dismal stories,
Do but themselves confound,—
His strength the more is.
No lion can him fright,
He'll with the giant fight,
But he will have the right
To be a pilgrim.

Hobgoblin nor foul fiend
Can daunt his spirit;
He knows he at the end
Shall life inherit.
Then fancies fly away;
He'll fear not what men say;
He'll labor night and day
To be a pilgrim.

Words: John Bunyan, 1678
Tune: MONKSGATE
Arranged: Ralph Vaughan Williams

◆ ◆ ◆

Rise, my soul, to watch and pray,
From thy sleep awaken;
Be not by the evil day
Unawares o'ertaken.
For the foe,

Well we know,
Oft his harvest reapeth
While the Christian sleepeth.

Watch against the devil's snares,
Lest asleep he find thee;
For indeed no pains he spares
To deceive and blind thee.
Satan's prey
Oft are they
Who secure are sleeping
And no watch are keeping.

Watch! Let not the wicked world
With its pow'r defeat thee.
Watch lest with her pomp unfurled
She betray and cheat thee.
Watch and see
Lest there be
Faithless friends to charm thee,
Who but seek to harm thee.

Watch against thyself, my soul,
Lest with grace thou trifle;
Let not self thy thoughts control
Nor God's mercy stifle.
Pride and sin
Lurk within
All thy hopes to scatter;
Heed not when they flatter.

But while watching, also pray
To the Lord unceasing.
He will free thee, be thy stay,
Strength and faith increasing.

O Lord, bless
In distress
And let nothing swerve me
From the will to serve thee.

Words: J. B. Freystein, 1697
Tune: STRAF MICH NICHT, *Hundert Arien*, Dresden, 1694

Rise up, young men of God!
Have done with lesser things.
Give heart and mind and soul and strength
To serve the King of kings.

Rise up, young men of God!
The kingdom tarries long.
Bring in the day of brotherhood
And end the night of wrong.

Rise up, young men of God!
The church for you doth wait,
Her strength unequal to her task;
Rise up, Christ makes her great!

Lift high the cross of Christ!
Tread where his feet have trod.
As brothers of the Son of Man,
Rise up, young men of God!

Words: William P. Merrill, 1867–1954 (alt. D. Bond, 2006)
Tune: FESTAL SONG, William H. Walter, 1825–1893

Stricken, smitten, and afflicted,
See him dying on the tree!
'Tis the Christ by man rejected;
Yes, my soul, 'tis he, 'tis he!
'Tis the long expected Prophet,
David's son, yet David's Lord;
By his Son God now has spoken:
'Tis the true and faithful Word.

Ye who think of sin but lightly
Nor suppose the evil great
Here may view its nature rightly,
Here its guilt may estimate.
Mark the sacrifice appointed,
See who bears the awful load;
'Tis the Word, the Lord's Anointed,
Son of Man and Son of God.

Here we have a firm foundation,
Here the refuge of the lost;
Christ's the Rock of our salvation,
His the name of which we boast.
Lamb of God, for sinners wounded,
Sacrifice to cancel guilt!
None shall ever be confounded
Who on him their hope have built.

Words: Thomas Kelly, 1804
Tune: O Mein Jesu, Ich Muss Sterben, *Geistliche Volkslieder*,
Paderborn, 1850

That man is blest who, fearing God
From sin restrains his feet,
Who will not stand with wicked men,
Who shuns the scorners' seat.

Yea, blest is he who makes God's law
His portion and delight,
And meditates upon that law
With gladness day and night.

That man is nourished like a tree
Set by the river's side;
Its leaf is green, its fruit is sure,
And thus his works abide.

The wicked like the driven chaff
Are swept from off the land;
They shall not gather with the just,
Nor in the judgment stand.

The Lord will guard the righteous well,
Their way to Him is known;
The way of sinners, far from God,
Shall surely be o'erthrown.

Words: Psalm 1, Psalter, author unknown, 1912
Tune: IRISH, *Hymns and Sacred Poems*, Dublin, 1749

◆ ◆ ◆

The Church's one foundation
Is Jesus Christ her Lord,
She is His new creation

By water and the Word.
From heaven He came and sought her
To be His holy bride;
With His own blood He bought her
And for her life He died.

Elect from every nation,
Yet one o'er all the earth;
Her charter of salvation,
One Lord, one faith, one birth;
One holy Name she blesses,
Partakes one holy food,
And to one hope she presses,
With every grace endued.

The Church shall never perish!
Her dear Lord to defend,
To guide, sustain, and cherish,
Is with her to the end:
Though there be those who hate her,
And false sons in her pale,
Against both foe or traitor
She ever shall prevail.

Though with a scornful wonder
Men see her sore oppressed,
By schisms rent asunder,
By heresies distressed:
Yet saints their watch are keeping,
Their cry goes up, "How long?"
And soon the night of weeping
Shall be the morn of song!

'Mid toil and tribulation,
And tumult of her war,

She waits the consummation
Of peace forevermore;
Till, with the vision glorious,
Her longing eyes are blest,
And the great Church victorious
Shall be the Church at rest.

Yet she on earth hath union
With God the Three in One,
And mystic sweet communion
With those whose rest is won,
With all her sons and daughters
Who, by the Master's hand
Led through the deathly waters,
Repose in Eden land.

O happy ones and holy!
Lord, give us grace that we
Like them, the meek and lowly,
On high may dwell with Thee:
There, past the border mountains,
Where in sweet vales the Bride
With Thee by living fountains
Forever shall abide!

Words: Samuel Stone, 1866
Tune: Aurelia, Samuel S. Wesley, 1864

The Law of God is good and wise
And sets his will before our eyes,
Shows us the way of righteousness,
And dooms to death when we transgress.

Its light of holiness imparts
And knowledge of our sinful hearts,
That we may see our lost estate
And seek deliv'rance ere too late.

To those who help in Christ have found
And would in works of love abound
It shows what deeds are his delight
And should be done as good and right.

When men the offered help disdain
And willfully in sin remain,
Its terror in their ear resounds
And keeps their wickedness in bounds.

The law is good; but since the fall
Its holiness condemns us all;
It dooms us for our sin to die
And has no pow'r to justify.

To Jesus we for refuge flee,
Who from the curse has set us free,
And humbly worship at his throne,
Saved by his grace through faith alone.

Words: M. Loy, 1863
Tune: ERHALT UNS, HERR, *Geistliche Lieder*, Wittenberg, 1543

The Lord, Great Sovereign, shall appear,
His wand'ring sheep he'll bring,
From distant lands, through surging seas,
To shout before their King!

Deceitful shepherds, false and vain,
Have led his flock astray;
God's enemies he'll trample down,
Their lies he will repay.

With trumpet blast, the Lord appears,
His arrows flashing round;
He shields his flock, destroys his foes;
Glad vict'ry shouts will sound.

He makes his children mighty men,
They bend the battle bow;
So in God's strength, against the proud,
His foes they overthrow!

Restored, victorious, gathered in,
Their enemies o'ercome;
God's children worship round his throne,
And in his name they run!

God's bless'd, redeemed, and chosen ones,
His children shout and sing!
"All praise to Christ, the Cornerstone,
Triumphant, glorious King!"

Words: Douglas Bond, 2001
Tune: St. Magnus, Jeremiah Clarke, 1701

The Son of God goes forth to war,
A kingly crown to gain;
His blood red banner streams afar:
Who follows in His train?
Who best can drink his cup of woe,

Triumphant over pain,
Who patient bears his cross below,
He follows in His train.

That martyr first, whose eagle eye
Could pierce beyond the grave;
Who saw his Master in the sky,
And called on Him to save.
Like Him, with pardon on His tongue,
In midst of mortal pain,
He prayed for them that did the wrong:
Who follows in His train?

A glorious band, the chosen few
On whom the Spirit came;
Twelve valiant saints, their hope they knew,
And mocked the cross and flame.
They met the tyrant's brandished steel,
The lion's gory mane;
They bowed their heads the death to feel:
Who follows in their train?

A noble army, men and boys,
The matron and the maid,
Around the Savior's throne rejoice,
In robes of light arrayed.
They climbed the steep ascent of Heav'n,
Through peril, toil, and pain;
O God, to us may grace be given,
To follow in their train.

Words: Reginald Heber, 1827
Tune: ALL SAINTS NEW, Henry S. Cutler, 1872

◆ ◆ ◆

Though I can speak in tongues of fire
But love is not my chief desire,
And I'm not patient, humble, kind,
I'm nothing—nor will heaven find.

His gracious gifts Christ gives to me
So I, like him, might perfect be,
And know, and speak, and serve, and give,
And, like my loving Savior, live.

He knew and loved me ere he laid
The world's foundation, and he bade
Me come rejoice, and drink, and dine—
His love the flame that burns in mine.

In faith and hope, love perseveres,
No anger and no rudeness hears;
This love, like Christ's, will never cease
And leads to heaven's joy and peace.

We see in part, like children here,
So dull and pale, as in a mirror.
But face to face one day we'll know
The depth of Jesus' love below.

True love is patient, love is kind;
It's faith and hope in One refined;
The greatest thing of all is love,
For perfect love endures above.

Above I'll know, as Christ has known,
The depth of kindness he has shown;

In heav'n I'll see him face to face,
With eyes undimmed, his love embrace!

Words: Douglas Bond, 2006
Tune: GIFT OF LOVE, American folk tune, arranged by Hal Hopson, 1972

Douglas Bond, author of a number of books for young people, lives with his wife, two daughters, and four sons in Washington state. He is a ruling elder in the Presbyterian Church in America (PCA), has a master's degree in education, heads the English department at Covenant High School, and was awarded the regional *Teacher Award* for excellence in teaching young people how to write. Bond lectures on literature, writing, and church history, and leads literary and church history study tours in Europe. Visit Bond's website at www. bondbooks.net.

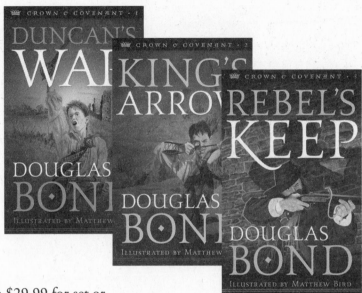

ALSO BY DOUGLAS BOND

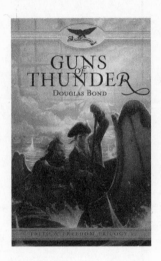

Price: $11.99 each
To order, visit www.prpbooks.com or call 1(800) 631-0094

In this first book of the new Faith and Freedom Trilogy, the M'Kethe clan finds itself in pre-Revolutionary War Connecticut weathering a storm of religious and political upheaval. Ian M'Kethe is forced to make a choice in the face of enormous odds, as tensions mount between the colonists and the French with their Indian allies. Forging an unlikely friendship with Watookoog, an Indian, Ian risks everything and gains something he thought he had lost forever.

The Faith & Freedom Trilogy, sequel to the Crown & Covenant Series, chronicles new generations of the M'Kethe family who find freedom in eighteenth-century America. Adventure is afoot as Old World tyrannies clash with New World freedoms. Bond weaves together fictional characters with historical figures from Scottish and American history.

Visit www.bondbooks.net for more information!

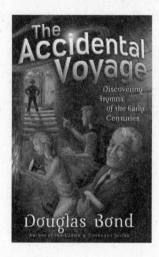